*Marvelous
Old Mansions
and other
Southern Treasures*

Marvelous Old Mansions

and Other Southern Treasures

by Sylvia Higginbotham

John F. Blair, Publisher
Winston-Salem, North Carolina

Published by John F. Boair, Publisher

The paper in this book meets the guidelines for

permanance and furability of the

Committee on Production Guidelines for

Book Longevity of the Council on Literary Resources

Cover photographs clockwise from top left: Chretien Point Plantation, Louisiana; Richards D.A.R. House, Mobile, Alabama;

Stanton Hall, Natchez, Mississippi. Photograph used in the background on the front and back covers: The Telfair Mansion, Savannah, Georgia

Library of Congress Cataloging-in-Publication Data

Higginbotham, Sylvia.
    Marvelous old mansions : and other southern treasures / by Sylvia Higginbotham.
        p.   cm.
    Includes bibliographical references and index.
    ISBN 0-89587-227-7 (alk. paper)
    1. Architecture, Domestic—Southern States—Guidebooks. 2. Architecture,
Colonial—Southern States—Guidebooks. 3. Greek revival (Architecture)—Southern
States—Guidebooks. 4. Architecture, Modern—19th century—Southern States. I. Title.

NA7211 .H53 2000
728'.0975'09034—dc21

                                                            00-044447

Design by Debra Long Hampton

Composition by The Roberts Group

Printed in Canada

To my husband, Weldon "Joe" Higginbotham, and our daughters, Saxonie Eicholtz of Louisville, Kentucky, and Shaye Erazo of Miami, Florida

Contents

Introduction

In the eighteenth and nineteenth centuries, planters and merchants built marvelous old mansions across the South. These mansions served two purposes: to emphasize the social position of their owners by showing that they knew how to live well and could afford to do so, and to provide the utmost comfort for families and friends of these wealthy men.

This book focuses on some of the most interesting and/or historically significant homes built during those two centuries in nine Southern states. Because New Orleans and the East Coast already had well-established communities in the eighteenth century, some of the featured homes in these areas come from that century. However, the region's golden age of building came during the antebellum period, primarily between 1830 and 1860.

Greek Revival was the architectural style of preference from the mid-1830s until the outbreak of the Civil War in 1860. Due to the scarcity of architects in more remote areas, owners often planned their own homes. Building was done by those who lived on the property or by local carpenters, with itinerant craftsmen coming through on occasion to do the more detailed work. Often, it took many years to complete a home, even if the craftsmen stayed in residence until the building was completed.

The builders of these showplaces, who were filled with faith and hope, surely could not have conceived of the ways lifestyles in the South were about to change with the coming of the Civil War. The war wreaked havoc on or resulted in the destruction of many of the architectural treasures. After the war, the grand old homes of the South were sometimes considered a liability. There was a scarcity of able-bodied men who could still muster the strength or the money to keep up the homes, so condemned signs became a common sight in the 1860s.

The financial situation in the South improved in the 1870s and 1880s, and a new style in homes emerged. The old antebellum styles were ignored as the Victorian look with its frills and filigree came into fashion. Further blows came to Southern architecture with World War I and the Great Depression. During these tumultuous times, little attention was paid to the dilapidated houses that were often more than a hundred years old. As the century progressed, many of the mansions were torn down in the name of "progress"—progress being a parking lot or acres of concrete surrounding a mall.

When the nation began to struggle to its economic feet in the late 1930s, jobs were more plentiful, so American women longed for ways to enhance their feminine wiles and bring romance back into their lives. In 1939, as if on cue, Miss Scarlett O'Hara of Tara sashayed down the stairs at Twelve Oaks and into the heart of Rhett Butler—and into the hearts of millions of moviegoers. *Gone With the Wind* became an American movie classic and, in the process, did its part to change the way things were.

Suddenly, the women of America had a new hero in Rhett, a new heroine in Scarlett or Melanie—some chose the kind and mellow Melanie over the conniving and feisty Scarlett—and a new interest in the old homes of the South. Some of these old homes were in their own neighborhoods, perhaps reeling and peeling from years of neglect. But interest was sparked, and once again the great houses of the South were back in vogue.

It took a few years for preservation to catch on, though it got a big boost when the Mount Vernon Ladies' Association purchased and undertook the restoration of George Washington's Mount Vernon. More organizations joined the preservation bandwagon, among

them the Daughters of the American Revolution, the United Daughters of the Confederacy, and state chapters of various societies for the preservation of antiquities.

In the 1930s, historic properties were documented by the Historic American Building Survey (HABS). In 1949, the National Trust for Historic Preservation was chartered to provide leadership and to encourage public interest and participation in historic properties. In 1966, a new law authorized the establishment of the National Register of Historic Places within the Department of the Interior.

The National Register of Historic Places includes properties "that embody the distinctive characteristics of a type, period, or method of construction, or that represent the work of a master, or that possess high artistic values, or that represent a significant and distinguishable entity whose components may lack individual distinction." We used this register extensively in our research and most of the homes included are on that register. Some are also on the prestigious National Historic Landmarks list.

Today, these historical homes have universal appeal, not only for those who enjoy the architecture but also for those who appreciate the art involved in creating the decorative molding and elaborate hand-carved woodwork. And of course, there's keen interest in the engineering ingenuity of these magnificent structures. It is amazing to know that the unsupported, spiraling wooden staircases still stand after all these years.

Hundreds of these marvelous old mansions are private residences and are not accessible to the public. We've chosen to concentrate on the homes that can be seen, if not daily, at least during annual home tours, or pilgrimages, or by appointment.

Many of these treasures that are open to the public practice the art of Southern hospitality. The owners of these homes have a deep appreciation for the home's historical value and want to share it with others. We have included the homes that we believe are the most accessible and most hospitable and accommodating to the public.

When homes are located in towns or cities, we offer a brief overview of the community. Country homes stand alone.

In such places as Natchez that host annual pilgrimages or tours of historic homes, local mansions are open on a rotating basis during the event. If you happen to arrive on a day when the home you want to see is not on that day's tour schedule, there will be plenty of others to see. If you have a strong preference for a particular home and can't stay a day or two until it rotates back on again, call in advance for a schedule. All pilgrimage events provide printed schedules of dates and times well in advance.

Contact telephone numbers are listed in this book.

And speaking of telephone numbers, please be advised that area codes change frequently. We made many calls to "wrong numbers" because the area codes listed in research materials had changed. If this happens with a number in this book, please know that we made every effort to give correct numbers, but changes may have occurred after the book went to press.

It is always a good idea to verify pertinent information before you arrive at homes you wish to see. Please know that even though the descriptions say "open daily," that normally does not mean major holidays. Most historic sites are closed for Thanksgiving, Christmas, and New Year's Day. Expect to pay from $4 to $8 for individual admission to a home tour; some group rates are less. Groups are advised to make advance arrangements.

With each state's listing, we included sidebars about historic attractions that might also be useful if you're traveling in the area. The sites we've featured in the sidebars are those we think lovers of old houses will enjoy, such as colorful gardens, living-history villages, or towns with many historic sites that make it conducive to join a walking tour.

Thanks ever so much to all the people in each state who helped with information, tours, and encouragement. Special thank-yous go to

Carolyn Sakowski, president of John F. Blair, Publisher; Debbie Geiger, of Geiger & Associates PR, in Tallahassee; Susan Coggins Hammond of Savannah; Margaret Maraist Ritchey and Mary Jane Bauer of Lafayette, Louisiana, and Debbie Fleming Caffrey of Breaux Bridge, Louisiana, for letting me stay in their homes while I scouted the region; Ami Simpson of Alabama State Tourism; E. Patrick McIntyre, Jr., of the Alabama Historical Commission; Kelly Grass of Florida Tourism Marketing; Shelley Knox of the Tallahassee Convention & Visitors Bureau; Mason Sheffield of the Florida Division of Historical Resources; Faye Richardson of Natchez Pilgrimage Tours; Renè Adams of Dunleith; Laura Godfrey of the Natchez Convention & Visitors Bureau; historian Carl Butler from Columbus, Mississippi; the Louisiana Office of Tourism; the New Orleans Metro Convention & Visitors Bureau; the Lewises of Melhana Plantation in Thomasville, Georgia; the Charleston, South Carolina, Area Convention & Visitors Bureau; Ann Possner of the Historic Columbia Foundation, in Columbia, South Carolina; South Carolina Parks, Recreation and Tourism; the ladies of Poplar Grove Plantation near Wilmington, North Carolina; Kay Montgomery Tyler of Sherwood Forest Plantation on the James River in Virginia; Julie Grimes and Jay Hollomon of the Virginia Tourism Corporation; the Tennessee Antebellum Trail staff; Barbara Parker of the Tennessee Department of Tourist Development; Leslie Miller of the Raleigh Convention & Visitors Bureau; The Thomas Jefferson Memorial Foundation; the National Trust for Historic Preservation in Washington; Stephen W. Skelton, South Carolina Archives and History Center; and the many others who invited me to their homes, spoke with me on the phone, sent information and photographs, and were generally kind and helpful. Thank you.

Sylvia Higginbotham
Columbus, Mississippi
September 2000

The publisher would like to especially thank our interns, Brantley DuBose and Erin Styers, for their tireless efforts in checking for factual accuracy.

Alabama

The Alabama that I know, especially in the rural areas, is a state populated with gentle people. It's the land of Atticus Finch and Boo Radley from *To Kill a Mockingbird*; it is the home of the Alabama Shakespeare Festival, the only American theater invited to fly the same flag used by England's Royal Shakespeare Company. It's a state of beaches that segue into the scenic vistas of the Appalachian chain. And, it is a state filled with old Southern mansions waiting to welcome you.

The houses in Alabama are located in the "Heart of Dixie" in the Sunbelt where extremely warm summers are the norm. The influence of the climate is in evidence in many of Alabama's mansions. Front porches, wide halls that help stimulate breezes, and punkahs—a type of fan that is pulled with a rope to create a breeze over the dining table—were standard in many Alabama homes built before 1860.

Although many of Alabama's grandest homes were lost during the Civil War or in the name of progress in later decades, the majority of those left standing are lovingly preserved.

For information on attractions and events in Alabama, call the Alabama Bureau of Tourism and Travel at (800) 252-2262.

Mobile

Located at the southernmost tip of Alabama, Mobile follows St. Augustine, Florida, as the second oldest settlement founded by Europeans in the United States. Spaniards originally explored this area in 1559, but it was Pierre Le Moyne, Sieur D'Iberville, who actually established a small colony here in 1702. In an effort to bring stability to the colony, King Louis XIV sent a shipload of young women to wed the lonely young Frenchmen who manned this remote garrison known as Fort Condé.

However, French ingenuity did not deter the English, who still managed to hoist the Union Jack over Fort Condé. The flying of the British flag proved temporary when the French regained control of the area.

After more than a hundred years of fighting Spaniards, Indians, and the elements, the French ceded the town of Mobile to England. But the fighting was not over, for Spain came into power again in 1780. United States troops finally took control in 1813, and Alabama was admitted to the Union in 1819.

Influences from its French, Spanish, and English heritage are still found today in Mobile's architecture and attitudes. One example of this influence is Mobile's annual celebration of Mardi Gras. Although the Krewe parades most people associate with a Mardi Gras celebration did not begin until 1869, Mobile's observance of Mardi Gras actually began in 1703 when the settlement was under French rule. Mobile has rigorously celebrated Mardi Gras since about 1830, so Mobilians say their town celebrated Mardi Gras long before New Orleans.

Mobile is known as a city of flowers. Each spring, the azaleas offer a profusion of vibrant color, a perfect backdrop for touring the city's historic mansions, although many are private residences not open for tours. For those who want to visit the homes that are open to the public and see the exteriors of the city's other lovely homes and their gardens, each spring Mobile offers The Azalea Trail, a thirty-seven-mile, self-guided driving route that leads visitors through Mobile's oldest residential areas. The first Trail opened in 1930. Maps are available at the Fort Condé Welcome Center. Signs in the downtown area direct you to Fort Condé.

For information, call the Mobile Convention & Visitors Corporation at (334) 208-2000 or 1-800-5-MOBILE; their fax number is (334) 208-2060; their website is www.mobile.org.

Oakleigh Mansion

LOCATION: 350 OAKLEIGH PLACE, MOBILE, AL 36604

TELEPHONE: (334) 432-1281

FAX: (334) 432-8843

WEBSITE: www.historicmobile.org

Resting regally among the tree-canopied streets in the Oakleigh Garden District is the Oakleigh Mansion, Mobile's official period-house museum. Begun in 1833, the house was finished in 1838, though it was remodeled for another owner in the mid-1850s.

Oakleigh's half-timbered, T-shape design takes advantage of the breeze from the Gulf of Mexico. The porches in the center and on the front of each side wing enjoy the view of Oakleigh's three-and-one-half-acre lawn. An asymmetrical door on the second-floor veranda was a popular style in Mobile homes of this period. The winding, slightly off-center exterior stairway, which curves from the ground floor to the veranda, is another feature unique to Mobile homes.

Because of the simplicity of detail in its unusual design, Oakleigh stands out as an important architectural treasure. Although its architectural style is Greek Revival, the house does not have many of the frills seen in houses of the period.

When Oakleigh was constructed, the

Oakleigh Mansion
PHOTO BY A. CULPEPPER / COURTESY OF MOBILE CONVENTION AND VISITORS CORPORATION

plantation's acreage bordered the Mobile River. Cotton broker James W. Roper, a native of South Carolina, built the house on what had been a Spanish land grant. Eventually, the plantation was replaced by a neighborhood that grew up around Oakleigh. Today, this popular public home, which is the focal point of the Oakleigh Garden District, serves as the headquarters of the Historic Mobile Preservation Society.

It is a treat to visit this lovingly restored home and see the fine period furniture, the sterling silver, the china, and the gilt mirrors, which grace the old marble fireplaces. Oakleigh also offers a tour of the garden on the property. The garden is unusual because it is a "sunken garden" placed where the clay was dug to make the bricks for Oakleigh's walls. There is a gift shop on the ground floor.

The mansion is owned by the city of Mobile and managed by Historic Mobile Preservation Society. Along with the mansion, the complex includes the Cox-Deasy Cottage, which is a raised Creole cottage, typical of the houses used by middle-class city dwellers along the Gulf Coast during the 1850s. Furnished in simple nineteenth-century pieces, you can tour this cottage at no additional charge. Its authenticity complements Oakleigh, and together, the two dwellings offer a more complete view of life in Mobile in the mid-1800s.

The complex serves as a setting for artistic and educational programs throughout the year and is available for private functions. Visitors particularly enjoy the opulent Christmas-season decorations and the brilliant floral displays in March.

Open Monday through Saturday for tours; an admission is charged.

*B*ragg-Mitchell Mansion

LOCATION: 1906 SPRINGHILL AVENUE, MOBILE, AL 36607

TELEPHONE: (334) 471-6364

FAX: (334) 478-3800

WEBSITE: www.braggmitchell.com

This stately showplace in Historic Mobile reeks of Old South mystique, with Spanish moss dancing from the limbs of its ancient trees. The

Bragg-Mitchell Mansion
COURTESY OF MOBILE CONVENTION AND VISITORS CORPORATION

house gets its name from two families who previously owned the mansion.

Three Bragg brothers, whose family was originally from North Carolina, were instrumental in making the house what it is today. Judge John Bragg, who also served in the United States Congress, built the house in 1855. His brother Alexander, an architect, helped to design the house. Another brother, Confederate general Braxton Bragg, for whom Fort Bragg is named, was a frequent guest. The Mitchell name comes from Mr. and Mrs. A.S. Mitchell, who first restored the house in 1931.

During the Civil War, because of the fear of invasion, the stately old oaks around the home were cut down to give the Confederate artillery free range to shell Federal troops. Judge Bragg later re-planted the trees, using acorns from the original trees. The re-planted trees, now full and lovely, form a canopy over the grounds and home.

During the war, Bragg took his exquisite furnishings to his twelve-thousand-acre cotton plantation, located south of Montgomery. As it happened, the Yankees burned the "safe" country house and the fine furnishings, while

Bellingrath Gardens

The sixty-eight-acre former estate of Walter and Bessie Bellingrath was opened to the public in 1932, and now encompasses over nine hundred acres. The couple returned from a European tour in 1927 and began transforming a rustic fishing camp into a showplace with the aid of Mobile architect George B. Rogers.

The gardens have a distinctly English flavor, with meandering pathways, a formal rose garden, fountains, and water cascades. A riverfront "grotto" served the couple as the focal point for visitors arriving by boat.

Bellingrath Gardens

Walkways of old English flagstones were originally nineteenth-century sidewalks in nearby Mobile. The stones had arrived as ballast in the thousands of British ships used to transport Alabama cotton to mills in England. Mrs. Bellingrath made a deal with the city of Mobile. She would replace the flagstones used in the city with concrete sidewalks, if she could have the flagstones.

A rustic bridge crosses Mirror Lake and leads up to overlooks and a waterfall. Beyond a gazebo made of old wrought iron provides shelter.

The gardens are renowned for year-round color, especially in March when more than 250,000 azaleas bloom. An extensive November chrysanthemum showing is followed by a nightly light display the entire month of December.

Although it requires a separate a ticket, you can also tour the fifteen-room mansion, which was built

in 1935. Although the dates of the house's construction fall after the guidelines for coverage of this book, a tour of this English Renaissance home allows you to see the best of the old and new designs familiar to the Gulf Coast.

Open daily except Christmas; an admission is charged.

Location: 12402 Bellingrath Gardens Road, Theodore, Alabama 36582

Located twenty miles south of Mobile, Bellingrath Gardens may be reached by taking I-10 West from Mobile to Exit 15A.

Telephone: (334) 973-2217 or 1-800-247-8420

Fax: (334) 973-0540

Website: www.bellingrath.org

the home in town still stands tall and proud today.

The thirteen-thousand-square-foot, Greek Revival mansion with Italianate influences features sixteen fluted columns. One interesting feature is an asymmetrical front door. Because of this alignment, the iron-lace balcony is not over the front door, but at the center of the house. Of particular note inside is the faux mahogany in the grand dining room. Actually made of heart pine, the doors and wainscoting were hand-painted to look like mahogany. One also notices that the ceilings are fifteen feet high.

Among the period pieces displayed in the dining room are a pair of cobalt blue Sèvres urns, a sterling tea service, and hand-carved Chippendale chairs. Placed on the National Register of Historic Places in 1972, the Bragg-Mitchell House is now part of the Exploreum Museum Complex.

Open for tours Monday through Friday and Sunday afternoon; an admission is charged.

Condé-Charlotte House

LOCATION: 104 THEATRE STREET, MOBILE, AL 36602

TELEPHONE: (334) 432-4722

FAX: N/A

WEBSITE: N/A

The somewhat genteel look of this impor-

Condé-Charlotte House
COURTESY OF MOBILE CONVENTION AND VISITORS CORPORATION

tant old home may be deceiving. A 1940 restoration revealed the outline of four small, six-foot by eight-foot cells in the thick brick floor, for a part of the house once served as the city's first official jail. Although the structure was begun in 1822, it became a residence for the family of New Jersey master builder Jonathan Kirkbride in 1850.

The first-floor gallery features sturdy Tuscan columns. The Corinthian columns on the second-floor gallery give the facade a Greek Revival look, though the structure as a whole is reminiscent of the Federal style.

Partial restoration began when the Historic Mobile Preservation Society purchased the house in 1940. When The National Society of Colonial Dames of America in the State of Alabama bought the home later, they completed the restoration.

The Colonial Dames chose to use the house to showcase the history of Mobile by having each room pay artful tribute to a country whose flag formerly flew over Mobile. The rooms are decorated to reflect a particular period in the host country's history. The Colonial Dames have reconstructed and authentically furnished a 1763 English Council Chamber, a 1780 Spanish courtyard, an 1813 Federal dining room, an 1815 French sitting room, an 1825 French bedroom, and two 1860 Confederate "salon" parlors, where men may have met to discuss the forthcoming War Between the States. This unique house museum is a treat to see.

Open for tours Tuesday through Saturday; an admission is charged.

Richards D.A.R. House

LOCATION: 256 NORTH JOACHIM STREET, MOBILE, AL 36603
TELEPHONE: (334) 208-7320
FAX: (334) 208-7321
WEBSITE: pending

When Captain Charles Richards built this brick Italianate townhouse in 1860, little did he know that his prized home would someday become a bastion of Victorian elegance in twenty-first-century, downtown Mobile.

From the street, the first evidence of the fine detail work in this house is the elaborate

Richards D.A.R. House

ironwork on the facade, which is called iron lace. The four seasons are represented in the ironwork's motif. The porch floor features gray and white marble squares.

Enter the Richards D.A.R. house and note the etched Bavarian glass in the side panels surrounding the door. Next, see the unusual suspended staircase, the Carrara marble mantels, and the crystal chandelier in the formal dining room. Period furnishings appear even grander in the high-ceilinged rooms and huge double parlors.

Today, the Richards D.A.R. House is the star of the DeTonti Square Historic District. It is maintained by the city of Mobile and administered and staffed as a house museum and gift shop by the six Mobile chapters of the Daughters of the American Revolution.

Open for tours every day but Monday; an admission is charged.

Eufaula

The architectural styles of the Old South are well represented in Eufaula. The town sits on a bluff over the Chattahoochee River, an area chosen in 1823 by planters from Georgia who were seeking more fertile soil. Along with the money that came from the cotton grown in this rich soil came big houses and local businesses. By the 1840s and 1850s, Eufaula was booming.

During the Civil War, the residents of Eufaula were loyal secessionists who sent six companies to fight for the Confederate cause. After the war, Eufaula's loss of cotton production was devastating to the local economy. By 1880, the venerable town was again prospering because of textile mills and railways.

Today, historic tourism and outdoor recreation are the big businesses in Eufaula. The town is a mecca for bass fishermen who come to try their luck at Lake Eufaula.

Your first stop in Eufaula should be the neoclassical Shorter Mansion. Although not included in this book because it was built in 1884 and remodeled to its present grandeur in 1906, it is still an elegant and elaborate house, with eighteen Corinthian-capped columns and an outstanding, ornate frieze beneath the roof.

Shorter Mansion houses the Eufaula Historical Museum and serves as headquarters for the Eufaula Heritage Association. Located at 340 North Eufaula Avenue, the mansion is open year-round. There is an admission. For additional information, call the Eufaula Tourism Council at 1-800-524-7529.

Fendall Hall

LOCATION: 917 WEST BARBOUR STREET, EUFAULA, AL 36027
TELEPHONE: (334) 687-8469
FAX: (334) 687-8469
WEBSITE: www.preserveala.org (Alabama Historical Commission's website)

It is a safe bet that the restoration of Fendall Hall is historically accurate because the Alabama Historical Commission now owns the house. The commission has restored the house to reflect the period during its 1880-1916 occupancy.

Completed in 1860, Fendall Hall was built by E.B. Young, a banker and merchant, and Ann Fendall Beall Young. This unusual house has a strong Italianate influence, but its style is more eclectic than most Italianates. The couple chose the Italianate townhouse style because of its popularity in the years between 1850 and 1870. The house remained in the Young family for five generations, until 1972.

As you enter the foyer, notice the black-and-white marble floor. Between viewing the striking floor and the Waterford crystal

Fendall Hall
COURTESY OF FENDALL HALL

chandelier, be sure not to miss the marvelous Victorian-era murals, hand-painted in the 1880s by a traveling French artist called Monsieur LeFranc. These murals decorate the entry hall, parlor, and dining room. The murals are a must-see if you're in the area, for they are considered to be among the finest in the country. In the early twentieth century, the hallway murals were covered with wallpaper. The wallpaper has been removed, and the murals in all three rooms have been carefully restored.

Other than the fine Victorian furnishings and decor, Fendall Hall offers another interesting feature for a house of its age—indoor plumbing that worked by using attic cisterns.

Open for tours on Monday through Saturday; closed on state holidays; an admission is charged.

Montgomery

Montgomery is a state capital that was once, for a short time, also a national capital. The state of Alabama chose Montgomery as its capital in 1846. When Jefferson Davis was sworn in as president of the newly formed Confederate States of America (CSA) in 1861, Montgomery was named the Confederate capital. It remained the capital for three months before Richmond, which was more strategically located, was chosen. In some circles, Montgomery is still called the "Cradle of the Confederacy."

About one hundred years after being named CSA capital, Montgomery made national news as the birthplace of the civil rights movement. Today, it is home to the Civil Rights Memorial, which has averaged 17,000 visitors per month since its 1989 dedication.

Montgomery is also the home of the Alabama Shakespeare Festival, the Montgomery Museum of Fine Arts, and the Scott and Zelda Fitzgerald Museum.

One of the newest and best attractions in Montgomery is Old Alabama Town. It's a walk-through historic district that provides a good glimpse of life in the 1850s. It begins with a tête-à-tête under a scuppernong arbor. For information, contact the Montgomery Convention and Visitors Development at (334)

261-1100 or 1-800-240-9452, or visit the visitors center, located at 300 Water Street, inside historic Union Station.

*F*irst White House of the Confederacy

LOCATION: 644 WASHINGTON AVENUE,
   MONTGOMERY, AL 36104
TELEPHONE: (334) 242-1861
FAX: N/A
WEBSITE: www.montgomerychamber.com

When William Sayre built this historically significant structure in the 1830s, it was a simple frame house, comfortable but unassuming. It was remodeled into an Italianate-style house in the 1950s.

Now sitting across the street from the Alabama State Capitol, which is an awesome structure in itself, this house was the ideal residence for the Jefferson Davis family. For the three months in 1861 that Montgomery was the Confederate capital, the Davises made their home at the corner of Bibb and Lee Streets. In 1920, the house was moved to 664 Washington Avenue by dividing the structure into three parts and placing the parts on wooden logs and rolling them uphill for almost eleven blocks.

Many guests, who later became well-known

First White House of the Confederacy
COURTESY OF MONTGOMERY AREA CHAMBER OF COMMERCE

historical figures, were received in the downstairs parlors. The second-floor bedrooms and a nursery were reserved for the first family.

Today, the home is much the way it was when the Davis family resided in Montgomery. It is furnished with period antiques, a few of the Davises' possessions, and Civil War memorabilia.

Open Monday through Friday for tours; free admission.

Selma

Located in southwestern Alabama, Selma is a lovely town of about twenty-four thousand people. Because its location on the Alabama River made it a transportation center, Selma was once home to the state's cotton aristocracy. Today, Selma is better known for the 1965 voting rights march across the Edmund Pettus Bridge. Martin Luther King, Jr., led the march, which proved to be a pivotal factor in our nation's struggle for equal voting rights. The fifty-four-mile route has been named an All American Road and a National Historic Trail. Every year in early March, The Bridge Crossing Jubilee commemorates the Selma to Montgomery march.

On a visit to present-day Selma, you can browse along Water Avenue, a restored antebellum riverfront warehouse district complete with old brick streets. The district is a must-see in Selma, as are the shops and restaurants at the Riverfront Market.

Selma's Old Town Historic District is the largest historic district in the state, with more than 1,200 antebellum and Victorian structures, dating from the 1820s. The St. James Hotel, which was built around 1837, was recently restored to its grand 1830s style. The hotel now stands as a tribute to its original era.

The annual Selma Pilgrimage is a popular

Sturdivant Hall
COURTESY OF ALABAMA BUREAU OF TOURISM AND TRAVEL/ KARIM SHAMSI BASHA

springtime event, and a good time to see some of the grand old homes not otherwise accessible. For information, call the Selma Chamber of Commerce at (334) 875-7241 or 1-800-45-SELMA.

Sturdivant Hall

LOCATION: 713 MABRY STREET, SELMA, AL 36701
TELEPHONE: (334) 872-5626
FAX: N/A
WEBSITE: www.SelmaAlabama.com

The late Edward V. Jones, the architect of the White House in Washington, D.C., called Sturdivant Hall "the finest Greek Revival neoclassical antebellum mansion in the Southeast." Built in 1853 by Thomas Helm Lee, this grand home is Greek Revival in proportion, but the ornate cast-iron balcony on the second story and the side portico denote an Italian influence. Sturdivant Hall was built at a cost of $69,000, a princely sum in 1853, but unbelievably low by today's standards.

The front of the house features six Corinthian columns, a recessed portico on the first and second stories, and a center cupola. The decorative plasterwork and moldings feature a motif of intertwined grape leaves and vines. The period furnishings are American, with many pieces original to the Sturdivant family, who gave the city $50,000 in 1957 to house their collection of antiques. Because of their generosity, the historic house museum, which is owned by the Sturdivant Museum Association, bears their name.

Other interesting features include servant pulls that each have a different tone and a collection of antique dolls. A gift shop is located in the original kitchen of the home. Formal gardens feature native foliage and flowers, which are at their best in the spring.

Open for tours Tuesday through Saturday; an admission is charged.

Demopolis

Demopolis officially got its start in 1817, when aristocrats who were fleeing France, settled here. The French immigrants designed a "city of the people" and planned to cultivate vineyards and olive groves. As it happened, the French aristocrats had no talent for farming and less tolerance for the climate, so they soon gave up and abandoned the property.

On the other hand, Southern planters found the soil in the area ideal for growing cotton. Bumper cotton crops have been produced in the Black Belt region of Alabama since the mid-1820s. The prime location along the river basin aided the cotton planters. Today, Demopolis welcomes visitors who come in from the Tennessee-Tombigbee Waterway or the highway. These visitors leave with an appreciation for the town's historic value and its appeal as a New/Old South town.

For information, contact the Demopolis Chamber of Commerce at (334) 289-0270.

Gaineswood

LOCATION: 805 SOUTH CEDAR, DEMOPOLIS, AL 36732
TELEPHONE: (334) 289-4846
FAX: (334) 289-1027
WEBSITE: www.demopolis.com/gaineswood/

Gaineswood has been called the grandest Greek Revival home in Alabama. Once you see it, you will know why. The superb house was originally a two-room cabin built by United

Gaineswood
COURTESY OF ALABAMA BUREAU OF TOURISM AND TRAVEL/
KARIM SHAMSI BASHA

States Indian factor General George Gaines in 1821.

In 1843, the cabin and surrounding property were sold to Nathan Bryan Whitfield, a North Carolina native with many talents. A cotton planter, Whitfield used his wealth and creative abilities to implement his plans for a grand mansion. Over a span of eighteen years, he enlarged the cabin into his dream home, improvising when the mood struck him and money was available. The house now reflects the genius of the man who planned it, as well as his affinity for spaciousness and freedom of movement

The result of all the enlarging and remodeling of Gaineswood is that its domes and roof resemble Thomas Jefferson's Monticello, though other descriptions have called it "a plantation palace." Gaineswood boasts four exterior colonnades, with each side offering a different look. On the roof, Whitfield also added a circular platform, surrounded by a balustrade.

While the exterior is impressive, the interior is resplendent. Whitfield was particular about details, and he thoroughly researched the work on his house, using Greek Revival art and architecture handbooks as his guides.

If he couldn't find what he wanted, he had it made, often using the talents of the slaves on his plantation. It is believed that slaves did much of the decorative plasterwork, and a letter written by Whitfield indicates a slave named Issac [sic] made the columns.

Prominent throughout the interior are the transoms, where you'll see art glass depicting mythological scenes. Whitfield even ordered silver doorknobs and French hand-blocked wallpaper.

In a clever design move, Whitfield made the parlor and dining room exact replicas of each other. A hall divides the two, but each has identical plaster ornamentation and a domed ceiling. Atop each dome is a circular window lantern.

The huge drawing room measures twenty by thirty feet. Twenty-eight fluted columns and pilasters surround the room. The coffered ceiling has ornate plaster medallions. The identical vis-à-vis mirrors on each side of the room endlessly reflect the room's features, creating the illusion of infinity.

Like Jefferson, Whitfield was a Renaissance man of his time. Musically, you can see this in the hand-cranked barrel organ he designed and had built.

Apparently Whitfield was also an engineering genius. He used a team of mules walking around a shaft in circles to power the workshops where much of the work for the house was done.

When the house was not finished in time for his son Bryan's wedding, Whitfield compensated for an unfinished wall in the drawing room by stretching a big piece of canvas across the area and painting a row of columns. It became a *trompe l'oeil* colonnade.

Whitfield died in 1868, but Gaineswood remained in the family until the 1920s. Two other families owned the house before it was purchased by the state of Alabama in 1966. The Alabama Historical Commission (AHC) restored the home from 1971 to 1975.

The magnificent Gaineswood has been open to the public as a house museum under AHC stewardship since 1975. Listed as a National Historic Landmark, the house contains original furnishings returned by Whitfield descendants. There is a gift shop on the premises.

If you can see only one house in Alabama, it should be Gaineswood.

Open daily for tours; an admission is charged.

Bluff Hall
COURTESY OF ALABAMA BUREAU OF TOURISM AND TRAVEL/
KARIM SHAMSI BASHA

Bluff Hall

LOCATION: 405 NORTH COMMISSIONERS
AVENUE, DEMOPOLIS, AL 36732
TELEPHONE: (334) 209-0282
FAX: (334) 289-9644
WEBSITE: N/A

Named because it sits on a bluff of the Tombigbee River, Bluff Hall was built by slave labor in 1832, at a time when something called a "civil war" could not be imagined.

The sturdy Federal-style brick house was Allen Glover's wedding gift to his daughter. The home evolved into a modified Greek-Revival style after later additions around 1840.

The two-and-one-half-story brick, stuccoed facade features Doric columns on the portico and delicate carved scalloping on the bargeboards and under the eaves. The door is centered, with a semi-elliptical fan on top and round-arched sidelights. Corinthian columns are used as design elements in the drawing room.

Owned by the Marengo County Historical Society, the house has been restored with furnishings from the Empire and mid-Victorian periods. Special highlights include the symbol of a "debt-free home," which you can find by looking in the newel post's amity button as you head upstairs. There is also a room of memorabilia from the French aristocrats who came to settle the Vine and Olive Colony.

Open for tours Tuesday through Saturday; an admission is charged.

Eutaw

Eutaw is a quaint, small town, built around a courthouse square. It is also a treasure trove of antebellum houses. In fact, twenty-five of Eutaw's structures are listed on the National Register of Historic Places. Although many of these homes are private residences not open to the public, it is still a charming place to visit.

There is a Visitors Center in the Vaughn-Morrow House at 310 Main Street, but the center is not open consistently. For information, call the Eutaw Chamber of Commerce at (205) 372-9002.

Kirkwood

LOCATION: 111 KIRKWOOD DRIVE, EUTAW, AL 35462
TELEPHONE: (205) 372-9009
FAX: (205) 372-0602
WEBSITE: www.kirkwoodplant.com

Begun in 1850, Kirkwood was not quite completed at the outbreak of the Civil War. The beginning of the war ended Foster Mark Kirksey's plans to have one of the South's most splendid plantation homes. His plans eventually came to fruition, but long after Kirksey was gone.

After the home languished for many years following the departure of the last Kirksey heir, a lawyer and his wife from Washington, D.C., toured the home and decided they had to buy the antebellum, Greek Revival-style Kirkwood. They spent the next fifteen years restoring it. Their efforts won an Honor Award from the National Trust for Historic Preservation, and Kirkwood received a listing on the National Register of Historic Places. Kirkwood has also won the Great American Homes Award for Bed & Breakfast Restoration, has been recognized in national and regional publications, and was featured on Bob Villa's "American Homes" television show.

As you come into Eutaw from the west, you're sure to spot this imposing mansion,

Kirkwood

standing proud and picture-perfect on the left side of the street. It has eight massive Ionic columns, and the cupola sits perched atop the house like a high hat.

Antiques of the period are used throughout. One of the highlights is an exquisite Waterford chandelier. The houses includes many Kirksey family antiques and memorabilia, including some of the family letters and documents that were found in an old trunk in the attic.

Today, new owner Sherry Vallides is in residence operating Kirkwood as a daily tour home and a bed-and-breakfast inn.

Open daily for tours; an admission is charged.

Birmingham

Founded in 1871, Birmingham is considered a young town. Since its birth, this city of close to a million people has made great strides, first as a steel town and now as a banking, medical, commercial, and service center for the South. Now Alabama's largest city, Birmingham is surrounded by great green hills, which are actually small mountains.

The downtown area offers shopping, dining, and sites, such as the most impressive Birmingham Civil Rights Institute and the Birmingham Museum of Art. You'll find good antiques shops in and around the area of Five Points.

The only antebellum house in or near Birmingham is Arlington, which is about thirty years older than the town. For information on Birmingham, call the Birmingham Convention & Visitors Bureau at (205) 458-8000 or 1-800-458-8085.

Arlington

LOCATION: 331 COTTON AVENUE,
BIRMINGHAM, AL 35211
TELEPHONE: (205) 780-5656
FAX: N/A
WEBSITE: N/A

When Judge William S. Mudd began construction of his Greek Revival-style mansion, the only nearby community was the tiny town of Elyton. Judge Mudd went on to become one of the ten founders of the city of Birmingham, and the new city grew up around Arlington.

The actual date of construction is uncertain. According to some reports, the house was actually built in 1822 and enlarged to its present size in 1842. When it was first built, Arlington was pure Greek Revival in style. It had six giant square columns. Both the columns and the entablature were paneled. Sidelights surrounded the doors. A later owner, Robert Munger, added Colonial Revival features inside and out when he renovated the home at the turn of the century. Munger also added a second-story balcony in front and a rear portico.

The one thing that may have saved Arlington from destruction during the Civil War was its use by Union general James Wilson. He used it as his headquarters when his troops were in the area. From Arlington, General Wilson issued the orders to burn the University of Alabama at Tuscaloosa and to destroy the iron furnaces in the area.

Mooresville

Mooresville is situated between Decatur and Huntsville. It seems a bit of a dichotomy to find a tiny town that is older than the state itself so close to Alabama's sprawling space-age city of Huntsville. The town of Mooresville, which was incorporated in 1818, provides the rare treat of seeing a place where time seems to stand still. In Mooresville, you'll find that the puny trees planted by the settlers around 1818 are now giant oaks that serve as canopies over the old buildings.

All twelve of Mooresville's square blocks are listed on the National Register of Historic Places. Here, there's a great amount of pride in preserving the past. All the buildings are still in use today.

The first weatherboard house was built by Robert Donnell, a staunch Presbyterian minister who later served as minister of the nearby red brick church. The church was built around 1820. An original chandelier that survived the Civil War still hangs in the church, though the slave balcony was boarded up after the war.

After a split in the church's congregation, a new church, which became a Church of Christ, was built in 1854. It was from the pulpit of this little church that James A. Garfield read from the Bible while his troops were camped nearby during the Civil War. Garfield later became president of the United States. Another former president named Andrew Johnson once worked as a tailor's apprentice in Mooresville.

You'll also find an 1828 stagecoach inn and a post office that still features original mailboxes used in the mid-1800s.

You can purchase a booklet called "A Walking Tour of Mooresville" at the post office. For more information, contact the Alabama Mountain Lakes Association (phone numbers are listed below.)

Group tours are by appointment.

Location: Located between Decatur and Huntsville, take the Mooresville exit off I-565.
Telephone: (256) 350-3500 or 1-800-648-5381
Fax: N/A
WEBSITE: N/A

Arlington
COURTESY OF ALABAMA BUREAU OF TOURISM AND TRAVEL

After the city of Birmingham built up around the illustrious Arlington, the city purchased the home in the 1950s. Renovation began shortly thereafter, when fifty prominent citizens donated funds for renovation. Today it is a tour home and museum that displays an extensive collection of textiles, silver, paintings, decorative arts, and Southern-made furniture, as well as fine English pieces.

Open daily for tours, except Monday; an admission is charged.

Valley Head

The small town of Valley Head is sometimes overshadowed by nearby Ft. Payne and even Mentone, but it's a special place of its own. Located in the northeast mountain region of Alabama, north of Ft. Payne, it is just off I-59. Valley Head is thirty-five miles south of Chat-

tanooga, Tennessee. For more information about Valley Head and the vicinity, contact the DeKalb County Tourism Association at (256) 845-3957.

Winston Place

LOCATION: P.O. BOX 165, VALLEY HEAD, AL 35989
Located in downtown Valley Head, take Exit 231 off I-59, and go east on Ala. Hwy. 117.
TELEPHONE: (256) 635-6381 OR (888) 4-WINSTON
FAX: (256) 635-1904
WEBSITE: www.virtualcities.com

Three generations of the same family have lovingly maintained this massive old mansion. If the house wasn't enough to attract visitors, there's the added perk of its location at Valley Head. The area is known for its mountains and natural beauty, and at Winston Place, Lookout Mountain seems to soar up from just behind the Greek Revival-style house. It also has plenty of porches from which to view the mountains.

Long before owner Leslie Bunch's grandfather bought the house from Mary Tutwiler, it was a place with strong family ties to England. The Duke of Marlborough and Winston Churchill are included in the family tree. The descendants of the three Winston brothers who

Winston Place

came to "the colonies" in the late 1600s in search of adventure include Dolley Madison, Patrick Henry, and William Overton Winston, the lawyer who built Winston Place in the 1830s.

During the Civil War, about thirty thousand uninvited guests arrived at the rambling white-frame mansion. High-ranking Union officers occupied the house, while Union troops camped on the lawn. Union general Jefferson Cullman Davis, a cousin of CSA president Jefferson Davis, planned strategy for the Battle of Chickamauga here.

A new feature in the house is a line of textiles from Crown Crafts, which chose Winston Place to introduce a line of comforters, linens, decorative pillows, and such. Winston Place served as inspiration for the vintage colors used in these products. The products look perfectly at home in the antique bedrooms of this great old family home, which is now a bed-and-breakfast inn.

Winston Place may be toured with advance reservations; an admission is charged.

Florida

In a state known for bright sun, white sand, and azure water, antebellum mansions are not a priority. Perhaps as a result, they are not in great supply. When people in neighboring states were building mansions, Florida was still wet and wild. It wasn't admitted to the Union until 1845.

Floridians cherish their 1,800 miles of coastline and seemingly endless inland rivers and waterways. Add year-round warmth, the entertainment industry of Disney, world-class golf, nature trails and parks, shopping meccas, and you can see why the state attracts millions of annual visitors and a plethora of retirees who seek Florida's own special brand of gold for their golden years.

The Sunshine State offers thousands of beach cottages and upscale private and public accommodations. Victorian structures are abundant, and the art-deco districts around Miami are flourishing. However, because the format of this book concentrates on mansions built during the seventeenth and eighteenth centuries, there are less entries for this state than the other Southern states. Although Florida has many grand mansions, such as Villa Viscaya in Miami and Ca D'zan in Sarasota, these home were built during the early twentieth century.

For information on Florida's myriad attractions, call the Florida Attractions Association at (850) 222-2885 or 1-888-735-2872.

Tallahassee

Tallahassee is a capital city that has managed to maintain its charm. You'll find politics aplenty, but you will also find unexpected pleasures: lush parks, towering and flowering trees, unspoiled historic districts, and an old capitol restored to its former glory, complete with festive striped awnings.

According to legend, Tallahassee was established as the capital in 1823, when South Florida was still relatively undeveloped. The story goes that two explorers set off—one on horseback from St. Augustine, the other by boat from Pensacola—to find a central location for the seat of government. They met at a lovely site that the Creek and Seminole Indians called "talla hassie." This is it, the two explorers said, and indeed it was.

One of the grand mansions in the city, The Columns, which was built around 1830, now houses the Tallahassee Area Chamber of Commerce. It is the oldest surviving building within the original city limits of Tallahassee.

The capital city is proud of its outstanding amenities, and the tourism office will be pleased to tell you more about everything from museums to mansions. Contact the Leon County Tourism Development Council at (850) 413-9200 or 1-800-628-2866.

The Knott House

LOCATION: 301 EAST PARK AVENUE, TALLAHASSEE, FL 32301
TELEPHONE: (850) 922-2459
FAX: (850) 413-7261
WEBSITE: The Knott House is listed on the Florida Department of State's website (www.dos.state.fl.us) under "historic sites."

This house has a rare distinction for a Southern house built in the mid-1800s. It is believed that the house was built in 1843 by George Proctor, a free black carpenter. Attorney Thomas Hagner and his wife Catherine were the original owners of this gracious, Classical Revival house. Used as a boardinghouse during the Civil War, Union brigadier general Edward McCook read the Emancipation Proclamation from the front steps of this building, thus ensuring that black Floridians knew of their freedom.

The house also had another connection to African-American history. In the 1890s, the medical practice of Dr. George Betton was housed here, and Florida's first black physician, William Gunn, received early training from Dr. Betton.

The William V. Knott family purchased the eight-thousand-square-foot house in 1928. William Knott was Florida's first state auditor,

Knott House
COURTESY OF TALLAHASSEE CONVENTION
AND VISITORS BUREAU

and he later served successive terms as comptroller and state treasurer. His wife Luella was a poet, a musician, and a local temperance leader.

During their ownership, the Knotts added columns to the front of the house and filled the house with their unique collection of Victorian furniture. Today, four massive columns still support a center portico that covers a pediment with a small balcony over the front door. Four shuttered windows run across the front on the first and second stories.

Luella was an artistic woman who wrote light-hearted and humorous poetry to her antique furniture. She would then tie the poems to the furniture with festive satin ribbons. Perhaps this was her way of keeping an upbeat outlook while the country was in the turmoil of the Great Depression.

After the couple's death, their son, John Charles "Charlie" Knott, inherited the house. After his death, Charlie bequeathed the house and everything in it to the people of Florida for use as a house museum. The house is now restored to its 1928 appearance, complete with the Victorian furnishings that sport Luella's whimsical poems.

The state of Florida operates the Knott House Museum for the education and enjoyment of the public. A daylily garden and a gift shop are on the site.

Open for tours on Wednesday, Thursday, Friday, and Saturday; check for tour times, as they vary; admission is free.

*B*rokaw-McDougall House

LOCATION: 329 NORTH MERIDIAN STREET,
   TALLAHASSEE, FL 32312
TELEPHONE: (850) 891-3900
FAX: (850) 891-3902
WEBSITE: N/A

It took four years—from 1856 to 1860—to build this house, but it has changed little since that time. Peres Bonney Brokaw came south from New Jersey in 1840. In Tallahassee, he and a partner operated a successful livery stable. Brokaw married in 1850 and began construction of this house six years later. He eventually became prominent in city and state governments.

One of the Brokaw daughters, who married a McDougall, inherited the house. Thus the house is known as the Brokaw-McDougall House.

The Brokaw-McDougall House is a Classical Revival/Italianate two-story frame structure. It features a cupola and a porch running the width of the front. The second story duplicates the first, except it has windows instead of French doors. Six Corinthian columns support the roof. Sidelights and a transom surround the front door. Inside, the high ceilings and heart-pine floors show off the furniture and decorative arts.

According to local legend, a New York landscape architect designed the gardens before the Civil War. It is surmised that he may have suggested the planting of the four live oak trees that still stand. The Florida Federation of Garden Clubs, in cooperation with the Historic Tallahassee Preservation Board, spent two years restoring the gardens.

The house was sold to the state of Florida in 1973 and is now used for receptions and as

Brokaw-McDougall House
COURTESY OF TALLAHASSEE CONVENTION AND VISITORS BUREAU

offices for the Historic Tallahassee Preservation Board. Tours may be arranged in advance, but if you arrive by chance and a staff member is available, they will offer you a casual tour.

Casual tours on occasion; admission is free.

Goodwood Museum and Gardens

LOCATION: 1600 MICCOSUKEE ROAD,
 TALLAHASSEE, FL 32308
TELEPHONE: (850) 877-4202
FAX: (850) 877-3090
WEBSITE: www.goodwoodmuseum.org

This house looks somewhat Victorian, though it predates the Victorian period. Built in the 1830s by Bryan Croom, Goodwood's looks are deceiving, for the house is much larger than it appears. The central hall is about fifty-five feet in length.

The estate known as Goodwood was

Goodwood Museum and Gardens
COURTESY OF GOODWOOD MUSEUM AND GARDENS

assembled in the early 1830s by Hardy Croom of North Carolina. His plans for a full-time Florida residence were dashed when he, his wife, and all three of their children perished in the sinking of their steamship while en route to Florida. Hardy's brother, Bryan, completed the main house and established it as the centerpiece for his extensive Florida landholdings. To enhance his new home, Bryan Croom ordered the doors and windows from New York. After the materials arrived, he, a master carpenter, and skilled laborers did all of the work themselves.

In the 1850s, Goodwood was a successful plantation with cotton growing on its 2,400 acres. After the Civil War, agriculture declined and acreage was sold. By the 1880s, only 160 acres remained.

When Fanny Tiers bought the property in

1911, major renovations began. Fanny wanted her home to be more "Southern," so she eliminated the Italianate elements, such as the wrought-iron grillwork around the front porch. Across the front, she added slender columns, which support an open gallery or porch. She also replaced the plain square cupola with an octagonal one.

Inside, ornate modeled plaster rosettes set off the chandeliers. There are also frescoed ceilings in the two sitting rooms on the main floor. Gilt mirrors and window cornices enrich the Victorian decor.

In 1925, Goodwood became the home of Florida state senator William C. Hodges and his wife and mother. In 1990, Tom Hood, Goodwood's last owner, bequeathed the house and lovely, impressive gardens to Goodwood Museum and Gardens, Inc., a nonprofit foundation established to provide for the restoration, care, maintenance, support, and success of Goodwood as a museum and public park.

Today the house is restored to its appearance in the early 1900s, though restoration is an ongoing process.

Open for tours Thursday and Friday; an admission fee is charged.

Old Capitol Museum

Florida has a history unique to the United States. Long before the United States came into its own, Florida attracted European explorers who were charting a new world. They were apparently enchanted with this long stretch of land with water almost everywhere.

From 1763 to 1783, the British divided the land in northern Florida. The result was two capitals—one in St. Augustine, the other in Pensacola.

Territorial legislators grew weary of conducting business in two places several hundred miles apart, so they choose Tallahassee as a central location. When Florida became an American territory after a treaty with Spain in 1821, the region was still wild and unsettled. Tallahassee became the official capital in 1824, and government business was transacted in a log cabin for two years before a temporary capitol was constructed. In 1839, the United States Congress appropriated $20,000 to build a suitable capitol. The new building was completed in 1845, the year Florida became a state. By the 1880s, an economic boom was underway, and the capitol needed repair. It was updated and renovated. Running water was installed, a small cupola was placed on top, and later, boldly striped awnings were added.

Around the turn of the century, "capital removal" became a political issue, and the site for the capital city was finally put to a vote. Tallahassee won out over St. Augustine, Jacksonville, and Ocala. The legislature appropriated $75,000 to do a second renovation on the capitol and to expand the statehouse. Architect Frank Pierce Milburn was hired to create a new look for the old capitol. He added a copperized iron dome, a "subdome" of colorful art glass, and other elements that enhanced the architectural look of the building. The renovation was completed in 1902.

The Old Capitol Museum restored to its 1902 appearance
COURTESY OF MUSEUM OF FLORIDA HISTORY

By 1923, Florida was still growing, and money was once again allocated for another renovation of the capitol. This time the architect was Henry J. Klutho, a proponent of Frank Lloyd Wright's Prairie School of design. He doubled the usable space, stayed within the prior classic design lines, and added the double-curved staircase and marble wainscoting. The building served the state well until 1977, when a skyscraper became the new state capitol. The grand old capitol was given a new life as a museum.

The bright, white "Pearl of Capitol Hill," with its majestic dome, has been beautifully restored to its 1902 grandeur. It now stands as a proud example of the good life so valued by Floridians. Inside, Florida's political history is traced in an eight-room exhibit area. Throughout the building, artifacts that helped shape Florida, turn-of-the-century furnishings, and important historical documents are on display.

The Old Capitol Museum, located in downtown Tallahassee on South Monroe Street, is open daily; there is no admission fee. For information, call (850) 487-1902.

Gamble Plantation
COURTESY OF BRADENTON AREA CONVENTION AND
VISITOR'S BUREAU / PHOTO BY JACK ELKA

$\mathcal{G}$amble Plantation

LOCATION: 3708 PATTEN AVENUE, ELLENTON,
  FL 34222
  Ellenton is located off I-75, near Bradenton.
TELEPHONE: (941) 723-4536.
FAX: (941) 723-4538
WEBSITE: N/A

If you know history, you probably know about Judah P. Benjamin, the secretary of state of the Confederate States of America. Jefferson Davis supposedly said that Benjamin was his most trusted confidant.

A brilliant man, Judah Benjamin entered Yale University at the age of fourteen and shortly thereafter began the study of law. In May 1865, when it became apparent that the Confederacy would suffer defeat, Benjamin supposedly destroyed all papers left in his charge concerning the Confederacy. He did this to prevent them from being confiscated by the Yankees.

By May 15, Benjamin had crossed the Suwannee River, with Union troops searching for him. He arrived in central Florida on May 20 and hid at Gamble until friends secured a boat for him. On May 23, he sailed for England, where he went on to have a distinguished career as a barrister and served as counsel to the queen.

Built between 1843 and 1850, the house on Gamble Plantation was the centerpiece of Major Robert Gamble's large sugar plantation. The plantation also produced sugar cane, molasses, citrus, wild grapes, and olives. As it happened, although only sixteen acres of the original plantation remain, this structure is the only surviving pre-Civil War plantation house in south Florida.

After the Seminole Indian War in 1842, the area around the Manatee River was opened to settlement. After acquiring 3,500 acres, Gamble brought 150 slaves from his Tallahassee plantation to build the house and clear the land. Much of the mansion was constructed with a primitive form of concrete called "tabby," which is a mixture of water, shells, and limestone.

The walls are two-feet thick, and the house

Cypress Gardens, Winter Haven

Although the time of its creation is later than the guidelines for this book, it did not seem proper to write about Florida and not mention Cypress Gardens—one of the state's favorite attractions. Founded in 1936, this place of beauty and awe predates the world of Disney.

Located in central Florida's Winter Haven, which is about an hour from the Disney parks in Orlando, this attraction began as a sixteen-acre public garden on the banks of lovely Lake Eloise. The gardens have evolved into a 200-plus-acre wonderland, featuring more than 8,000 varieties of plants from almost 100 countries. The thousands of tropical plants and subtropical plants, which bloom year-round, can be enjoyed from two miles of colorful, winding paths.

Cypress Gardens also offers crystal-clear lagoons, sparkling waterfalls, bronze sculptures, Italian fountains, and the natural beauty of ancient cypress trees, draped in mystical Spanish moss. As a symbol of Florida's commitment to Southern hospitality, beautifully gowned Southern belles, complete with parasols and big hoop skirts, welcome visitors as they stroll leisurely around the grounds.

Sharing billing with this floral extravaganza is the world-famous water-ski team, which performs

Gazebo Hill at Cypress Gardens

amazing feats of skill and athletics. Four shows are scheduled on Lake Eloise each day. Some shows even feature hang-gliding demonstrations. You can also see an ice-skating show and the Wings of Wonder exhibit, which features more than one thousand beautiful butterflies. There's surely something of interest for all ages.

The park in Winter Haven is open daily. There is an admission charge, so call 1-800-237-4826 or (863) 324-2111 for fees and discounts.

is designed to remain cool even in hot Florida. The two-story house features a facade with eighteen gigantic columns. The columns support the roof and upper verandas, which extend around three sides of the building. The outdoor kitchen is attached by a breezeway.

In 1925, the Judah P. Benjamin chapter of the United Daughters of the Confederacy (UDC), bought the mansion and donated it to the state of Florida to be used as a state historic site. It now stands as a memorial to Benjamin's famous escape from Florida.

The home is furnished in the style expected of a successful sugar planter in the mid-nineteenth century. It contains some Continental pieces, as well as some American-made furniture. A guided tour of the mansion explains the life and times of a Florida planter in the days of Indian uprisings and early statehood.

Open for tours Thursday through Monday; an admission fee is charged.

❧

Historic Haile Homestead

LOCATION: 8500 SW ARCHER ROAD, GAINESVILLE, FL 32608

Historic Haile Homestead is on the north side of the road approximately three miles west of I-75. After you pass Tower Road on SW Archer, it is 0.9 mile to the homestead.

TELEPHONE: (352) 372-2633

FAX: (352) 278-3931

WEBSITE: N/A

Known as Kanapaha Plantation, this house may not be a grand mansion by some standards, but it is an important Florida plantation that dates back to the 1850s. Kanapaha Plantation literally tells the story of the Haile family and of the settlement of north central Florida. It seems the Haile family had a habit of recording things by writing on the walls. One wall writing dated January 1886 says: "Bitter cold. Thick ice lasting from Friday 7th until Thursday 14th. Oranges are all frozen, ground frozen from 8th to 13th. The long-est and most severe spell of cold since we came here in 1854."

Thomas Evans Haile, his wife Serena, their relatives (Mrs. Haile's family, the Chestnuts, and Thomas's brother and mother), their children, and about four hundred slaves moved from Camden, South Carolina, to Alachua County in 1854. Haile had heard about Florida's climate and favorable growing season.

The Hailes built a house that is described as "cracker style," though it seems more traditional, almost Southern Georgian. Patterned after the family home in Camden, the simple home, which was built to last, showcases fine workmanship and creative use of native materials, including heart pine.

Built on the Hailes' 1,500-acre tract, the ten-room, one-and-one-half-story structure has about seven thousand square feet of living space under one roof. Supported by six sturdy wood columns, the roof extends over the front porch. Fourteen-foot ceilings, large windows, and louvered shutters help keep the house cool in summer.

When the Civil War came, the Hailes were staunch Confederates. Thomas and his son joined the cause, and on one occasion two members of the Confederate treasury train spent a night here as they fled to the Gulf Coast. After the war, many of the freed slaves chose to remain as tenant farmers.

After the senior Hailes died, the plantation remained with their children, who used it for family gatherings and entertaining. In 1976, the house was used in the film version of Marjorie Kinnan Rawlings' story, "Gal Young Un." After that, the property underwent a rebirth. In

St. Augustine

Founded in 1565 by the Spanish, St. Augustine still reflects its Spanish heritage in its architecture, street names, food, and art. Some of the city's historic sites include the Castillo de San Marcos National Monument, the oldest stone fort in the United States; the Fountain of Youth Discovery Park, where it is said Ponce de Leon sought everlasting youth; the Mission of Nombre de Dios, where Pedro Menendez de Aviles first set foot on Florida's shore in 1565; and the Spanish Quarter Village, a living-history museum, which interprets life in colonial St. Augustine around 1740.

Although it may not seem grand compared to some of the other houses in this guide, and it pre-dates the guidelines for this book, it seems appropriate to mention The Gonzalez-Alvarez House. The "Oldest House," as it is known, is the area's oldest surviving Spanish Colonial home. For more than a hundred years after Aviles first landed in 1565, the community was repeatedly raided and burned by both the English and pirates. The earliest confirmed date for the house's existence is documentation of a funeral here in 1727. However, archaeological evidence indicates that the site has been occupied since the early 1600s.

After the British took over St. Augustine, Major Joseph Peavett owned the house. The life of his widow, Mary (or Maria), was the basis for the novel, Maria, by Eugenia Price. Maria's second husband ran up so many gambling debts that the house had to be sold at auction in 1790. A Spaniard, Geronimo

The Gonzalez-Alvarez House
COURTESY OF ST. AUGUSTINE HISTORICAL SOCIETY

Alvarez, purchased the house. His family occupied the house for almost a hundred years.

In 1918, the St. Augustine Historical Society acquired the property. Today, the Oldest House Museum Complex includes the house, two other museums, including the only exhibit about St. Augustine's four hundred years of history, a gallery with rotating exhibits, and a museum store.

Open daily except Thanksgiving, Christmas, and Easter; an admission is charged.

Location: 271 Charlotte Street, St. Augustine, FL 32084

Telephone: (904) 824-2872

Fax: (904) 824-2569

Website: www.oldcity.com/oldhouse/

1992, the Alachua Conservation Trust and the Haile family devised a plan to open the house to the public as an interpretive center. Today, the home is sparsely furnished to allow visitors to see the wall writings. The limited furnishings that are on display came from the Haile family. Development of the property is still ongoing, but the house is now fully restored. Tours are available by appointment only at this time.

Tours by appointment; an admission fee is charged.

Kingsley Plantation

LOCATION: 11676 PALMETTO AVENUE, JACKSONVILLE, FL 32226

Located one-half mile north of the St. Johns River Ferry Landing on Rt. AIA, near Jacksonville. Please call for directions, as the site is not listed on all maps.

TELEPHONE: (904) 251-3537

FAX: (904) 251-3577

WEBSITE: www.nps.gov

Kingsley Plantation, located on Fort George Island, is unique in many ways. While documents don't provide conclusive evidence for the house's construction date, a letter from the plantation's owner at the time points to its completion date as 1798. The house has an un-usual floor plan—the two-story middle section had four corner rooms that were accessible only by outdoor porches, allowing excellent ventilation. The home, as it stands today, has a more Victorian look, as the main house was remodeled during the 1870s.

However, the most unusual aspect of this plantation might be a later owner, Zephaniah Kingsley, for whom the plantation is named. Born in Bristol, England, in 1765, Zephaniah was reared in Charleston, where his father was a prosperous merchant. The young Kingsley began a career as a West Indies merchant and participant in the slave trade before his move to Spanish Florida in 1803, where he became a planter.

During a trip to Cuba in 1806, Kingsley bought a Senegalese woman, Anta Madgigne Jai. He brought Anta back to his plantation at Laurel Grove, an area presently known as Orange Park. Anna, as her name became, presided over the household as Kingsley's wife and the mother of four of his children. Anna became a free person, a businesswoman, and a plantation owner. Apparently, even though he had once been part of the slave trade, Kingsley was alarmed by prejudice against people of color.

When Laurel Grove was destroyed during the Patriot's Rebellion in 1813, Kingsley moved into the plantation on Fort George

Island and maintained his status as a wealthy planter and respected citizen. Here, with the hard labor of approximately seventy slaves, the planation produced Sea Island cotton as its cash crop.

Kingsley advocated the Spanish system of society in which there were enslaved persons, free people of color, and white free people, and under this system he and his wife thrived economically. He was considered a student of the classics, yet he was also a nonconformist who scorned organized religion. Despite his unorthodox views, he was still a prominent and popular man in society.

In 1837, with Florida now an American territory, he moved his family to the island of Haiti. He became concerned for their livelihood in Florida if anything should happen to him. New ideas on society and race relations that had moved south with the new Americans coming into Florida had made business difficult for people such as Anna. Haiti was the only free colony in the hemisphere at the time, and the family was settled on large farms of indentured servants, who were Kingsley's former slaves. Kingsley died in New York in 1843. Anna returned to Florida before the Civil War and died in Jacksonville a few years after the war was over.

Speculation still abounds about Zephaniah Kingsley and his years at Kingsley Plantation. Through the work of preservationists and researchers with the National Park Service, the Timucuan Ecological and Historic Preserve strives to learn more and share more with the visiting public about this fascinating man's life and times. In 1955, the plantation became part of the Florida State Park system, and in 1991, it became part of the National Park Service. It is the oldest standing plantation house in Florida.

Today, the planter's residence is the visitor center. You can also tour the kitchen house, the barn, and twenty-three of the original tabby slave cabins. A historical garden demonstrates crops from the plantation era.

Open daily; admission is free.

Georgia

For most of the more than seven million people who live within its borders, Georgia is the promised land, and it's easy to understand why. The state has almost everything you'd want: beaches, mountains, glitzy cities, and quaint, small towns, where people still greet you warmly and seem genuinely glad to see you. The song "Georgia On My Mind" often brings tears to natives who have left the state, usually out of necessity.

From the islands around Savannah to the gold mines of Dahlonega in the mountains, Georgia is indeed golden. Even, the dome on Georgia's state capitol is golden. The dome is topped with gold mined from Dahlonega, the site of one of the first gold rushes in North America.

And then there's Atlanta—fast-paced, forward thinking, and constantly changing. It's the metropolis of the Southeast, the mecca for Southern arts, and the home of the internationally watched CNN. The most amazing thing about Atlanta is that it rebuilt itself in a short time. During the Civil War, the city was burned almost beyond recognition.

But even with all the high tech and high art, Georgia has not forgotten its Southern roots. It is proud to claim Margaret Mitchell, who gave us the epic *Gone With the Wind,* and just as proud of Flannery O'Connor, who told us that a good man is hard to find.

The state also reveres its historic properties. Although many old homes are private residences and inaccessible to the public, many other seventeenth- and eighteenth-century homes are available for touring. The Old South is alive and flourishing in such places as Macon, Madison, Milledgeville, and Washington. Georgia is worthy of a long road trip, so make your plans to visit.

For a free copy of the travel directory, "Georgia On My Mind," call 1-800-847-4842.

LaGrange

Founded in 1828, LaGrange is a good example of what a prosperous textile operation meant to a town. Textile money brought cultural amenities as well as jobs. Paved brick streets, the tolling of the carillon bells, and the marvelous old family homes that line the streets around LaGrange College lend an old-world charm to the town.

And while you're here, be sure to ask about the "Nancy Harts." During the Civil War, every capable woman of LaGrange, married or single, enlisted in a military company which they named the "Nancy Harts" after a famous Revolutionary War heroine. The stories about this full-fledged militia unit are quite entertaining.

For information, contact the LaGrange/Troup County Chamber of Commerce at (706) 884-8671.

Bellevue

LOCATION: 204 BEN HILL STREET,
　LAGRANGE, GA 30240
TELEPHONE: (706) 884-1832
FAX: (706) 882-8012
WEBSITE: www.lagrangechamber.com

When lawyer and statesman Benjamin Harvey Hill built his home on a twelve-hundred-acre estate in the center of lush forests

Bellevue

and farmlands in the early 1850s, he knew it was a superb Greek Revival mansion. He did not know that one day it would earn the coveted and prestigious designation of National Historic Landmark.

In the years the Hills occupied Bellevue before moving to Athens, they entertained lavishly. Many of their guests were nationally known, including Confederate president Jefferson Davis. Because of his ties to Davis, Hill was arrested at his home, in his own bedroom.

Hill served in the Georgia legislature and the United States House of Representatives before his election to the United States Senate. As a senator, Hill was called the "silver tongued orator." It was said that he influenced President Rutherford Hayes to withdraw Federal troops from the South after the Civil War.

In 1869, Judge Jesse McLendon bought

Westville Village, Lumpkin

For those who love history and want to experience things the way they were, it's always 1850 in Westville Village. Located in Lumpkin, which is just across the state line not far from Eufaula, Alabama, Westville is a functioning living-history village. Here, authentic, original buildings depict the early days of rural Georgia.

The fifteen-block village encompasses fifty-eight acres and showcases about thirty restored buildings, most of which were moved from other locations. The moving process began in 1968, and the museum village opened in 1970. The site is a project of the Westville Historic Handicrafts, Inc., a nonprofit educational corporation.

Westville is a perfect village for strolling and listening to the sounds of country life. The clang of the blacksmith's hammer is a surprisingly comforting sound, and the crunch of old wagon wheels on a dirt road is something you may never hear again. You can see ladies quilting or making candles, soap, and even syrup. If you're lucky, you can try your hand at a timeless craft.

Westville's purpose is to demonstrate and keep alive the crafts of pre-industrial America. It also offers a living-history lesson to all who are interested. Westville is located in southwestern Georgia,

Craftsmen in front of McDonald House at Westville Village
COURTESY OF WESTVILLE

on U.S. 27 about thirty-five miles south of Columbus. For more information, call (912) 838-6310.

Bellevue. The McLendon family occupied the home until the 1930s. Bellevue stood vacant until it was purchased by the Fuller E. Callaway Foundation in the 1940s. In 1942, the foundation presented Bellevue to the LaGrange Woman's Club, which owns and maintains the mansion today.

Bellevue has all of the expected amenities and elements of a Greek Revival-style home: Ionic columns, wide porticos on three sides of the house, and two stories. The impressive white house comes into view from a block away.

Inside, you'll find wonderful hand-carved

cornices over doors and windows, black marble fireplaces, and ornate ceiling medallions. In the foyer, custom-made wallpaper duplicates the original, which had deteriorated over the years.

Most of the furnishings are period, although none, with the possible exception of a piano in the parlor, are original to the house. Oriental rugs are used in some downstairs rooms, but original heart-pine floors are also visible. Elaborate woodwork sets off the high ceilings and spacious rooms.

Open for tours Tuesday through Saturday; an admission fee is charged.

Thomasville

Finding a place like Thomasville is an unexpected surprise; though once there, you won't be surprised to learn that the town won the 1998 Great American Main Street Award. The main street's attraction is that one feels the timelessness of the place. Old storefronts sport new awnings; Bradford pear trees along the wide sidewalks offer shade from the hot Georgia sun; and shops of all kinds are ready to sell you almost anything you need. My trip there with a magazine editor from New York City allowed me to see the town and appreciate Southern hospitality from her perspective. She couldn't believe people were so friendly that they made shopping a pleasure.

Back in 1887, *Harper's Magazine* named Thomasville "the best winter resort on three continents." Those are not bad accolades for rural Georgia. Since the late 1800s, Thomasville has been celebrated as a place of comfort and culture. It was about that time that wealthy Northern industrialists bought the remaining estates and transformed them into "pleasure plantations," where they spent winters languishing in the warm Southern sun. They used the plantations for quail hunting, horseback riding, and other outdoor sports. Some of the Northern families are still here today. There are approximately seventy very private plantations still in the area.

One plantation that is not private is Melhana, the Grand Plantation, where bed-and-breakfast guests are pampered in the best tradition of the Old South. First built in the 1820s and further developed in the late 1800s, Melhana, with its world-class restaurant and amenities, is truly a special place.

For information about Thomasville, contact the Welcome Center at (912) 227-7099 or 1-800-704-2350. For information about Melhana Plantation, call (912) 226-2290 or 1-888-920-3030.

Pebble Hill Plantation

$\mathcal{P}$ebble Hill Plantation

LOCATION: P.O. BOX 830, THOMASVILLE, GA 31799

Pebble Hill is located five miles south of Thomasville on Ga. Hwy. 319 South

TELEPHONE: (912) 226-2344

FAX: (912) 226-0780

WEBSITE: www.pebblehill.com

Pebble Hill Plantation was begun in the 1820s by planter and politician Thomas Jefferson Johnson. When Johnson's daughter inherited the estate, she enlarged the cotton operation. In 1850, she replaced the original house with a much finer house designed by the English architect John Wind. Northern industrialist Howard Melville Hanna purchased Pebble Hill in 1896. The house was inherited by his daughter Kate and later by Kate's daughter, Elisabeth "Pansy" Poe.

This massive plantation house is certainly one of the finest in the South. In 1850, it was a fine neo-classical house of modest proportions. When Hanna's daughter Kate inherited the house in 1901, she indulged her love for building by adding an east wing. This wing included a one-hundred-foot-long loggia. Kate also directed the construction of most of the outbuildings at Pebble Hill, including stables, a "million dollar" dairy barn, a carriage house, gatehouses, guesthouses, and service buildings.

After the house burned in 1934, it was rebuilt in 1936 on an even bigger and better scale. It is now a sprawling classical-style house, with eight Doric columns across the front and an inset entrance. There are galleries on the first and second floor. It has been said that Pebble Hill exhibits a "stately but comfortable grandeur."

Over the years, the house has hosted many famous guests, including J.P. Morgan, several of the Rockefellers, President and Mrs. Dwight Eisenhower, the Duke and Duchess of Windsor, and more recently, former President and Mrs. Jimmy Carter. It is a house made for entertaining with a country flair. Since guests were usually outdoor enthusiasts, even the art reflects the owners' love of nature. The main drawing-room walls feature murals of local wildlife. The murals were cut from an original painting to fit the existing panels. Judging from the size of the panels, the painting must have

Marvelous Old Mansions

been huge. Elsewhere, paintings of horses and hounds, bronzes, and Audubon prints are prominent. Fine antiques are used throughout the house, though it is not exclusively furnished in antiques.

"Miss Pansy," who died in 1978, established the plantation as a museum open for public tours. About 25,000 visitors tour the plantation each year.

Today it is owned and maintained by the foundation established by Mrs. Poe. In 1997, Pebble Hill Plantation was featured on the Art & Entertainment Channel's *America's Castles*.

Although closed in September, the plantation is otherwise open for tours Tuesday through Sunday; an admission fee is charged.

Savannah

If General James Oglethorpe and the group who settled Savannah in 1733 could see it now, they would be amazed. What is most amazing is that their plan to build residential and commercial buildings around public squares has not merely survived, but flourished. Savannah is indeed Georgia's colonial capital and crown jewel.

Young Savannah became a trade area for surrounding settlements, and port traffic from England soon followed. Eli Whitney's invention of the cotton gin in 1793 made Savannah the principal port for cotton plantations across the state. Savannah soon became a bastion of great wealth and grand homes. Many of the plantations from the 1820s were destroyed during William Tecumseh Sherman's fiery and famous march through Georgia. Thankfully, Savannah was spared. According to local legend, General Sherman was so captivated by Savannah that he could not torch it. Instead, in December 1864, he sent a telegram to President Abraham Lincoln offering him the city of Savannah as a Christmas gift.

Savannah's two-and-one-half-square-mile, tree-filled Historic District is a history lover's dream. Although many historic homes are private residences, you can still see and photograph their exteriors on a walking tour. One fine example of the Greek Revival style is the Champion-Harper-Fowlkes House at 230 Barnard Street.

Since the original version of *Cape Fear,* which starred Robert Mitchum, was filmed in Savannah in 1962, other film companies have followed suit. Some of the many films shot in Savannah are *Forrest Gump, Something to Talk About, Glory,* and, of course, *Midnight in the Garden of Good and Evil.* Although many natives of Savannah did not care for the way the latter depicted their city, Savannah now hosts about 14,000 visitors a day, so expect to encounter crowds almost everywhere.

Jekyll Island Club Historic District

In the 1880s, John Eugene DuBignon and his brother-in-law, Newton Finney, decided to take advantage of the southern resort boom and market this barrier island, which is located six miles off the southern coast of Georgia, as an exclusive hunting club.

In 1886, DuBignon sold the island to the newly formed, exclusive Jekyll Island Club, a club whose powerful and wealthy members included J.P. Morgan, Joseph Pulitizer, William K. Vanderbilt, and Marshall Field. Members prized the island for its isolation, landscape, and moderate climate, but they made sure they brought their exclusive lifestyle with them. Several members built "cottages," which they considered simple. Each house, however, had fifteen to twenty-five rooms.

When the clubhouse was opened in 1887, chefs and waiters from the best restaurants in New York were recruited to staff the facility. It has been said that when the club members dined together, one sixth of the world's wealth was gathered in one room.

Although the Depression took its toll on some of the members, it was finally the shortages of supplies and labor during World War II that caused the club to close. Members left the island in 1942 and the state of Georgia purchased the island in 1947. Today it is a state park with resort amenities. The one-hundred-acre National Historic Landmark District is operated by the Jekyll Island Authority through the Division of Museums and Historic Preservation. You can take one of the various guided tours of the historic district, or you can take a self-guided tour.

Although many of the homes were built after the period covered in this book, there are several that were built in the 1880s. The DuBignon Cottage was built in 1884. This house was built in the Queen Anne style with the characteristic asymmetrical plan, wrap-around porch, and detailed brackets on the second-floor porch. Today the interior and exterior are restored to their 1896-1917 appearance. The house contains period-room exhibits and is part of the guided tour.

The Moss Cottage, also known as the Macy Cottage, was built in 1896. It is representative of the Shingle Style, which was in fashion during the last quarter of the nineteenth century. It is a combination of several earlier traditions. From the Queen Anne Style, it adopted the wide porch, shingled surfaces, and asymmetrical plan. From the Colonial Revival Style came the gambrel roofs, rambling lean-to-additions, and classical columns. The Shingle Style was prevalent at the seaside resorts along the Northeast coast, so it was natural that the Jekyll Island Club members would bring this style with them.

The Clubhouse is still magnificent. It too is a good example of Queen Anne architecture, with its wrap-around porches, towers, and decorative features, such as spindles and lattice work. When it was completed in 1897, it had indoor plumbing. Telephone service was added in 1898, electricity in 1903, and an elevator in 1916. It was modified to serve as a contemporary resort in 1986, but the exterior and first floor look almost as they did when it first opened.

Although the structures described above are the ones that qualify for this book, the historic district offers numerous other restored sites. In addition to taking either the guided tour or the self-guided walking tour, another way to view the island is to rent a bicycle. The easy-to-ride biking paths, with little elevation change, offer a way to enjoy the extensive unspoiled natural areas as well as the historic buildings.

Open daily; an admission is charged for the guided tour.

Location: Jekyll Island Museum & Historic
    Preservation, 381 Riverview Drive, Jekyll
    Island, GA 31527
Telephone: (912) 635-2119
FAX: (912) 635-4420
Website: www.jekyllisland.com

Savannah has a grand selection of historic bed-and-breakfast inns, some with walled gardens. The Gastonian, which has received rave reviews from a number of publications, is a favorite. Raves and awards have also come to the Kehoe House, the Eliza Thompson House, and the Ballastone Inn.

For information, contact the Savannah Convention & Visitors Bureau at (912) 944-0456 or 1-800-444-2427.

The Green-Meldrim House

LOCATION: ON MADISON SQUARE AT 14 WEST
MACON STREET, SAVANNAH, GA 31401
TELEPHONE: (912) 233-3845
FAX: (912) 232-5559
WEBSITE: N/A

Architects agree that this National Historic Landmark is the finest surviving Gothic Revival house in the South. What makes it so important is the attention to detail paid by the architect. In 1833, an Englishman named Charles Green moved to Savannah. In 1853, Green hired John Norris, a New York architect known for his Greek Revival and Romantic designs, to build his Savannah home.

The mansion combines Gothic Revival design with the best materials, a fact quite obvious upon entering the imposing cast-iron entrance. Interesting features include windows that slide into hidden wall pockets, silver-plated hardware, and a domed, spiral staircase illuminated by a skylight. When it was built, the mansion was considered the epitome of luxury because it had indoor bathrooms and running water. Although you might think that's why General Sherman commandeered it as his headquarters when he arrived in Savannah, in reality, Green is said to have invited General Sherman to use his house.

Many unusual architectural features set this house apart. The front entrance features three sets of doors. The heavy outer double doors fold in and form a small closet on either side of the entrance. The second set of doors has glass inserts for light. The third set is louvered for ventilation. The black walnut woodwork on the interior is intricately carved. The house also contains superb crown moldings and marble mantels in each room. The graceful curved stairway is a trademark of the architect.

St. John's Episcopal Church has owned the home since 1943. It is lovingly cared for and serves as the church's parish house.

Open for tours Tuesday, Thursday, Friday, and Saturday, except December 15-January 15 and the two weeks prior to Easter; donations are appreciated.

Isaiah Davenport House

*I*saiah Davenport House

LOCATION: 324 EAST STATE STREET,
   SAVANNAH, GA 31401
TELEPHONE: (912) 236-8097
FAX: (912) 233-7938
WEBSITE: N/A

Built in 1820, the Davenport House is recognized as one of the great Federal houses in America. Its somewhat somber brick exterior leads to a surprising interior of fine architectural details. Master builder Isaiah Davenport built the house for himself, which may be why it is so rich in fine woodwork and plasterwork. Davenport, a native of Rhode Island, came from a shipbuilding family.

The creamy yellow parlor with its high ceilings features ornate molding and woodwork. There are recessed columns near each window. An arch of molding connects the columns, with a pier mirror in between. A crystal chandelier is suspended from a ceiling medallion. Period furniture, including pieces by Chippendale, Hepplewhite, and Sheraton, are featured, as well as a superb collection of Davenport china.

By the 1930s, this once great structure had become a tenement, divided into many small apartments. Oilcloth covered the filthy floors, bare bulbs hung from electric cords, and wallpaper hung in tatters. By 1955, plans were under way to demolish the structure to make way for a parking lot. A group of outraged ladies raised $22,500 to save the house, and the Historic Savannah Foundation was born. The foundation has since come to the rescue of numerous other worthy structures around the city.

In the basement of the home is the foundation's museum shop, which features specialty items unique to Savannah and to Isaiah Davenport's time. Proceeds from the shop support the preservation projects of the foundation.

Open daily for tours; an admission fee is charged.

Juliette Gordon Low House

LOCATION: 10 EAST OGLETHORPE AVENUE,
SAVANNAH, GA 31401
TELEPHONE: (912) 233-4501
FAX: (912) 233-4659
WEBSITE: N/A

Juliette Gordon Low House

This three-story Regency-style townhouse gets a lot of attention for its historical significance. The house was begun in 1818 for James M. Wayne, who was the mayor of Savannah at the time but later became a Supreme Court justice. The house's architect is unknown.

In 1831, Wayne sold his home to his niece Sarah Gordon and her family. Their granddaughter Juliette married Englishman William McKay Low. Juliette Gordon Low's philanthropic work with Girl Guides led to the establishment of the Girl Scouts of the USA.

In 1965, the house, which is located in the heart of Savannah's Historic District, was the first Savannah site to be declared a National Historic Landmark. One special feature is a small porch with four Tuscan columns. A double-door set within a recessed arch opens to the balcony above. The house sits on a raised basement with brownstone steps leading to the door.

The interior of the house, with its fine classical moldings and plasterwork, is a lovely example of quiet elegance. Restored to its 1886 splendor, the interior is Victorian, complete with documented colors and a curved leather club fender in front of the fireplace in the library. Sliding doors connect double parlors, which each have a grand crystal chandelier. Another prominent feature of the house is a massive bookcase in the library.

The house remained in the Gordon family until it was purchased by the Girl Scouts in 1953. Affectionately called "the Birthplace," the house is now visited by thousands of Girl Scouts and their families from across the country. There is a museum shop on the site.

Open for tours every day except Wednesday, except for the first two weeks in January; an admission fee is charged.

The Owens-Thomas House

LOCATION: 124 ABERCORN STREET,
SAVANNAH, GA 31401
TELEPHONE: (912) 233-9743
FAX: (912) 233-0102
WEBSITE: www.telfairmuseumofart.org

The Owens-Thomas House

This National Historic Landmark is one of the five houses in Savannah's Historic District that was designed by William Jay. These five houses are called the "little palaces." Like its sisters, this house is considered one of the country's finest examples of the English Regency period. The Owens-Thomas House is perhaps the best example of Jay's work because it is the only structure still unaltered. It is also the only early nineteenth-century townhouse complex in Savannah that still has its original slave quarters and carriage house intact.

Built between 1816 and 1819 for cotton broker Richard Richardson and his wife, who was William Jay's sister-in-law, the property stretches the depth of a full city block. After the Richardsons lost their home in 1820, it became an elegant boarding house. In 1830, George Welchman Owens, a politician and lawyer, bought the property for $10,000. It remained in the Owens family until 1951, when Owens's granddaughter bequeathed it to the Telfair Academy of Arts and Sciences.

After entering through an iron gate, you proceed through the small front garden and up steps that curve gently on either side of the portico, which is supported by Ionic columns. The entrance, which is an alcove doorway protected by the slightly curved portico, sits shyly behind these columns. Two uniform windows flank each side of the entrance. A Palladian window, with two tall windows on each side, sits atop the portico.

Inside, gilt-topped Corinthian columns, situated on marbleized bases, serve as an entryway to the brass inlaid staircase, which leads to the second floor. The parlor features two concentric circles of Greek frets, surrounded by a somewhat curved molding. The molding is bordered by plasterwork designed to look like folds of fabric draped over a circular room.

The house also has an elaborate plumbing

system, which called for rain-fed cisterns, "flushing water closets," sinks, bathtubs, and a shower. So innovative for 1819!

Owens family furnishings are predominant, though other Savannah antiques are also used. While not changed architecturally, the house recently underwent an extensive preservation process. There is a museum shop on the premises.

Open daily for tours; an admission fee is charged.

The Telfair Mansion
Courtesy of Telfair Museum of Art

The Telfair Mansion

LOCATION: 121 BARNARD STREET, SAVANNAH, GA 31401
TELEPHONE: (912) 232-1177
FAX: (912) 232-6954
WEBSITE: N/A

The Telfairs of Savannah played an important part in the city's history. The patriarch Edward Telfair, who would go on to serve three terms as governor, first came to Savannah to join his brother in an import-export business. He later made his fortune as a cotton and rice planter. He and his wife Sarah had nine children. When Edward died in 1807, he left his six surviving children—Josiah, Thomas, Alexander, Margaret, Sarah, and Mary—very wealthy.

In 1818, Alexander commissioned English architect William Jay to design and build a "town villa" that the family could use during Savannah's social season. The result is now considered one of the country's most important examples of Regency architecture.

In 1875, after the death of Mary Telfair, the last surviving family member, the mansion, its furnishings, its books, and a thousand shares of railroad stock were willed to the Georgia Historical Society.

In 1883, the mansion was remodeled and enlarged into what became the first art museum in the Southeast. The architect for the project was German-born Detlef Lienau, who had trained in Paris and lived in New York City. Lienau maintained the integrity of William Jay's previous work while adding an attic, a three-story west wing on the rear of the house, a sculpture gallery and rotunda, and statues. When the museum opened in May 1886, Jefferson Davis was among the dignitaries who attended.

Today, several rooms, including a dining room, a drawing room, and a kitchen are restored and furnished with Telfair family pieces. Some of William Jay's signature design features are seen in the curved doors and walls of the drawing and dining rooms. You can see the famous "bird girl" sculpture that graced the cover of the book, *Midnight in the Garden of Good and Evil*, in the drawing room. Of special note is the octagonal receiving room, which is now a restored period room.

Today, this National Historic Landmark houses the Telfair Museum of Art's excellent collection of nineteenth- and twentieth-century American, French, and German impressionist paintings, as well as sculpture and other decorative art. The first painting purchased by the museum, *Relics of the Brave*, hangs in the rotunda gallery, along with Jean-François Raffaelli's *La Demoiselle d'Honneur*. The Telfair Museum of Art is an umbrella organization, comprised of the Telfair Academy of Arts and Sciences and the Owens-Thomas House.

Open daily; an admission fee is charged.

Macon

Macon is a protected place nestled in a lush valley, hemmed in by the Piedmont plateau to the north and the beginnings of the coastal plain to the south. There's no mistaking that it was once a rich river town, for elegant antebellum and Victorian mansions line the streets. The town was incorporated in 1826 and grew to adulthood on the west bank of the Ocmulgee River. Its founders wisely planned large garden parks and wide streets.

The 5,500 individual sites and ten historic districts included on the National Register of Historic Places are an indication of Macon's historic importance; practically the entire town is on the register. Macon delights history lovers, especially once they see that more restoration is under way.

Take a drive down College Street if you care to enjoy a selection of the town's mansions. The 1842 Inn, located at 353 College Street, is a gracious, rambling Greek Revival structure that is now an internationally acclaimed bed-and-breakfast.

Another point of interest is the Middle Georgia Historical Society, located in the Sidney Lanier Cottage at 935 High Street. Lanier, a gifted linguist, mathematician, lawyer, musician, and poet, was born in this 1840 house. A soldier in the Confederate army, he served five months in a Federal prison camp, where he developed consumption. Lanier died in 1881 at the age of thirty-nine. The home is open for tours from Monday through Saturday; a museum shop is on the premises.

For information, call the Macon-Bibb

Convention and Visitors Bureau at 800-768-3401 or (478) 743-3401.

The Cannonball House

LOCATION: 856 MULBERRY STREET, MACON, GA 31201
TELEPHONE: (478) 745-5982
FAX: (478) 745-5944
WEBSITE: www.cannonballhouse.com

The Cannonball House

This house was meant to survive. Otherwise, it would have been demolished in 1864 when a Union cannonball went through a column, entered the parlor, and landed in the hall. Probably much to the dismay of General George Stoneman, the damage from the cannonball was not as extensive as he would have liked.

The house was built around 1853 for Judge Asa Holt. Although it is Greek Revival in style, it is more narrow than most classical houses, perhaps because it is a townhouse. Four tall Corinthian columns support the extended roof over the portico. A railed balcony is perched on the second story of the great white house.

The interior of the Cannonball House has an interesting history. The Sidney Lanier Chapter of the United Daughters of the Confederacy saved the house from becoming a parking lot in the early 1960s. Two parlors in the house recreate the original meeting rooms of the first two secret sororities for college women, Al-

pha Delta Pi (1851) and Phi Mu (1852). These two sororities were founded at Wesleyan College and met in parlors of the Wesleyan College building. When Wesleyan moved its campus, the furniture from these parlors was moved to the Cannonball House, along with wall hangings, books, and correspondence. Because the same architect designed both buildings, the dimensions matched exactly, allowing for exact replicas. Other rooms have period furnishings and artifacts.

The former servants' quarters and the outside kitchen now serve as a Confederate Museum, complete with soldiers' uniforms, weapons, and items relating to Macon's history. Currently, the house is owned and operated by the Friends of the Cannonball House, Inc. A museum shop is also located on the premises.

Open Monday through Saturday for tours; an admission fee is charged.

The Hay House

LOCATION: 934 GEORGIA AVENUE, MACON,
  GA 31201

TELEPHONE: (478) 742-8155

FAX: (478) 745-4277

WEBSITE: www.georgiatrust.org

William Butler Johnston was not a typical nineteenth-century Southerner. He obtained his substantial wealth through investments in banking, railroads, and public utilities, rather than from the agrarian cotton economy. In 1851, he married Anne Clark Tracy, twenty years his junior, and the two embarked on an extended honeymoon in Europe.

During their trip, the Johnstons visited hundreds of museums, historic sites, and art studios. They collected fine porcelains, sculptures, and paintings as mementoes of their Grand Tour. More significantly, they were inspired by the Renaissance architecture that they observed while they were in Italy. Upon their return to Georgia, Mr. Johnston traveled to New York City, where he commissioned the architectural firm of T. Thomas and Son to provide the plans and specifications for their new home.

After five years of construction, the Johnston family took up residence in their stately mansion in January 1860, on the eve of the Civil War. The Johnstons' Italian Renais-

The Hay House

sance Revival *palazzo* boasted technological innovations such as indoor plumbing, hot and cold running water, central heating and ventilation systems, and an indoor kitchen. Further, the residence was decorated and furnished in accordance with wealth and good taste, and it became known as "The Palace of the South."

The Johnstons created a setting for elegant social events, but it was daughter Mary Ellen and her husband, Judge Felton, who elevated the setting to a high-profile stage for a seemingly endless array of card parties, suppers, and dances. As social and political leaders in Macon, the Feltons established a standard for gracious living that would span the turn of the century and endure for a generation.

After the deaths of Judge and Mrs. Felton in 1926, the Felton heirs sold the house to P.L. Hay, an insurance magnate who lived in Macon. The Hays substantially redecorated the house to reflect the changing character of

Marvelous Old Mansions

twentieth-century living, and the house continued to be recognized as a local landmark for gracious living throughout the Hay ownership.

After Mrs. Hay's death in 1962, her heirs operated the house as a private house museum until 1977, when ownership of the house was formally transferred to the Georgia Trust for Historic Preservation. The house has been operated by the Trust since that time and has been designated as a National Historic Landmark. The house contains four floors of living space crowned by a three-story cupola. Stained glass windows, exquisite plasterwork, gold leafing, grained woodwork, and fine marbleized finishes decorate the rooms, and hidden within the house is the secret room rumored to have held the Confederate gold.

Open daily for tours; an admission is charged.

The Woodruff House

LOCATION: 988 BOND STREET, MACON, GA
  31201
The Woodruff House is located on the campus of Mercer University.
TELEPHONE: (478) 744-2715
FAX: N/A
WEBSITE: N/A

The Woodruff House looks like a Greek temple reigning over Macon from a hill on the campus of Mercer University. Formerly called Overlook, this great Greek Revival structure was built in 1836 for a railroad financier and banker. The architect was Elam Alexander of Macon.

This outstanding classical house has colonnades and porticos on three sides. The massive oak door is superb. It has four panels with hand-carved acorns and other adornments, with a lion's head located in the center of the door.

After the first owner fell upon hard times, he sold the house to Joseph Bond. Described as an "outstanding gentleman," Bond was also the largest cotton producer in the state of Georgia. In February 1857, he set a world's record for selling cotton when he sold 2,200 bales for $100,000. He would have been set for life except that his life was cut short. According to a local historian, after Bond reprimanded an

Woodruff House

overseer for mistreating a slave, the overseer shot and killed him.

The home also has two connections with the Jefferson Davis family. Winnie Davis celebrated her sixteenth birthday at a ball held in this home. The other connection came in 1886, when a Confederate reunion was held in Macon, with some ten thousand people in attendance. During the reunion, the mansion was the site of a reception, held in honor of former CSA president Jefferson Davis.

In 1905, the O'Neill family bought the grand mansion and named it Overlook. After the house was restored by the city of Macon and the Robert Woodruff Foundation, it became the property of Mercer University. At that point, it was renamed the Woodruff House in honor of its major benefactor from Atlanta.

Open during the annual Macon Cherry Blossom Festival, and for tours by appointment; an admission fee is charged.

Milledgeville

Milledgeville was writer Flannery O'Connor's hometown. It was here that she wrote her major works, and unfortunately, it was here that she died of lupus before reaching middle age. It seems probable that a town like Milledgeville could influence great works. It surely influenced state politics from 1804 un-til 1868, when it served as Georgia's capital. Other than Washington, D.C., it is the only city in the United States that was specifically laid out to serve as a capital.

Indeed, Milledgeville is the center of Georgia's antebellum history. Recognized as a Main Street City, the town has important historic structures and townspeople who appear to cherish them. It is also the home of Georgia College & State University.

For information, call the Milledgeville/Baldwin County Convention & Visitors Bureau at (912) 452-4687 or 1-800-653-1804.

The Old Governor's Mansion

LOCATION: 120 SOUTH CLARKE STREET,
  MILLEDGEVILLE, GA 31061
TELEPHONE: (912) 445-4545
FAX: (912) 445-3045
WEBSITE: www.gcsu.edu/acad_affairs/
  ce_ps/mansion/default.html

This National Historic Landmark is one of Georgia's most historically significant buildings. It was the residence of Georgia's governors during three crucial periods of the state's history: the antebellum period, the Civil War, and Reconstruction. During these years, the state's history was being drastically altered, and Milledgeville, the capital city, was the center of political power. Architectural experts

The Old Governor's Mansion
COURTESY OF GEORGIA DEPARTMENT OF INDUSTRY, TRADE, AND TOURISM

consider this building to be one of the country's most perfect examples of High Greek Revival architecture.

Completed in 1838, this building served as the residence of eight of the state's governors until 1868, when the capital was moved to Atlanta. Rich in history, it was the first executive mansion constructed for Georgia's governors. The exterior walls are beige-pink painted over stucco. The original color was likely a pale beige, natural colored stucco. Architect Charles Cluskey designed the building with its classic pediment to top the portico, which is fronted by four massive Ionic columns. Georgia granite was used on the floor and steps. Granite also tops the door, window sills, and column caps. Beautiful New England and Italian marble accentuate the interior fireplace mantelpieces.

Once inside, you can see the amazing central domed rotunda. The fifty-foot-high ceil-ing of recessed plaster has highly decorative moldings that are emphasized by their striking gilt finish. A skylight at the top of the dome provides natural light. An octagonal room just off the rotunda serves as the governor's office.

Much to the chagrin of Georgians, Union general William T. Sherman occupied the mansion briefly in 1864, during his infamous March to the Sea campaign. The general occupied Milledgeville with thirty-thousand Union troops after the destruction of Atlanta.

Today, the Old Governor's Mansion is a historic house museum, furnished in period antiques. Since 1889, the mansion has been a part of Georgia College and State University, the state's first public women's college.

Open for tours daily except Monday; an admission fee is charged.

Stetson-Sanford House

LOCATION: CORNER OF JACKSON & WEST
HANCOCK STREETS, MILLEDGEVILLE, GA
31061
TELEPHONE: (912) 452-4687 OR 1-800-
653-1804
FAX: N/A
WEBSITE: N/A

Built around 1825, the Stetson-Sanford House boasts a style sometimes referred to as "Milledgeville Federal." Englishman John

Marlor designed a beautiful Palladian double portico with double pilasters on the bottom floor and small columns on the top floor. Fanlights on both floors feature eagles spread for flight, while dogwood blossoms decorate the lead dividers. The two-story clapboard house also has a basement and an attic.

The Stetson-Sanford House remained in the same family for about one hundred years before Misses Fannie White and Mary Jo Thompson opened a nationally acclaimed tearoom and restaurant. At that time, the house was located on Wilkinson Street.

In 1966, the house was conveyed to the Old Capital Historical Society and moved to its present site at the corner of Jackson and West Hancock Streets.

Architectural historians say that the house blends vernacular eighteenth-century and Classical Revival styles. The blending is also evident in the decorative touches. The parlor's woodwork shows a fine example of woodgraining. Furnishings are Empire and Victorian. An elliptical cantilevered stairway dominates the main hall.

The house now serves as the headquarters for the Old Capital Historical Society.

Tours are available through the Convention and Visitors trolley on Tuesday through Saturday, or by appointment Monday and Saturday; an admission fee is charged.

Washington

Resting quietly in the midst of Georgia's rich cotton belt, the town of Washington is a treasure trove of grand mansions associated with the prosperous planters of the Old South.

With cotton money flowing freely, fine houses sprang up with regularity. Many owners or their wives indulged their whims with alterations and additions to their homes. Some added another story; many added porticos and other features. As a result, today it is not always easy to identify the architectural style of the mansions in Washington, Georgia.

Founded in 1780, Georgia's town of Washington was the first incorporated town named after George Washington. About forty Greek Revival structures still stand in the town, but most are private residences. Among the places open to the public is the Mary Willis Library, which was built around 1888. It features fine Tiffany windows. You can also visit the Washington-Wilkes Historical Museum, which is housed in an 1835, eighteen-room townhouse. At the museum, you can see local and county exhibits, Civil War relics, and Indian artifacts.

For information about historic Washington, contact the Washington Chamber of Commerce at (706) 678-2013.

Robert Toombs House

LOCATION: 216 EAST ROBERT TOOMBS
AVENUE, WASHINGTON, GA 30673

TELEPHONE: (706) 678-2226

FAX: (706) 678-7515

WEBSITE: pending; contact Washington
Chamber of Commerce.

Robert Toombs House
COURTESY OF THE ROBERT TOOMBS HOUSE STATE
HISTORIC SITE

When Robert Toombs purchased the house in 1837, it was already about forty years old. However, Toombs certainly left his stamp on the house that now bears his name. In 1850, he added the Doric-columned facade and portico. In 1854, he further enhanced the Greek Revival look by changing the windows and doors. In the 1870s, Toombs added Victorian wings on the east and west sides.

Toombs also left his stamp on Georgia and the Confederacy. The lawyer and planter served in the state legislature, the United States Congress, and the United States Senate. Known for his fiery oration and strong Southern sympathies, he made a name for himself on January 24, 1860, when he voiced his secessionist feelings on the Senate floor by yelling: "Defend yourselves; the enemy is at your door!"

When Georgia seceded from the Union the following year, Toombs served five months as the Confederacy's secretary of state before resigning to accept the commission of brigadier general in the Army of Northern Virginia. He had hoped to be president of the Confederacy, but Jefferson Davis was the people's choice.

Toombs later resigned his commission and returned to Georgia, where he complained vigorously about the Confederate government. To escape arrest from Federal troops, Toombs lived abroad for two years after the war.

After Toombs's death, his younger brother purchased the house. The house remained in the Toombs family until 1973, when it was sold to the state of Georgia. The Robert Toombs House is now a State Historic Site operated by the Georgia Department of Natural Resources. The site offers a complete interpretive program that tells the story of the house's feisty namesake and shows the way he lived. Many of

Toombs's furnishings and documents are on exhibit in the house. Visitors are encouraged to view a video portraying the elderly Toombs telling his story to a young reporter.

Open Tuesday through Sunday; an admission fee is charged.

Madison

Madison has been a favorite of visitors since the early 1800s, when an issue of *White's Statistics of Georgia* called it, "the most cultured and aristocratic town on the stage route from Charleston to New Orleans." The Madison Historic District, one of the first designated historic areas in Georgia, is considered one of the finest in the state.

In its early days, the town prospered, and fine homes were built to reflect the town's wealth. When the rest of the Georgia delegation seceded from the Union, Senator Joshua Hill of Madison, a strong Unionist, resigned his seat rather than secede. Later, Hill made a gentleman's agreement with a Union general to save the town's houses from destruction.

Today downtown Madison looks much as it did decades ago, with brick sidewalks and tree-lined streets accenting the old buildings that have been restored to house new shops. For information, contact the Madison Welcome Center at (706) 342-4454 or 1-800-709-

7406. You can also visit their website at www.madisonga.org.

Heritage Hall

LOCATION: 277 SOUTH MAIN STREET, MADISON, GA 30650
TELEPHONE: (706) 342-9627
FAX: N/A
Website: N/A

This grand Greek Revival structure is just two blocks from the downtown square. Although Heritage Hall is one of the few homes open to the public, a stroll around Madison to see other historic homes is recommended. You can also tour the Rogers House and Rose Cottage.

It is hard to miss Heritage Hall, for it is the only white house with six massive columns

Heritage Hall
COURTESY OF MORGAN COUNTY HISTORICAL SOCIETY

Marvelous Old Mansions

across the front and rocking chairs on the portico. The columns have an unusual twist: four round columns are flanked by two square piers. The same design is repeated at the entry.

Dr. Elijah Evans Jones built Heritage Hall for his wife Elizabeth, sometime around 1833–35. Amazingly, in all the ensuing years, the mansion has had only four owners, all of whom apparently treasured the house. The only evidence of anything less than reverence for the house is the "window writing" on a few panes, where girls etched the names of their romantic interests.

As is typical in Greek Revival homes, the house has high ceilings, eight fireplaces, and the "four over four" floor plan.

Lovely furnishings, from Empire through Victorian periods, are displayed in each room. As with many old Southern homes, a resident ghost is said to keep things interesting. It is rumored that a young woman holding a baby appears on the hearth in the "ghost bedroom."

Heritage Hall was a family residence until 1977, when the granddaughter of its last owner, Sue Reid Walton Manley, donated the home to the Morgan County Historical Society. The society maintains the home today.

Open daily for tours; an admission fee is charged.

Athens, Georgia

When naturalist John Muir visited Athens in 1867, he described it as "a remarkably beautiful and aristocratic town," and a place where "marks of culture and refinement" were apparent everywhere. If he could see the town today, he'd bestow the same accolades.

Incorporated in 1806, Athens is old by Southern standards. The town actually came to life because of the University of Georgia, which opened in 1801. Both cultural and economic development soon followed.

By 1864, prosperity had diminished due to losses suffered during the Civil War. Because General Sherman's troops were busy elsewhere in the state, the town itself remained intact. Thanks to strong local leadership, Athens survived Reconstruction, and prosperity returned.

Today, the city, with a population of just over 100,000 people, wins national awards and recognition for its livability. But Athens has not forgotten its important history. The city boasts thirteen neighborhoods that are listed on the National Register of Historic Places. For information, contact the Athens Convention & Visitors Bureau at (706) 357-4430 or 1-800-653-0603; or visit their website at www.visitathensga.com.

Church-Waddel-Brumby House

LOCATION: 280 EAST DOUGHERTY STREET,
ATHENS, GA 30601
TELEPHONE: (706) 353-1820
FAX: (706) 353-1770
WEBSITE: www.visitathensga.com/
welcomecenter.html

The oldest surviving residence in Athens, this house is an important example of the early architecture in Athens. It was built around 1820 as a Federal-style house. Although records indicate that it was built for mathematics professor, Alonzo Church, its first occupant was University of Georgia president Dr. Moses Waddel, who lived in the house until 1829.

After Dr. Waddel ended his tenure as university president, Mrs. Stephen Harris bought the house. It remained in her family—the Hardemans and the Brumbys—for over 130 years. Luckily, the graceful, stately two-story house was rescued from demolition by the Athens-Clarke Heritage Foundation in the late 1960s. Locals say that this house and the Taylor-Grady House were responsible for sparking interest in historic preservation in Athens. The Church-Waddel-Brumby House is now used as a house museum and welcome center. The house is furnished with period antiques, some of which are on loan from the Brumby family.

The truly outstanding gardens are tended by the Piedmont Garden Club. A gift shop is located on the premises.

Open daily for tours; admission is free.

Taylor-Grady House

LOCATION: 634 PRINCE AVENUE, ATHENS, GA
30601
TELEPHONE: (706) 549-8688
FAX: (706) 613-0860
WEBSITE: pending

Built in the early 1840s as a "summer retreat" for the family of cotton planter and merchant Robert Taylor, this house is by no stretch of the imagination a quaint little townhouse. This National Historic Landmark is indeed a grand Greek Revival mansion that could be as much a part of Athens, Greece, as Athens, Georgia.

Taylor, who earned the rank of general in the Georgia militia, moved from Savannah to Athens while his sons attended the University of Georgia. The family was so enamored with the town and their home, they became permanent residents.

In 1863, one of the Taylor sons sold the house to William S. Grady while Grady was on furlough from the Confederate army. Unfortunately, Grady died in battle and never lived there. His son, Henry Woodfin Grady, who

Taylor-Grady House
COURTESY OF ATHENS CONVENTION AND VISITORS BUREAU

was born in Athens, lived here while he attended the University of Georgia from 1865 to 1868. Henry Woodfin Grady went on to become the editor of the *Atlanta Constitution* in the 1870s. As editor of this major Southern newspaper, Grady became the chief spokesman for the New South. He was called the "master conductor" who orchestrated the reconciliation between the North and the South after the Civil War and Reconstruction.

Grady described his boyhood home as "an Old Southern home with its lofty pillars, and its white pigeons fluttering down through the golden air." The "lofty pillars" are actually thirteen Doric columns, which represent the thirteen original colonies.

Today, the house is owned by Athens-Clarke County and managed by the Junior League of Athens. Inside, the furnishings are primarily

period pieces, but there are also some reproductions, as well as earlier and later antiques. It stands as another prime example of the importance of historic home preservation.

Open for tours on weekdays, unless a special event is in progress (the house is rented out for special occasions); an admission fee is charged.

Roswell

Located on the lovely Chattahoochee River, Roswell was home to the Cherokee Indians before they were forced to travel the Trail of Tears. About the time the Cherokees were leaving, gold was discovered in northern Georgia, which brought settlers in droves.

Gold and settlers attracted the attention of Roswell King, who scouted the area for possible business ventures. Upon discovering the abundant natural resources, he began construction of a cotton mill in 1838. After the mill was built, homes, schools, and churches followed.

The lifestyle enjoyed by Roswell citizens changed drastically during and after the Civil War, because the cotton mill was burned. When Union troops arrived in town, a Frenchman who worked for the mill flew the French flag and claimed neutrality. It worked until Federal soldiers found "CSA"—Confederate States of America—on fabric produced at the mill. The mill was burned and the employees—mostly women and children, since the men were at war—were arrested, charged with treason, and sent north to uncertain fates.

After the war, textile mills operated in Roswell until the 1970s. By the time the textile industry hit a depressed period, other industry was well established, thus insuring that Roswell would remain prosperous. Today it is an address of choice for residents of the metro Atlanta area. For more information, contact the Historic Roswell Convention & Visitors Bureau at (770) 640-3253 or 1-800-776-7935.

Bulloch Hall

LOCATION: 180 BULLOCH AVENUE, ROSWELL, GA 30075
TELEPHONE: (770) 992-1731
FAX: (770) 587-1840
WEBSITE: N/A

Bulloch Hall was built in 1840 by Major James Stephens Bulloch, an early settler of Roswell and grandson of Governor Archibald Bulloch. The house has a full pedimented portico supported by four Tuscan columns. The floor plan is a "four square," which features a central entrance hall with an equal number of rooms on each side. Architects say that this house is one of the South's few examples of

Bulloch Hall
COURTESY OF JANICE SANBORN

true temple-form architecture. It is constructed of hard and durable hand-sawn heart pine.

One of the most historically significant events ever held at Bulloch Hall was the 1853 wedding of Mittie Bulloch to Theodore Roosevelt of New York. Miss Mittie gracefully descended the hall stairway and joined her intended in front of the fireplace in the dining room. Little did they know that their union would produce one son, Teddy, who would become a United States president and another son, Elliot, whose daughter Eleanor would marry her distant cousin, Franklin D. Roosevelt.

Bulloch Hall is owned by the city of Roswell and managed by Friends of Bulloch, Inc. Ongoing exhibits at the house include the Bulloch-Roosevelt display; the Wood-Wing Museum Room, which features furniture and memorabilia from the Wood and Wing

Dickey Plantation, Stone Mountain

Recreating this twenty-building plantation site was no easy feat, but it was masterfully done. The untrained eye cannot detect that the buildings have been moved. The manor house, now the focal point of the guided tour of the site, was constructed in Dickey, Georgia, around 1840. It was moved to its present site in 1961, after it had been the residence of the same family for more than one hundred years.

The fourteen-room, 6,200-square-foot Greek Revival house, now solidly ensconced in its suburban Atlanta surroundings, features matching porticos at the front and rear—each supported by four massive, curved brick columns. Also of interest are the twin outside stairways that curve gracefully upward to the front entrance, in a welcoming-arms motif. The home is built on a raised basement.

Featuring a breathtaking barrel-vaulted ceiling, the entrance hall leads to several rooms, including the dining room. In the dining room, a large Federal banquet table is set up with formal china and silverware, as though guests are expected. In its heyday, food for the guests was brought from the cookhouse to the warming kitchen, and then served when needed.

After dinner, it was customary for the ladies to excuse themselves to rest and visit in the Empire-style ladies' parlor, while the gentlemen went to their own parlor for cigars, libations, and talk of politics.

All the plantation buildings, including the children's dining room and the summer dining room, are part of the tour. The plantation buildings, overseer's house, and the manor house were scouted, moved, researched, and restored. An expert in period furnishings carefully selected all of the authentic antiques.

Along with the plantation tour, the park features a steam train, an antique auto and music museum, a riverboat complete with paddlewheel, and the Confederate Memorial. The memorial is a mountain-side carving of three equestrian figures who were chosen because they best represent the Old South: Confederate States of America president Jefferson Davis, General Robert E. Lee, and General Thomas J. "Stonewall" Jackson.

Georgia's Stone Mountain Park and its authentically recreated antebellum cotton plantation is located sixteen miles east of Atlanta on U.S. 78. It is open daily, and an admission fee is charged. For more information, call (770) 498-5600.

families, who lived in the house for one hundred years; and the permanent exhibit, "Slave Life in the Piedmont," which is housed in the reconstructed slave quarters.

Open daily; an admission fee is charged.

Louisiana is practically two states in one: conservative, cowboy-influenced North Louisiana, which acts and feels like East Texas, and carefree, fun-loving South Louisiana, which is a place like no other in the world. Even the language is different. South Louisiana's sing-song dialect comes from the French Acadians who settled in the bayou country after the British expelled them from Nova Scotia in the 1750s. Their crime was refusing to swear allegiance to the British crown. The four thousand or so Acadians—who became known as Cajuns—certainly made their impact on the state, even the country.

The houses in Louisiana are almost as diverse as its people. The River Road, between New Orleans and Baton Rouge, boasts houses so grand they must be seen to be believed. Except for a few private mansions in the Garden District, New Orleans architecture, as exhibited in the townhouses of the French Quarter, is built more for utility than for show. The architecture of South Louisiana was influenced by the need to withstand the humidity and low-lying areas of the bayous. For information, call the Louisiana Office of Tourism at (225) 342-8119 or 1-800-33GUMBO.

New Orleans

Of all the American cities, New Orleans has the most European attitude and ambiance. It truly is "the city that care forgot," where *laissez les bon temps rouler*—"let the good times roll"—is a rallying call. New Orleans is Mardi Gras madness and Catholic confessions and many things between.

New Orleanians don't merely live life, they celebrate it, and they're never short on causes for celebration. The fine art of celebration has been practiced in New Orleans since the city came into existence in 1718.

Architecturally, New Orleans is as rich as the fabulous food served in its smorgasbord of restaurants. The French Quarter, or Vieux Carré, covers the seventy or so blocks between Canal Street and the Mississippi River. The Quarter is old New Orleans, filled with old brick and cypress buildings that sport ornate cast-iron balconies, or galleries, and quaint, colorful courtyards in the most unexpected places.

St. Charles Avenue leads to the Garden District, where grand mansions line the shady streets. Many of the Garden District houses are Greek Revival, best identified by double rows of columns, with Ionic below and Corinthian above. They are usually decorated with cast-iron railings.

The Louisiana section starts in New Orleans, because as any true New Orleanian will tell you, everything that's anything starts in "Nu'awlins."

For more information, contact the New Orleans Metropolitan Convention and Visitors Bureau at (504) 566-5003 or 1-800-672-6124. Their fax number is (504) 566-5021; their website is www.neworleanscvb.com.

Hermann-Grima House

LOCATION: 820 ST. LOUIS STREET, NEW
    ORLEANS, LA 70112
TELEPHONE: (504) 525-5661
FAX: (504) 568-9735
WEBSITE: www.gnofn.org/~hggh

This National Historic Landmark is unusual because it is a formal red-brick, Federal-style house, perched in the French Quarter where French Creole houses are in abundance. Except for the wrought-iron balcony railing and typical New Orleans-style courtyard in the back, this house reflects a more formal taste.

Inside, the spacious rooms open off a central hallway. In the parlor and dining rooms, you'll find crystal chandeliers, Corinthian columns dividing the parlor, and exquisite antique furniture and other lavish adornments that you don't often see in the houses in the Quarter that are open to the public.

Since most houses of this age in New Orleans sit on the street, it's unusual to see an elevated entrance. All of these aspects combined to make New Orleanians curious about the new "Yankee-style" house that had invaded their French- and Spanish-influenced city.

Samuel Hermann came to Louisiana from Germany in 1804 and settled near Baton Rouge. His success as a merchant, entrepreneur, and private banker encouraged him to move to the more cosmopolitan New Orleans. With the help of architect/builder William Brand, Hermann built his home here in 1831. Hermann was known for his lavish entertaining. At one party, he invited 350 people to a grand soirée for which he planned a fireworks display.

After the financial chaos surrounding the panic of 1837, Hermann suffered subsequent business failures. As a result, he had to sell his house to Felix Grima, a Creole gentleman. Grima was an attorney, a notary public, and a judge. In private life, Grima was a scholar and linguist, and he treasured the house. It was kept in the Grima family for five generations.

The house has been impeccably restored to show the gracious lifestyle of a prosperous Creole family in the years from 1830 to 1860. Many of the Grima and Hermann family antiques are exhibited in this house museum today.

Open for tours Monday through Friday; an admission fee is charged.

Gallier House

LOCATION: 1132 ROYAL STREET, NEW
    ORLEANS, LA 70116
TELEPHONE: (504) 525-5661
FAX: (504)-568-9735
Website: www.gnofn.org/~hggh

James Gallier, Jr., was a man who knew what was important in a house. A prominent architect, he designed and built many Garden District homes, as well as the French Opera House. When he built his own house from 1857 to 1860, it had many innovative features, including indoor running water, built-in closets, a ventilation system, and a skylight. Gallier's house was definitely ahead of its time.

The Gallier family was originally from Ireland, where the family name was Gallagher. James Gallier, Sr., was trained as an architect in England. When he moved from Ireland to England, he changed his name, perhaps hoping to win more acceptance in London society, with its inherent potential for architectural commissions. In 1832, he came to New York City. Disillusioned by the "confused" professional situation in New York, he moved to New Orleans. Working with Charles Dakin in New Orleans, James Sr. built Christ Church and the first St. Charles Hotel. He also built the Government Street Presbyterian Church in Mobile, Alabama. Good architects were much in demand.

James Gallier, Jr., also a notable architect like his father, completed his own house on Royal Street in 1860. Indulging his preferences as architect/builder, James Jr. built a narrow townhouse with an Italianate, stucco facade that he had stippled and scored to look like stone. The "sidehall" townhouse features a long hall. The hall opens onto a double parlor that is deep rather than wide. Corinthian columns with gilded tops separate the twin rooms. Furniture is placed in groupings in the two heavily decorated rooms. These small groupings create intimate settings for quiet conversation or for listening to music. An interesting piece of furniture is the méridienne, which is a small sofa that has an arm on only one side to make sitting down easier for ladies wearing hoop skirts.

Upstairs, the children's bedroom is set up as though the four Gallier girls were playing house, complete with antique dolls and miniature furniture. This room is permanently decorated to reflect the summer lifestyle in the mid-nineteenth century. After the death of James Gallier, Jr., from unknown causes at the age of forty-one, his daughters kept the house in the family until 1917. The Gallier House is now run by The Woman's Exchange, which restored this National Historic Landmark in the style of the 1860s.

Open for tours Monday through Friday; an admission fee is charged.

River Road Plantations

After the traffic and busy pace of New Orleans, you'll probably be ready for the peace and quiet of the off-the-beaten-path plantations. Some may not be easy to reach, but they are well worth the effort once you arrive. History was made here, so do take the time to enjoy this most impressive part of the country.

The River Road is some 120 miles long on each side of the Mississippi River. It roughly parallels the river between Jefferson and East and West Baton Rouge Parishes. The route, which passes through eight parishes and numerous towns, runs close to two large urban areas: New Orleans and Baton Rouge. In 1850, two-thirds of America's millionaires were planters who had homes on the Great River Road between Natchez and New Orleans.

When planning your own trip, plan your route according to where you want to stay overnight. Once you're in the general vicinity of each plantation, signs will direct you.

Destrehan Plantation

LOCATION: 13034 RIVER ROAD (LA. HWY. 48), DESTREHAN, LA 70047

Destrehan is located only eight miles from New Orleans International Airport. It is one-half mile east of Destrehan Bridge.

TELEPHONE: (504) 764-9315

FAX: (504) 725-1929

Website: www.destrehanplantation.org

The oldest plantation intact in the lower Mississippi Valley is the remarkable Destrehan. It's located on the River Road, about an hour west of New Orleans. Completed in 1790, this imposing West Indies-style planter's home is a favorite tour house.

Destrahan was built in the colonial style, with major alterations made later. There is speculation that Destrehan and its neighbor, Homeplace, were built by Charles Pacquet, a free man of color. The courthouse records at Hahnville say that Pacquet, a "carpenter, woodworker, and mason," was hired to construct a house for Robert Antoine Robin DeLogny, a Creole planter. The records also show that Pacquet would be paid with a slave, a cow and its calf, fifty quarts of rice in chaff, fifty quarts of corn in husks, and $100 upon completion. After the house was completed, Pacquet swore that he had been paid in full.

Eight huge columns form a line across the

Destrehan Plantation
COURTESY OF LOUISIANA OFFICE OF TOURISM

front of Destrehan. The ground-floor walls are constructed of large bricks covered with plaster. This construction provided added protection if the nearby Mississippi River should flood. Typical of French Colonial homes of the period, the floor plan features three rooms across and two rooms deep. Rooms open into rooms, instead of using connecting hallways.

Until wings were built in 1810, galleries surrounded the house. Now there are galleries only across the front. The tall, wide roof provides great shade for the galleries on the ground and second floor. Jalousies that block the sun also help keep the interior of the galleries cool.

Major alterations began when DeLogny's son-in-law bought the house in 1802. For years, he made changes according to the style of the day or the needs of the family, which included fourteen children. The aristocratic Creole family of Destrehan entertained lavishly and often. Among their guests were the Duc d'Orleans, who later became the king of France; William C.C. Claiborne, governor of the Mississippi Territory; and even the notorious pirate Jean Lafitte.

When Destrehan was remodeled again in 1840, Greek Revival design elements were added. After being vacant and the target of vandals for years, the American Oil Company, which owned the property, donated the house and its four remaining acres to the River Road Historical Society in 1968. The society restored Destrehan to its present state. It is completely furnished with pieces from 1850 or earlier. These furnishings include an Empire sofa and chairs, a bayou bed, gaming tables, and an Aubusson rug.

Open daily; an admission is charged.

San Francisco Plantation

LOCATION: P.O. BOX DRAWER AX, RESERVE, LA 70084

From New Orleans, take I-10 West toward Baton Rouge; take Exit 206. At the dead end, make a right onto U.S. 61 (Airline Hwy.). Go to the fifth traffic light and make a left onto La. Hwy. 53 (Central Avenue). At the dead end,

make a right turn onto La. Hwy. 44 (River Road) and go 3.3 miles. The house will be on the right.

From Baton Rouge, take Exit 194 off I-10 and follow the signs to La. Hwy. 44 (River Road). Turn left and go about five miles to the house.

TELEPHONE: (504) 535-2341 OR 1-888-322-1756

FAX: (504) 535-5450

WEBSITE: www.sanfranciscoplantation.org

Three towns claim this plantation— Garyville, Reserve, and LaPlace—for its address has been attributed to all three. It's no wonder they all want to claim this 1856 "Steamboat Gothic," for it is an unusual and interesting architectural creation. The house is so distinctive that it inspired novelist Frances Parkinson Keyes to write "Steamboat Gothic," a story about a family she imagined lived here. The unusual style may have come from the fact that its builder, Edmond Bozonier Marmillion, loved the steamboats that plied the nearby Mississippi River and wanted his house to resemble the festive vessels.

The house has nothing to do with the city of San Francisco. Perhaps its name is a light attempt at humor directed toward the cost of the house's construction. In French, *sans frusquin* means "without a cent."

San Francisco Plantation
COURTESY OF LOUISIANA OFFICE OF TOURISM

Originally called St. Frusquin, the home was built around 1856. Even today, the grandeur of this house remains incomparable. The house is reminiscent of a Creole style because rooms open into other rooms rather than hallways. Another Creole characteristic is having the main living quarters on the second floor. There is a large gallery under the steeply pitched roof. Unlike other houses on the River Road, the ceilings are made of tongue-and-groove boards, rather than plaster. Other Creole-like features include stuccoed brick walls, brick floors, and French doors.

Between 1926 and 1932, the Army Corps of Engineers started construction on the levee and spillway stretching from Baton Rouge to New Orleans. The corps originally planned to build the levee right through San Francisco Plantation. Sidney Levet, Sr., a member of the Ory family who then owned the plantation, petitioned the governor of Louisiana to stop the destruction of the home. When the governor denied the request, Levet successfully worked to have the home declared a National Historic Landmark.

In 1973, Energy Corporation of Louisiana (ECOL) purchased the site for an oil refinery. The chairman of the corporation, Frederick B. Ingram, urged restoration and donated the building and eight acres to the San Francisco Plantation Foundation. When Marathon Oil Company purchased ECOL in 1976, it agreed to underwrite the cost of the restoration, which eventually exceeded one million dollars.

During restoration, paint scrapings and salvaged samples were used to match original paint colors as well as the beautifully marbleized and grained cypress moldings. Five beautiful ceiling frescoes, which were also discovered during restoration, have been carefully and authentically restored. Furniture in the house represents the period when the Marmillions owned the house. Included are important pieces by John Henry Belter and Prudent Mallard.

Open daily; an admission fee is charged.

Oak Alley Plantation

LOCATION: 3645 LA. HWY. 18, VACHERIE, LA 70090

From New Orleans, take I-10 west to the Gramercy Exit 194. Turn left on La. Hwy. 641 traveling south. Follow La. Hwy. 641 until it turns into La. Hwy. 3213. Continue over the Veteran's Memorial Bridge on La. Hwy. 3213. Turn left onto La. Hwy. 18 and travel 7.5 miles to Oak Alley.

From Baton Rouge, take I-10 east to Lutcher/Mississippi River Bridge Exit 194. Follow the same directions as listed for New Orleans.

TELEPHONE: (225) 265-2151 OR 1-800-44-ALLEY

FAX: (225) 265-7035

WEBSITE: oakalleyplantation.com

Oak Alley Plantation
COURTESY OF LOUISIANA OFFICE OF TOURISM

This National Historic Landmark is a majestic example of the classical vernacular style. Built between 1837 and 1839 by Jacques Telesphore Roman III, an affluent sugar-cane planter, this house may be the best known in the region.

The Greek Revival plantation gets its name from the allée of twenty-eight gigantic oaks, which stretch a quarter-mile between the house and the Mississippi River. These oaks were planted about one hundred years before this house was built. A French settler planted the trees in two rows of fourteen trees each. The rows were eighty feet apart. After planting the oaks, the settler then built a small house where the plantation manor now sits.

Perhaps because of the twenty-eight oaks, twenty-eight towering columns, each eight feet in circumference, frame the brick facade of the current mansion. The brick facade is actually sixteen-inch-thick brick walls covered with stucco that were apparently tinted a peach color. Consequently, the house has a warm and inviting look. The veranda, which extends thirteen feet from the brick wall, keeps the house shady and cool. Cross ventilation provided by the windows, doors, and twelve-foot ceilings also cool the house.

Jacques Roman was from a prominent Louisiana Creole family, which also included his brother Andrea Bienvenu Roman, who served as governor of Louisiana. The Romans enjoyed all the pleasures afforded by New Orleans society. Well-kept family records and correspondence confirm the graciousness of plantation life before the Civil War. The letters and documents also confirmed the overwhelming changes that occurred during and after the war.

Henri, the last Roman to live at Oak Alley, tried valiantly to save the place, but was forced to sell the house and property for $32,800. In 1866, when money was hard to find, that amount was a princely sum.

After several owners and subsequent hard times, the grande dame Oak Alley was boarded up and left alone for many years. The Andrew Stewarts, who purchased the house in 1925, became the last resident owners. Their renovation of Oak Alley was the first attempt in this area to restore the old plantation homes.

Mrs. Stewart created a nonprofit foundation, which assumed possession of the house and twenty-five acres at her death in 1972. The Oak Alley Foundation commissioned an extensive restoration and has invested about $350,000 in redecoration efforts to date.

The house has been restored to the 1830s period and furnished accordingly. The restoration effort included the re-upholstering of the living room's mahogany sofa and chairs.

One of the few items original to the house is the punkah, or "shoo-fly" fan used to shoo away bothersome insects and keep guests cool while they were dining.

Because Oak Alley so well represents the antebellum mansions of the Old South, many films and television shows have used it as a location site. Among these films was a version of *The Long Hot Summer,* starring Don Johnson, and *Primary Colors,* a film starring John Travolta and Emma Thompson, which is based on a novel about a Southern governor who becomes president.

Open daily for tours; an admission fee is charged.

St. Francisville

Some say that St. Francisville owes its life to the Mississippi River in more ways than one. In the 1770s, Capuchin monks selected the high point on the river as a place to bury their dead, because the graves would be safer from the river's marauding floodwaters. Early settlers followed suit and chose the "highlands" as a place to establish a settlement. St. Francisville's location on the river soon brought prosperity to the town through river trade and commerce.

Originally settled by Houmas Indians, then the Tunica tribe, by the sixteenth century, this region was attracting both Spanish and French explorers. The first formal settlement was a French fort in 1729. This was abandoned when

France lost the rest of Louisiana to Spain; France's vast territory east of the Mississippi went to England in 1763 and became known as West Florida.

In the 1770s, the Capuchin monks arrived, and for the rest of the century the area was dominated by Spain and England. In 1779, the governor of Spanish Louisiana ousted the British from the portion of West Florida that he called Feliciana, which means "happy land" in Spanish.

The strong-willed pioneers who carved their plantations out of the wilderness tended to be English-speaking Anglo-Saxons. They revolted against the Spanish twice after the Louisiana Purchase excluded their area—once in 1804 and again in 1810. In the 1810 coup, the Republic of West Florida existed for seventy-four days. This led to the desired annexation of the Felicianas to the United States by President James Madison. It became part of the state of Louisiana by 1813. Today, the eight Louisiana parishes (counties) are sometimes referred to as the "Florida parishes."

After its beginnings as a pioneer post, the town began to attract people who were determined to see their town prosper. By the early 1800s, St. Francisville was the major trade center for the region. Soon, St. Francisville became the center for fine architecture, culture, and education. Thanks to the land that was so suitable for growing sugar cane, cotton, and indigo, St. Francisville and the River Road did indeed flourish. The structures still standing today serve as confirmation of the high quality of life enjoyed in and around St. Francisville.

For information, contact West Feliciana Parish Tourist Commission, P.O. Box 1548, St. Francisville, LA 70775. Their telephone number is (225) 635-6330; their fax number is (225) 635-4626; their website is www.saint-francisville.la.us.

Rosedown Plantation

LOCATION: 12501 LA. HWY. 10, ST. FRANCISVILLE, LA 70775

Rosedown is located at 12501 La. Hwy. 10, twenty-five miles north of Baton Rouge, via U.S. 61 or La. Hwy. 10.

TELEPHONE: (225) 635-3332

FAX: N/A

WEBSITE: N/A

If you aren't watchful, you may pass right by Rosedown without actually seeing much of the house, but there is no doubt that there is something special at the end of the allée of old oak trees.

The architectural style of Rosedown is hard to categorize, for it is a little bit Georgian, more Greek Revival, with a modicum of Creole.

Whatever the style, Rosedown is a remarkable home in an extraordinary setting. It is even more valuable historically because its ownership remained in the original family from the time it was built around 1835 until 1955.

In 1828 when Martha Hilliard Barrow of Highland Plantation married Daniel Turnbull, the marriage combined two West Feliciana Parish plantation fortunes. The newlyweds left on a European honeymoon and stayed about six years. While in Europe, the couple studied and observed European houses and gardens. Upon their return in 1835, they commissioned a builder to carry out their plans. They wanted their house to be ". . .not necessarily monumental, but fine." Indeed it is one of the finest along the River Road, and its lush and lovely gardens are unmatched.

Martha Turnbull was an accomplished horticulturalist who oversaw the planting and nurturing of a thirty-acre garden. She loved the gardens of Versailles, and her own designs at Rosedown imitated grand continental gardens.

In 1844, the Turnbulls added two small wings to the rectangular main section. There were double galleries and plain Doric columns on each of two levels across the front.

After viewing Rosedown's marvelous gardens and exterior, a pleasant surprise awaits you inside. Visitors are treated to an authentic Southern mansion from the 1830s, complete with fine family pieces. Behind the delicate fanlights and sidelights, the entrance hall features a curving mahogany staircase, which appears to segue into the ceiling.

The furniture consists of Empire Regency, Rococo Revival, and Gothic Revival pieces. Duncan Phyfe chairs surround the Regency dining table. But, the most significant of Rosedown's fine furnishings is the Gothic Revival "Henry Clay" bedroom suite, complete with a fourteen-foot-high, richly adorned canopy over the bed.

The story behind the Henry Clay suite is that Clay's friends expected him to be elected president in 1844, so they commissioned Philadelphia cabinetmaker Crawford Riddell to create furniture that would grace the presidential quarters in the White House. When Clay was defeated, the furniture was left in a warehouse until Daniel Turnbull purchased it for $1,280. The purchase included the massive canopy bed, an armoire, six chairs, a bureau, an octagonal table, and two washstands. Turnbull had a separate wing built to accommodate the furniture, which was far too large for any existing room at Rosedown.

After Daniel Turnbull died in 1861, Martha lived on at Rosedown with their only surviving child Sarah and her husband, James Bowman. James's mother was Eliza Pirrie Bowman of Oakley, which is described in the next entry. After the Civil War, the family began using sharecroppers to maintain the plantation and provide for the ten Bowman children. Of those ten Bowman children, eight were girls. Five of the girls remained single and lived out their days at Rosedown, tending the gardens and house. When the last sister died in 1955, the place was then sold.

Open for daily tours; an admission is charged.

Oakley Plantation

LOCATION: P.O. BOX 546, ST. FRANCISVILLE, LA 70775

Oakley is located near St. Francisville on La. Hwy. 965. From Baton Route, take U.S. 61 north to La. Hwy. 965. Turn right and follow the signs. It takes approximately 30 minutes.

TELEPHONE: (225) 635-3739 OR 1-888-677-2838

FAX: (225) 784-0578

WEBSITE: www.crt.state.la.us

This tall four-storied house actually has two full stories, an attic, and a raised brick basement. The house reflects a definite West Indies influence. On both top floors, you'll see the jalousied galleries, which were designed to accommodate cool breezes.

Oakley's architecture may be described as colonial, but adapted to South Louisiana, with a hint of the Acadian style of the lower bayou parishes. Like many of the earliest homes around St. Francisville, Oakley has exterior staircases.

Construction of Oakley began in 1799, but owner Ruffin Gray died in 1810 before the house was completed. His widow, who had two children by Gray, married James Pirrie. The Pirries then had a daughter named Eliza. Eliza's need for a tutor brought the artist John James Audubon to Oakley in 1821. The Frenchman was hired to instill culture in the beautiful Eliza, who was expected to marry well. Audubon was hired to teach Eliza dancing, music, drawing, math, and French. He was then free to spend his afternoons on his own paintings and studies. Some of Audubon's most famous bird studies were done at Oakley. He painted thirty-two of his "Birds of America" series while here. He also painted a portrait of Eliza, which now hangs at the plantation Rosedown, where her son later lived.

Now a part of the Audubon State Commemorative area, Oakley was purchased by the state of Louisiana in 1947. It is painstakingly preserved and maintained. The Federal-period furnishings represent the time when Audubon was in residence

A tour of the house includes the artist's room and the children's rooms. The tour also affords the visitor a chance to see what early building construction was like. Of special importance is the extensive collection of early light fixtures. The fixtures date from the 1690s through the nineteenth century.

Oakley sits on one hundred acres of land that offer hiking trails, woods, streams, and an old barn filled with vintage farm equipment.

Open daily; an admission is charged.

The Myrtles Plantation

LOCATION: 7747 U.S. 61, ST. FRANCISVILLE, LA 70775

TELEPHONE: (225) 635-6277 OR 1-800-809-0565

FAX: (225) 635-5837

WEBSITE: N/A

The Myrtles is surrounded by more than towering old trees. Stories of ghosts and intrigue have hovered over this home since it was built in 1796.

Ghosts notwithstanding, the house has its own colorful history. Pennsylvania judge and businessman David Bradford, who was a general in George Washington's army, refused to pay a tax levied on alcoholic beverages. He left the army and became one of the ringleaders of the Whiskey Rebellion. For his involvement in this rebellion, he was branded a traitor and a warrant was issued for his arrest. He then became a fugitive from justice and headed down the Mississippi River, where he landed at Bayou Sara. In December 1794, he purchased 650 acres of land from the Spanish government for $1.25 an acre.

When General Bradford built The Myrtles, he made it identical to his home in Pennsylvania. He died in 1818, and his wife Elizabeth sold the plantation to their daughter Sarah Matilda and her husband, Judge Clarke Woodruff, in 1826. After the death of his wife and two small children from poisoning by his household servant, Chloe, Judge Woodruff left the home in 1834 and moved to New Orleans. There he built a new home and never returned to The Myrtles.

In 1836, Ruffin Gray Stirling and his wife purchased the home and began major renovations on the mansion. They added the main foyer, the southern section of the home, the wraparound porches on the front and back part of the house, the ornamental ironwork, and the single and double dormers upstairs. Stirling also hired several craftsmen from France to create the elaborate open-pierced plaster friezes that adorn the ceilings and the *faux bois* on the woodwork. Twin parlors feature twin Italian Carrara marble mantles, pier mirrors, and Baccarat crystal chandeliers.

Furnishings, which are mostly imported antiques, reflect the 1850s when The Myrtles was in its heyday. Today, the home is a bed-and-breakfast inn and is listed as "one of America's most haunted houses."

Open for daily tours; an admission is charged.

ℋoumas House Plantation

LOCATION: 40136 LA. HWY. 942, DARROW, LA 70725

From the New Orleans International Airport, take I-10 to Exit 179. Go south on La. Hwy. 44 to Burnside. Turn west on La. Hwy. 942. Houmas House is located at 40136 La. Hwy. 942, approximately 45 minutes from the airport. Although the house is actually located in Burnside, it has a Darrow mailing address.

TELEPHONE: (225) 473-7841 OR 1-888-323-8314

FAX: 504-474-0480

WEBSITE: www.houmashouse.com

The perfectly proportioned Houmas House was built in 1840. In the following years, it became the state's largest sugar plantation. As elegant as it is today, you'd never guess that when it was built in the 1700s it was only a four-room structure. Still a part of Houmas House, this original structure was built in the style of a French country house with a hint of Spanish influence.

Historically, the house is significant because

Houmas House Plantation
COURTESY OF LOUISIANA OFFICE OF TOURISM

it stands on land once occupied by Houmas Indians. It was purchased around 1812 by General Wade Hampton, a South Carolinian who operated the thriving sugar plantation as an absentee owner. Hampton's daughter and her husband, John Smith Preston, came to live at Houmas in 1840, when the Greek Revival house was completed.

The impressive two-and-one-half-story, classical-style house has six massive Doric columns across the front and on each side. Colonial influence is shown in the upper and lower galleries on three sides, the hipped roof, and dormer windows. This grand Greek Revival home is what Irishman John Burnside saw when he decided to buy Houmas House from the Prestons in 1858. Under Burnside's guidance, the plantation grew sugar cane on twenty thousand acres.

A confirmed bachelor, Burnside became the

"sugar prince of Louisiana." When a Union general was about to commandeer Houmas House as his headquarters during the Civil War, Burnside proclaimed his British citizenship and declared immunity. The house was spared.

After Burnside's death in 1881, his beloved home had two interim owners before the Crozat family acquired it in 1940. Their heirs still own and manage the home.

Furnishings reflect the 1840s, the time period considered the home's heyday. Important antiques collected by Dr. George B. Crozat of New Orleans are featured throughout the house. Many pieces were made by prominent Louisiana cabinetmakers. American Empire pieces, along with a Victorian parlor set, are included in the collection at Houmas House. The graceful spiral staircase is a work of art.

During tours, guides tell guests about some of the films shot on location here. One of them was *Hush, Hush, Sweet Charlotte,* starring Bette Davis.

Open daily for tours; an admission is charged.

*M*adewood Plantation

LOCATION: 4250 LA. HWY. 308,
NAPOLEANVILLE, LA 70390

To get to Madewood from New Orleans, take I-10 west to Exit 182 (if coming from Baton Rouge, take I-10 east to Exit 182). Cross

Madewood Plantation
COURTESY OF LOUISIANA OFFICE OF TOURISM

the Sunshine Bridge and continue on La. Hwy. 70, following "Bayou Plantations" signs to "Spur 70," where you turn left. Continue one mile to the stop sign and turn immediately left onto La. Hwy. 308, which parallels Bayou Lafourche. Madewood is on the left 2.2 miles south of Napoleonville.

TELEPHONE: (504) 369-7151 OR 1-800-375-7151
FAX: 504-369-9848
WEBSITE: N/A

Once you arrive at the lovely Madewood, you will have no doubt why it's called "the Queen of the Bayou." This National Historic Landmark is about as regal as a house can be.

Located on the Bayou Lafourche, Madewood was built by Colonel Thomas Pugh. Descended from a North Carolina family, Thomas increased the family's vast wealth by purchasing about fifteen Louisiana plantations.

In 1846, the Pughs commissioned the Irish-born, New York-trained architect Henry Howard of New Orleans to design the grand two-story, Ionic-columned, Greek Revival-style house. In typical classical style, a portico stretches across the front. One-story wings flank each side, making it one of the South's most perfectly proportioned plantation houses.

The name Madewood derives from the fact that the cypress used in the house's construction came from the property. The large, heavy bricks that adorn the house were made in the kiln at Madewood. It is even believed that the wood was cut and the bricks were made before the plans were drawn.

Madewood is the perfect place to experience the spaciousness and graciousness for which Greek Revival mansions are known, because the height of some of the ceilings soar up to twenty-five feet. The interior of Madewood is furnished in the style of the 1840s. The furnishings include some Louisiana pieces, an eight-piece John Henry Belter parlor suite, a fine Renaissance Revival desk, a Pleyel piano, and a Meissen mirror. Each of the twenty-one rooms contains fine art and antiques, much of it collected by owners Millie and Keith Marshall and the Marshall family. Keith Marshall collected many of the pieces of furniture when he studied as a Rhodes Scholar at Oxford University in England.

Movies shot on location at Madewood include *A Woman Called Moses,* starring Cicely Tyson and *Sister, Sister,* which starred Eric Stolz, Jennifer Jason-Leigh and Judith Ivey.

Madewood is a private residence and an award-winning bed-and-breakfast inn that has been featured in many prominent magazines and newspapers. The mansion is about seventy-five miles southwest of New Orleans and forty-five miles from Baton Rouge.

Open for daily tours; an admission is charged.

Nottoway Plantation

LOCATION: (P.O. BOX 160) 30970 LA. HWY. 405 (RIVER ROAD), WHITE CASTLE, LA 70788

From Baton Rouge, take I-10 west towards Lafayette. When you get on the Mississippi River Bridge, get in the middle lane. Take the very first exit off the bridge, which goes to Plaquemine on La. Hwy. 1 South. Follow La. Hwy. 1 South for 18 miles to Nottoway. Nottoway is approximately seven miles past Plaquemine on the left side of the highway

From New Orleans, take I-10 west towards Baton Rouge. Get off Exit 182 (Donaldsonville/Sunshine Bridge). Turn left on La. Hwy. 22 and go approximately one-half mile. Turn left onto La. Hwy. 70, heading for the Sunshine Bridge. After crossing the bridge, you

Nottaway Plantation
COURTESY OF LOUISIANA OFFICE OF TOURISM

must pay a fifty-cent toll. Stay in the right land. Go toward Donaldsonvile, remembering to stay in the right lane. After leaving Donaldsonville, stay on La. Hwy. 1 North for twelve miles to White Castle. You'll see Nottoway two miles past White Castle, on the right side of the highway.

TELEPHONE: (225) 545-2730

FAX: (225) 545-8632

WEBSITE: www.nottoway.com

From a distance, Nottoway resembles a gigantic, frilly white wedding cake. Upon closer inspection, you'll see it's not a wedding cake, but it is gigantic. In fact, Nottoway is the largest plantation house in the South. Its fifty-three-thousand square feet hold sixty-four rooms. Perhaps this massive size gave the house its nickname, "the white castle."

New Orleans architect Henry Howard be-

gan this showplace for his client John Hampden Randolph in 1859. It took ten years to complete. Randolph, who was descended from the Randolph family of Virginia, grew sugar cane on seven thousand surrounding acres. The style of the house is Greek Revival, blended with Italianate traces. Randolph told the architect he wanted "the finest house on the river," and he got it.

Twenty-two giant columns, made of hand-carved cypress, enclose the balconies on both stories. Ornate cast-iron filigree decorates the balustrades that connect each column. The house has two hundred windows, one hundred sixty-five doors, and six interior stairways. Because taxes were levied according to the number of closets in a structure, it was unusual to see many closets in houses built during this era. But, Nottoway has abundant closets. It even has bathrooms.

The massive grand white ballroom is unforgettable. It is located inside a rounded wing on the side of the house that faces upriver. The towering Corinthian columns call attention to finely carved lace moldings and the crystal chandeliers above. The solid maple floor is the only wood in the house that isn't cypress. The ballroom was designed so the seven Randolph daughters could dance on the galleries during their soirées. The Randolphs also had four sons.

When the Civil War broke out, John

Randolph took his slaves and went to work a cotton plantation in Texas to keep the family solvent. The teenage daughters were sent away to safer territory, but Emily Randolph remained on the plantation with the younger children. One of her daughters, Cornelia, kept a diary that documents Emily's courage during the war.

Although Nottoway was marked for destruction during the Civil War, a young Union officer, who had once visited in the home, is said to have "gallantly refused to fire upon a house occupied by women and children." The Randolphs eleventh child was born during the war.

Nottoway is impeccably furnished in period antiques. It is said that Nottoway inspired segments of *Gone with The Wind*. The drapes, which Scarlett O'Hara used to fashion a dress, were similar to the ones hanging in Nottoway's study. A gift shop and restaurant are on the premises. It now operates as a bed-and-breakfast inn.

Open daily for tours; an admission is charged.

*E*vergreen Plantation

LOCATION: 4677 LA. HWY 18, EDGARD, LA 70049

Evergreen Plantation is located on River Road, between Edgard and Vacherie.

The address for contacting New Orleans Tours is 610 South Peters, New Orleans, LA 70130.

TELEPHONE: FOR RESERVATIONS, CALL (504) 592-0560

FAX: (504) 587-1740

WEBSITE: N/A

Evergreen sits serenely on the west bank of the Mississippi River, near the towns of Edgard and Vacherie. It is a favorite of those who want the full plantation experience, including a chance to see the outbuildings so necessary to plantation life. Still standing at Evergreen are what are considered to be the South's best remaining examples of a plantation complex: the plantation kitchen, servants' quarters, *garconnieres, pigeonniers,* and the twenty-two slave cabins. These cabins are still located in their original double-row configuration at the end of a allée of giant oaks.

Evergreen was initially built for Christophe Haydel in the 1790s. In 1832, it was reconstructed in a Greek Revival style for Haydel's grandson, Pierre Clidamant Becnel, and his bride, Magdelaine Gesira Brou. The house remained in the family for about one hundred years. During that time it became an important twenty-five-hundred-acre sugar-cane plantation.

Though not an architect, the owner did a remarkable job of reconciling the traditional galleried house, which is so prominent in Louisiana, with a projecting pedimented portico. Two Doric columns, which match the columns supporting the hipped roof, support the portico. A belvedere sits atop the roof.

Also at the time of this reconstruction, doorways with fanlights and sidelights were added at the first- and second-floor gallery entrances. Stuccoed-brick Doric columns rise from the ground to the roof, supporting the wide gallery.

One of the most interesting exterior features is the exquisitely curved double stairway that leads to the upper gallery. It winds around the portico columns, with simple banisters providing the symmetry for this National Historic Landmark.

In 1946, Matilda Geddings Gray, of New Orleans and Lake Charles, purchased Evergreen. With architect Richard Koch, Mrs. Gray began the careful restoration of the mansion, its outbuildings, and gardens. The plantation remains in the Gray family today.

Fine period antiques are found throughout the house. The first floor features the 1840s period; the second floor, the 1850s. Some tables and four-poster beds are adorned with a pineapple and acanthus leaf motif. Evergreen is a private residence and is available for tours if you make advance reservations through New Orleans Tours. You can not tour the facility except as part of a motor-coach tour.

Available for pre-arranged tours; a fee is charged.

*M*elrose Plantation

LOCATION: LA. HWY. 119, MELROSE, LA 71452

From I-49 south of Natchitoches, take Exit 119. Follow La. Hwy. 119 along the Cane River to Melrose Plantation.

TELEPHONE: (318) 379-0055 OR 1-800-259-1714 (NATCHITOCHES PARISH TOURIST COMMISSION)

FAX: N/A

WEBSITE: N/A

Located on the Cane River fifteen miles south of Natchitoches (pronounced Nack-ah-tish), Melrose may be the only plantation in the South that was begun by a freed black woman. After the death of her first owner, Marie Therese Coincoin and ten of her fourteen children were sold to Claude Thomas Pierre Metoyer, a Frenchman. In 1780,

Metoyer freed Marie Therese. He eventually also freed the children he owned. It is suspected that Metoyer was the father of these children. Metoyer also deeded Marie Therese a small grant of land. By 1794, Marie Therese and her children owned six thousand acres, which they had obtained through land grants. On this estate, they, with the help of slaves they purchased, raised cotton, indigo, tobacco, and pecans.

Marie Therese did not forget the four children who were not fathered by Metoyer. She purchased the freedom of two of her other children and a least one of her grandchildren.

Today, eight structures make up the complex, including Yucca House, which was built in 1796. This National Historic Landmark complex also includes the African House, which was built in 1800. This structure served as a storehouse and a jail for rebellious slaves.

Louis Metoyer, a son of Marie Therese and Pierre, began the Louisiana colonial-style main house, which was completed by his son. The lower floor is brick; the upper story is made of cypress.

When Hypolite and Henry Hertzog bought the plantation in the 1840s, they added the twin *garconnieres* and a kitchen wing. The house was sold again in 1884 before Mr. and Mrs. John Hampton Henry bought it in 1898. "Miss Cammie" Henry replanted and extended the

Melrose Plantation
COURTESY OF LOUISIANA OFFICE OF TOURISM

gardens, rescued the buildings, and revived local handicrafts.

Known as a patron of the arts, Miss Cammie often invited artists and writers to spend time at Melrose. Her guests included William Faulkner, Sherwood Anderson, and Alexander Wolcott.

The folk artist Clementine Hunter spent ninety of her 101 years at Melrose. Initially a servant, Hunter watched Miss Cammie's artistic guests at work, and eventually learned to paint herself. Over the years, Hunter developed her own distinctive style. By the time she died in 1988, she had become a prominent Southern primitive artist. Some of her art is exhibited at Melrose.

Open daily for tours; an admission is charged.

Hodges Gardens

The "Garden in the Forest" in west central Louisiana is a delightful discovery for nature lovers. The rolling pine hills and forests encompass forty-seven-hundred acres of lush foliage, colorful flowers, multilevel gardens, and a shimmering lake—all set amid sheer landscaping genius.

This wonderland in the forest began in the early 1940s when A.J. Hodges, a pioneer conservationist involved in a reforestation project, took his work one step further. He and his wife Nona began an experimental arboretum. In the process, they discovered an abandoned stone quarry. They recognized the potential of adding the natural rock formations to their scenic garden. After years of investing time, talent, and money, the beautiful Hodges Gardens opened to the public in 1956. Today, it is the nation's largest privately operated horticultural parkland and wildlife refuge. It is owned and operated by the nonprofit A.J. and Nona Trigg Hodges Foundation.

On the grounds, visitors may tour the conservatory and greenhouses, where there are exotic collections of palms, orchids, bromeliads, ferns, cacti, bougainvilleas, and everyday plants. All varieties of plants seen here can be purchased in the greenhouse. Nestled among the native greenery and constantly colorful flowers, you will find growing houses, a modern rose garden, and a daylily garden. You can even find cascading waterfalls in the sixty-acre formal garden.

Winter gardens boast camellias, pansies, anemones, narcissus, and winter honeysuckle. Spring brings bountiful blooms: azaleas, dogwood, tulips, and magnolia. Summer's roses, daylilies, water lilies, crepe myrtles, and annuals make way for the colors of fall.

From the Lookout Tower, nature lovers have a panoramic view of the property and the wildlife. Hodges Gardens is just off U.S. 171, between Many and Leesville, Louisiana. For additional information, call (318) 586-3523.

Bayou Country

South Louisiana's "Cajun Nation," or Acadiana, is a remarkable place. It is part old-world graciousness and part new-fangled activity. It is alligators and hauté cuisine, Acadian-style houses and grand antebellum mansions. It is a gumbo pot of interesting and intriguing people, places, language, and lagniappe. "Lagniappe" (pronounced lan-yap) means "a little something extra," and that is exactly what you can count on in South Louisiana. The heart of Acadiana is Lafayette.

The best thing to do on a visit here is to stay a week or so, get a map, and explore the backroads that lead to fascinating places. For example, Lake Martin, near Breaux Bridge, is a place where you can park on the parish road and see alligators sunning in the bayou, and pelicans and egrets decorating the cypress trees in the murky swamp.

St. Martinville is another treasure, with its

As luck would have it, two museums depicting the life and times of the Acadians are in Lafayette Parish, the heart of Cajun country. This region is one of the few remaining places in America that still holds on to its unique heritage and culture. The oldest of these two living-history parks is Acadian Village, a folk-life museum that includes period homes exemplifying Acadian architecture. The homes are furnished with native Louisiana antiques, appropriate to the time of early settlement.

Ten acres of gardens and woodlands, complete with a chapel, village store, blacksmith shop, and the different styles of Acadian houses, surround the Acadian Village. Quaint bridges cross the bayou of this educational and cultural center for Acadian history. For more information, call (337) 981-2364.

Vermilionville is the newest Cajun and Creole Living History Museum and Folklife Village. It is also located near Lafayette, on the banks of the Bayou Vermilion. This twenty-two-acre Cajun settlement portrays a life of laughter, good times, and hard work. Cajuns are known to work hard and play hard, which is a part of their proud heritage.

If you like Colonial Williamsburg in Virginia, chances are you will appreciate Vermilionville. The village is dedicated to authenticity, recreating period artifacts and furnishings in each of the carefully constructed buildings. Craft demonstrations and interpretive workshops are available throughout the year, and the performance center has daily offerings, specifically featuring French Cajun music. There are also two cajun/creole cooking demonstrations each day, and French is spoken by the entire staff. There's a gift shop, too. Vermilionville is funded in part by a grant from the Louisiana Endowment for the Humanities. For information, call (337) 233-4077 or 1-800-99-BAYOU.

Evangeline legacy and the Petit Paris Museum on the historic St. Martin de Tours Church Square. North of Lafayette is Washington, where a rambling old schoolhouse has been converted into an antiques mall, one of the biggest in the South, once you count the gymnasium, classrooms, and lunchroom. South Louisiana is endlessly interesting, and a place that has won the heart of this writer.

For information, contact the Lafayette Convention and Visitors Commission at (337) 232-3808 or 1-800-346-1958. Their address is P.O. Box 52066, Lafayette, LA 70505.

Chretien Point Plantation

LOCATION: 665 CHRETIEN POINT ROAD, SUNSET, LA 70584

Chretien Point is located ten miles north of Lafayette. From Lafayette, take I-10 west to Exit 97. Drive north approximately eight miles, through Ossun, Vatican, and Cankton. Two and two-tenths mile north of Cankton, turn left on Parish Road #356, heading toward Bristol. Go one block, turn right on Chretien Point Road, and go one mile. The plantation is on the left.

From Lafayette take I-49 to Exit 11, going

toward Sunset. As you go through Sunset, you will be on La. Hwy. 93 heading south. Stay on this road for 3.8 miles, until you reach Bristol Road. Turn right, go one block and turn right again. Go one mile; the plantation is on the left.

TELEPHONE: (318) 662-5876 OR 1-800-880-7050

FAX: (337) 662-5876

WEBSITE: N/A

Chretien Point
COURTESY OF LOUISIANA OFFICE OF TOURISM

When cotton planter Hypolite Chretien obtained a fine tract of land via a Spanish land grant around 1776, he commenced to build a somewhat modest home. When his son, Hypolite II, married Miss Felicité Neda, the spirited daughter of a neighboring planter, the couple wanted a "suitable mansion," so construction of the existing Chretien Point began in 1831.

Builders Samuel Young and Jonathan Harris designed and monitored construction of the elegant Greek Revival-style dwelling, though the house was built by slave labor. Among its most outstanding features are brick walls that measure eighteen inches thick, and a hipped roof covering an upper and lower gallery. Each gallery features gracefully arched and inset doors and windows. Six solid Doric columns support the entablature.

Hypolite II did not have a long time to enjoy the house, because he died of yellow fever not long after Chretien Point was finished. Felicité

managed the plantation for years. When she moved to New Orleans in 1845, her son Hypolite III took over. It was Hippolyte III's son, Jules, who left the house vacant. Over the years, it became a storehouse for hay, while chickens, cows, and pigs roamed freely in and out of what had been one of the grandest of the Louisiana plantation homes.

In its heyday, Chretien Point was a thriving ten-thousand-acre plantation. Today it has been completely restored as it was in its the glory days, when cotton and sugar cane were responsible for the Chretiens' great wealth. Interior furnishings and décor are representative of the 1840s and 1850s.

Rumors abound about the early house guests at Chretien Point. Supposedly, it was a rendezvous site for the pirate Jean Lafitte and his female friends. It is said that some of the pirate's treasure may still be buried nearby. To-day, Chretien Point is a bed-and-breakfast inn.

Open for daily tours; an admission is charged.

$\mathcal{S}$hadows-on-the-Teche

LOCATION: 317 EAST MAIN STREET, NEW
IBERIA, LA 70560
TELEPHONE: (337) 369-6446
FAX: (337) 365-5213
WEBSITE: www.shadowsontheteche.org

Shadows-on-the-Teche
COURTESY OF LOUISIANA OFFICE OF TOURISM

Among the treasures of this special land is Shadows-On-The-Teche in New Iberia. The Shadows, as it's called by those who know and love it, was built in 1831 by sugar-cane and cotton planter David Weeks.

Weeks wanted a home where his wife and six children could be comfortable, cool, and stylish. He built it primarily in the style of the day, which was Greek Revival, but he did make a few alterations. The Shadows features eight, coral-colored brick Tuscan columns across the front. It also has porticos that stretch across the length of the house on the first and second floors. A third floor, with dormer windows, blends into the slate roof.

The Greek Revival influence ends with the first view of the front. The rest of the house takes on a French Colonial style, with French doors and an outside staircase. Roof-high lou-vers and latticework cleverly conceal the stair-case, which is located at one end of the porch. The other end of the porch features the same green louvers for the sake of symmetry.

Inside, the regional Louisiana-French style comes into play, with three adjoining rooms across the front and back. You can reach most of the main rooms, which are on the second floor, by the outside stairway or by an enclosed stairway at the rear of the house.

Breezes from the Bayou Teche, which bor-ders the back lawn, and cross ventilation pro-vided by high ceilings and the strategic placement of doors and windows keep the Shadows as cool as possible.

When the Shadows was built, the prosper-ous Weeks operated one of the largest, high-est-producing sugar plantations in the Teche country. After three years of construction, the

Weeks family moved into the Shadows in June 1834, but David did not. He boarded a steamboat on the bayou in May and headed to Yale Medical College in Connecticut to obtain treatment for a malady, now thought to have been cancer. Though his condition worsened, he shipped American Empire furniture home to the bayou. Mary wrote to him on June 28, 1834, describing the move and saying how she had hated to move in without him. Weeks died in August 1834 while still in Connecticut.

Mary Conrad Weeks stayed on at the Shadows, caring for and educating her children and decorating her home. In 1841, Mary Weeks married Judge John Moore, who was a member of the United States House of Representatives. They enjoyed the social life in Washington and the planter society of Louisiana.

During the Civil War, Union forces marched into New Iberia and claimed the Shadows as their headquarters. Mary was determined to remain in her beloved Shadows-on-the-Teche, despite the Union occupation. The officer took over the first floor, while Mary, her sister-in-law, her daughter-in-law, and three servants remained on the second. Mary died in her own bed on December 29, although she was planning to leave the house the next day to visit with her son's family.

When the family returned from living as refugees in Texas after the war, Mary's oldest son and his family made the Shadows their home until his death in 1895. The house was lived in sporadically from 1895 until 1922.

In 1922, Weeks Hall, a great-grandson of David and Mary, returned from Paris and became enchanted with the old homeplace. It was, and still is, resplendent sitting amid tall moss-draped oaks and azaleas, with the quiet sound of the bayou nearby.

Hall restored the house and entertained lavishly, all the while trying to find ways to secure the future of the Shadows. He secured it by giving the house to the National Trust for Historic Preservation, after he had accumulated a supporting endowment. Hall died in 1958, and the house is today a National Trust property.

Of particular note among its adornments is the bronze doré chandelier in the parlor. The random-width flooring is polished and perfect. In the dining room, a crystal chandelier hangs over a Sheraton dining table set with Vieux Paris dinnerware. Other Sheraton furnishings are placed throughout the house.

The Shadows also contains an amazing collection of family letters, photographs, and documents, which were found in forty trunks in the attic. This "find" makes Shadows-on-the-Teche one of the best documented tour houses in the country.

Open daily for tours; an admission is charged.

Mississippi is a state with a strong sense of place, thanks in part to native Mississippi writers such as Eudora Welty, William Faulkner, and the playwright Tennessee Williams. Their words bring to the forefront things usually taken for granted—the gentleness of the people, a lifestyle that allows time to recall stories often heard on shady front porches, and the proud old mansions where guests are still greeted in the traditional Mississippi way.

There are many mansions in Mississippi, most of which were built by cotton planters and a few prosperous merchants in the early to mid-1800s. When the gallant call of the Confederacy came at the beginning of the Civil War in 1861, men and boys left the plantations and fields to fight for the cause. Those who made it back after four arduous years came home to a starving South, with more than their lifestyles changed. The plantations that were spared the Union torches were in dire need of repair, but the need for other things, such as food and survival, was more pressing. Fields were burned or overgrown, and not enough people were left to work the crops.

Although things have now changed for the better in the Magnolia State, the grand old mansions are the exceptions to change. These architectural treasures still stand tall and proud, serving the state today as major tourist attractions.

Natchez has the largest concentration of antebellum homes, though you will find impressive selections elsewhere. For information on historic tourism in Mississippi, contact the Mississippi Department of Economic and Community Development, Division of Tourism, at 1-800-WARMEST. You're sure to receive a warm welcome.

Beauvoir
COURTESY OF COAST CONVENTION
AND VISITORS BUREAU

Biloxi

Long known as a resort town, Biloxi, as well as the entire Mississippi Gulf Coast, has changed considerably since the advent of casino gaming. Documentation shows that the Mississippi beaches have been a destination of choice for about three hundred years. During that time, this coveted land has flown the flag of eight countries. "The Coast," as Mississippians call it, is no longer the sleepy little seacoast where waves could be heard lapping the shore on a quiet night.

Even with its current resemblance to Las Vegas, the Gulf Coast, with twenty-six miles of white-sand beach and many good seafood restaurants, is still a lovely place. The Seafood Industry Museum is the best place to learn more about the colorful history of the golden Gulf coast. For information, call the Coast Convention & Visitors Bureau at (228) 869-6699 or 1-800-237-9493.

Beauvoir

LOCATION: 2244 BEACH BOULEVARD, BILOXI,
    MS 39531
TELEPHONE: (228) 388-9074 OR 1-800-
    570-3818
FAX: (228) 388-7084
WEBSITE: www.beauvoir.org

This tranquil seaside estate was the last home of Jefferson Davis, the only president of the Confederate States of America. Beauvoir, whose name means "beautiful view" in French, indeed offers a magnificent view of the water on the Mississippi Sound and the lush green lawn and giant trees that surround the house.

Beauvoir has been described as a "raised cottage," though it is not a cottage at all. A wealthy planter named James Brown built the house in 1852. Later, Sarah Dorsey, who was known for her wealth and intellect, purchased the home.

Jefferson Davis was captured and imprisoned for two years after the close of the war. He was charged with treason, but never brought to trial. He was finally released from prison on a one-hundred-thousand-dollar bail bond that was signed by twenty prominent men, who included Cornelius Vanderbilt and New York newspaperman Horace Greeley. Davis, however, was denied United States citizenship.

After his release from prison, Jefferson Davis traveled in Europe and then settled in Memphis to head the Carolina Insurance Company. It failed within a few years. He visited the Mississippi coast looking for a place to write his memoirs. On one trip, he visited Sarah Dorsey, a childhood acquaintance of his wife, Varina. Mrs. Dorsey invited Jefferson Davis to stay in the library pavilion. He paid her fifty dollars a month for rent. In 1879, Mrs. Dorsey sold the property to Davis for $5500. He wrote *The Rise and Fall of the Confederate Government* and *A Short History of the Confederate States* while he lived at Beauvoir.

After Davis died in 1889, his widow Varina Howell Davis refused to sell Beauvoir when she was approached about selling it for use as a hotel. She later sold it to the United Sons of Confederate Veterans (USCV) for much less money than she was offered for the hotel. Today, Beauvoir is a National Historic Landmark,

which is still owned by the Mississippi Division of the Sons of Confederate Veterans. In October 1978, President Jimmy Carter signed a bill to restore citizenship to Jefferson Davis posthumously. The bill passed the congress without a dissenting vote.

In 1941, restoration of Beauvoir was begun, and today the house museum remains much as it did when the Davises were in residence. There is a presidential library, Confederate museum, historic cemetery, tomb of the unknown Confederate soldier, and a gift shop on the premises.

Open daily for tours; an admission is charged.

Natchez

Located on the site of an ancient Indian village, Natchez was founded as a French settlement in 1716. In its early years, the little town on the bluff above the Mississippi River flew the French, Spanish, British, and territorial flag, before finally accepting the Stars and Stripes. But the town should not be likened to a fickle femme fatale. Indeed, not! While Natchez was trying to find itself, it simply followed power.

As with other towns during the Civil War, Natchez yielded when the large numbers of Union troops came to take over the town. After all, what could they do? By not resisting, the grand homes were spared. Perhaps it was fortuitous.

Great wealth was abundant in Natchez just before the war began, because the area's climate and geography were perfect for growing the major money crop—cotton. Enamored with their wealth and good fortune, planters built ornate testaments to their success, and no expense was spared. Materials and furnishings were brought up from New Orleans, and some items were even imported from Europe. In the mid-1800s, Natchez boasted more millionaires than any place in America, except New York City. Once again, good times were not to last.

Natchezians had just begun to recover from the War Between the States, when other national problems occurred—World War I, the Great Depression, and World War II. Again, economic hard times were the order of the day.

In 1932, the grand old homes of Natchez were in the same sad state of neglect as *Gone With the Wind*'s Tara when Scarlett returned to the homeland with Melanie and baby in tow. Just as the legendary Scarlett O'Hara turned to the soil in times of need, so did the ladies of Natchez. Their lush and lovely flower gardens reflected their dedication.

In 1931, Natchez was designated to entertain the State Federation of Garden Clubs, whose members wanted to see Natchez's famous old antebellum gardens. Since the old gardens had fallen into neglect and decay, the Natchez ladies decided to open their antebellum homes with their informal gardens instead. The delegates were so enthusiastic about the house tour that the Natchez women decided to open their houses to the world in 1932, and the Natchez Pilgrimage was born. Today, the venerable Natchez Pilgrimage, which is held twice a year, continues to showcase the city's marvelous mansions.

Because Natchez boasts about five hundred antebellum structures and many outstanding historic homes, we could not include them all. All those that are included are open to the public and listed on the National Register of Historic Places. The Natchez Convention & Visitors Bureau can give you complete information. Their telephone number is 1-800-647-6724. The new Natchez Visitor Reception Center, at the foot of the Mississippi River Bridge on U.S. 84, has maps and information about a variety of Natchez and Mississippi attractions. The center is open daily.

The Natchez Pilgrimage Tours has specific information about historic homes. You can contact them at 1-800-647-6742.

Auburn

LOCATION: 400 DUNCAN AVENUE, NATCHEZ,
MS 39120

TELEPHONE: (601) 442-5981 OR 1-800-647-6742

FAX: N/A

WEBSITE: www.natchezpilgrimage.com

Auburn

Auburn is one of the oldest houses along the Mississippi River. It is also the first house in the Mississippi Territory to be designed and built by an architect. Begun in 1812, it was built to house the family of Massachusetts-born lawyer Lyman Harding. He was one of several New Englanders who chose to live in Natchez as a plantation owner. Harding was also Mississippi's first attorney general.

Harding commissioned architect Levi Weeks, also a Massachusetts native, to design his home. Weeks, who had been involved in the building trade in New York City with his brother Ezra, added Palladian elements to Harding's house, as well as design details from his collection of "pattern books." Thus, the house is predominately Federal style with sophisticated Georgian millwork on the interior.

Auburn was originally a two-story, five-bay house whose most elaborate architectural feature remains a freestanding circular staircase. The massive medium-red-brick structure fea-

tures a front entrance of four tall Ionic columns that support a two-story portico. A balustrade composed of sawn, flat balusters borders the second-story portico. Fanlights over the front doors, sidelights, and floor-length windows add detail as well as lighting.

In 1827, the house was sold to Stephen Duncan, a physician, cotton and sugar-cane planter, and entrepreneur who came to Natchez from Pennsylvania and "married well"—twice—into local families. Duncan flanked the original house with two-story, recessed wings on either side, making it more spacious and opulent to better entertain the likes of Henry Clay and other state and national leaders. Another concern was to have more room to accommodate the twenty-three servants who maintained the home and family.

Duncan vehemently opposed the Civil War and gave no support to the Confederate cause.

He left Natchez in 1863 and remained in New York City until his death four years later. The impressive and architecturally superior Auburn remained in the hands of Duncan heirs until 1911, when they donated it to the city of Natchez for use as a recreational park. The house now sits on the perimeter of Duncan Park. It is managed and maintained by the Auburn Garden Club. Tours of the home showcase the fine period furnishings and design details.

Open daily for tours; an admission is charged.

D'Evereux

D'Evereux

LOCATION: 160 D'EVEREUX DRIVE,
   NATCHEZ, MS 39120
TELEPHONE: (601) 446-8169 OR 1-800-
   647-6742
FAX: N/A
WEBSITE: www.natchezpilgrimage.com

Even the name sounds like a novel. Located on a slight incline, with moss-laden oaks protecting it from the sun, the grand mansion looks like it could grace the cover of a romance novel. It seems almost too perfect to be real.

D'Evereux was built in 1840 for William St. John Elliot, who wanted a grand home for elegant entertaining. With its large rooms and wide galleries illuminated with twinkling candles, the house was a natural setting for its many parties. When the Civil War began, the parties ceased.

The house is pure, classic Greek Revival, with six fluted Doric columns supporting the entablature at the roofline. Central doors on both stories are recessed, and a delicate cast-iron balcony is located on the second level. A gallery stretches across the front, and four tall windows tower over the door. D'Evereux is a Natchez Pilgrimage tour home.

Open for tours on a limited basis from April to August; an admission is charged.

Dunleith Plantation

LOCATION: 84 HOMOCHITTO STREET,
   NATCHEZ, MS 39120
TELEPHONE: (601) 446-8500 OR 1-800-
   433-2445
FAX: (601) 446-8554
WEBSITE: www.natchez/dunleith.com

Dunleith Plantation

On the site now occupied by the dazzling Dunleith, there once stood a home with connections to royalty. Job Routh gave the house that was originally on this site to his daughter, Mary, whose husband was Charles Dahlgren. Dahlgren was a direct descendant of Sweden's King Gustavus Adolphus. He would later become a brigadier general in the Confederate army.

Unfortunately, the original house burned in 1855. Construction on a new house began soon after, and the Dahlgrens were the first owners of the new house. It was sold in 1859 to thoroughbred-horse breeder Alfred Davis, who renamed it Dunleith.

Today, Dunleith's forty acres of landscaped grounds create a perfect setting for this Greek Revival-style work of art. Dunleith is unique among Mississippi homes because it is the only house that is completely encircled by twenty-six massive Tuscan columns and double-tiered galleries.

Resembling a Greek temple, it is said to be one of the most photographed houses in America. It has also been a stately presence in the films *Huckleberry Finn* and *Showboat*. Photographers recognize that the grounds and formal gardens provide as many photo opportunities as the house, for Dunleith reigns over wooded bayous where Spanish moss-draped trees segue into lush green pastures.

When you enter through the doors of Dunleith, you find a wide hall that runs the depth of the house. Two large rooms adjoin each side of the hall. To the left are outstanding double parlors, where the furnishings now include fine Belter carved parlor furniture.

The dining room features French Zuber wallpaper that spent World War I in a cave in Alsace-Lorraine. The wallpaper was placed in the cave for protection, and the only vestiges of the time spent there are a few mildew spots, barely visible to the unsuspecting eye. The wallpaper was printed from woodblocks carved in 1855.

Dunleith is now a privately owned, award-winning bed-and-breakfast inn, with eleven rooms in the courtyard wing and eight rooms in the main house. Breakfast is served in the restored poultry house, where old brick walls and rich warm woods create a homey atmosphere.

Tours are conducted daily; an admission is charged.

Longwood
COURTESY OF NATCHEZ PILGRIMAGE TOURS

*L*ongwood

LOCATION: 140 LOWER WOODVILLE ROAD,
    NATCHEZ, MS 39120
TELEPHONE: (601) 442-5193 OR 1-800-
    647-6742
FAX: (601) 446-8687
WEBSITE: www.natchezpilgrimage.com

The time when grand mansions were built routinely ended in 1861, at the beginning of what loyal Southerners called the "War of Northern Aggression." In many parlors and at many a political podium, some of the most affluent landowners maintained that the war was fought over the issue of states' rights and nothing more. But, the issue of slavery was of paramount importance to planters. Without a labor force, the plantations that brought all the wealth were not economically feasible.

Haller Nutt, the builder of Longwood, felt dif-
ferently about the war than most Southern planters. He took a strong Unionist position, a stance that was not popular in the South in those days.

Haller's father, Dr. Rush Nutt, was also a cotton planter and geologist, who experimented with various strains of cotton seeds. At one time or another, Haller Nutt owned plantations in Mississippi and Louisiana, which encompassed more than forty thousand acres of rich land. As a result, he could well afford to build the thirty-two-room Longwood.

In 1859, Haller Nutt hired famed Philadelphia architect Samuel Sloan to design and oversee the construction of his six-story octagonal dream house. Sloan sent skilled craftsmen, who completed the massive exterior in 1861. White Moorish columns and arches fronted all eight sides of the red-brick house. The Byzantine dome, which featured sixteen clerestory windows, was a source of wonder and awe. The rest of the home also featured a highly advanced lighting and ventilation system.

As the war got underway in 1861, the Yankee construction crew returned home to Pennsylvania, leaving the interior of the massive Longwood unfinished. It became known as "Nutt's Folly."

Dr. Nutt, his wife, and their eight children moved into the nine-room basement. Their fortune went up in smoke as both the Confederate and Federal armies burned the cotton fields.

Haller Nutt died of pneumonia in 1864, but the Nutt family continued to live in the cool, rambling basement until 1968.

Longwood was indeed a brilliant design and still is a treat to see. On the top floors, construction crates are still visible to the many visitors who come to gaze in amazement at the lovely, still unfinished, Longwood. This National Historic Landmark is owned and maintained by the Pilgrimage Garden Club.

Open daily for tours; an admission is charged.

*M*agnolia Hall

LOCATION: 215 SOUTH PEARL, NATCHEZ, MS 39120

TELEPHONE: (601) 442-6672

FAX: (601) 443-9065

WEBSITE: N/A

This beautiful mansion was built in 1858 by Thomas Henderson, a wealthy planter, merchant, and cotton broker. It has the distinction of being the last grand Natchez house to be built before the Civil War—and grand it is. It is one of the finest examples of the Greek Revival style in Natchez and features a well-proportioned portico with massive Ionic columns. The brick house was stuccoed, painted brown and scored to imitate the brownstone so popular in the northeast at the time. Magnolia Hall derives

Magnolia Hall

its name from the plaster arabesques of magnolia leaves and blossoms that adorn its ceilings.

Thomas Henderson was a sixty-year-old widower when he built his new mansion on the site of his family home, Pleasant Hill. He moved the old house by having it rolled on logs to its present site a block away.

The Hendersons were a prominent pioneer family. Thomas Henderson's father, John, had left his native Scotland in 1770. He owned numerous plantations in Natchez, wrote the first book published in the Natchez Territory, and helped found the Presbyterian Church in Natchez in 1807. In 1853, Thomas Henderson was elected vice-president of the American Colonization Society, an organization formed to free slaves and return them to Africa. His descendants have been involved in the civic, business, religious, and political life of the area since that time.

During the Civil War, the family and the house suffered. The servant wing of Magnolia Hall was damaged by a shell from a Union gunboat that bombarded the town from the Mississippi River several blocks to the west. Thomas's two sons fought for the Confederacy. One was wounded, the other taken prisoner. Thomas himself died at Magnolia Hall before the war ended.

The house contains many original Henderson pieces and artifacts. It is owned and maintained by the Natchez Garden Club. Magnolia Hall houses a museum featuring costumes reminiscent of the antebellum period, displays of historical importance, a collection of antique dolls, and a gift shop.

Open daily for tours; an admission is charged.

Melrose

LOCATION: ONE MELROSE PLACE, NATCHEZ, MS 39120

TELEPHONE: (601) 446-5790

WEBSITE: www.nps.gov (the National Parks website)

Between 1841 and 1848, prominent planter and lawyer John T. McMurran built this lovely, red-brick, white-columned Melrose. The house was part of a veritable compound, complete with an outdoor kitchen. Kitchens were often

Melrose
COURTESY OF NATCHEZ PILGRIMAGE TOURS

in separate buildings for several reasons. This arrangement kept the mess, such as plucking chickens, out of the house, kept the heat from the house, and protected the house from fire. Within close proximity to the kitchen were the dairy, slaves' quarters, stables, and a carriage house.

After the Civil War, McMurran sold Melrose to George Malin Davis, who later gave Melrose to his daughter as a wedding gift. Davis's grandson, George Malin Davis Kelly, who moved to Melrose in 1901, began the trend to restore rather than remodel. When the young Kellys came to Natchez for their honeymoon, they fell in love with the house and decided to stay and restore the home.

Amazingly, the block-printed floor cloths in the hall are still intact, along with the original chandelier by Cornelius and Baker of Philadelphia, and the woodgrained, or *faux bois*, doors. The parlor furnishings are rosewood Victorian pieces, including an unusual "courtship" sofa. The elaborate scroll and floral patterns carved on the rosewood furniture in the parlor were the inspiration for Gorham Sterling's "Melrose" pattern. Additionally, the house also contains a rare grand piano and a Charles White sideboard.

This National Historic Landmark has been a Natchez showplace since its construction. Now, Melrose is a stellar attraction for the Natchez National Historical Park. Congress authorized the creation of the park in 1988, but it did not begin operation until 1990 when Melrose was acquired. The park was established to preserve and interpret the history of Natchez, which it does through Melrose and the William Johnson House.

Open daily for tours; an admission is charged.

Monmouth Plantation

LOCATION: 36 MELROSE AVENUE, NATCHEZ, MS 39120

TELEPHONE: (601) 442-5852 OR 1-800-828-4531

FAX: (601) 446-7762

WEBSITE: www.monmouthplantation.com

This National Historic Landmark was once the home of Mexican War general John Anthony Quitman, who later became governor of Mississippi and a United States congressman. Built around 1818 on a sloping Natchez hill, Monmouth symbolizes the gracious lifestyle for which the Old South was known. It also provides an elegant respite for visitors and overnight guests who enjoy strolling the twenty-six acres of landscaped grounds.

Monmouth is Greek Revival in style, though other homes of the style and period are almost delicate in comparison to the sturdy, fortress-like mansion.

In 1853, the Greek Revival portico was added and the original handmade-brick wall was covered with eggshell stucco and then scored. Today, the wall is white, except for certain times of the day when it appears to have a pink cast. Four strong, square columns support the portico.

A "formal mood" best describes the interior of Monmouth. Ice-blue silk covers the Rococo-revival furniture in the double parlor. The furniture is made even grander by the subdued light from a Waterford crystal chandelier. Full and fanciful swags, bordered with rich fringe, adorn the windows.

The bedrooms feature period furniture, with tester and half-tester beds bathed in fabric that usually matches the color of the walls. Monmouth is, in a word, romantic. It is a favorite of those who film in the Magnolia State.

Monmouth Plantation
COURTESY OF MONMOUTH PLANTATION

For example, actors and crew were in residence at Monmouth during the filming of John Grisham's *A Time to Kill.*

Monmouth is the only property in Mississippi listed on the prestigious National Trust's Historic Hotels of America. The bed-and-breakfast inn is large enough to qualify as a small hotel. There are seven bedrooms in the mansion itself, and a total of thirty-one rooms in the nine buildings that make up the site. There is also a gift shop on the premises.

Open daily for tours; an admission is charged.

Rosalie

LOCATION: 100 ORLEANS STREET, NATCHEZ, MS 39120

TELEPHONE: (601) 445-9137

FAX: SAME AS TELEPHONE NUMBER

WEBSITE: www.natchezpilgrimage.com

The indomitable, red-brick Rosalie, like Auburn, is a grand example of the Federal style. Both have four columns across the front double-tiered porticos. The noticeable difference is that Auburn's columns are the more ornate Ionic, while Rosalie features the less frivolous Doric pattern. Rosalie also lacks the recessed wings. Now owned by the Mississippi State Society of the Daughters of the American Revolution, Rosalie was built on a bluff near the Mississippi River in 1823.

Lumber trader and sawmill owner Peter Little supposedly had Rosalie built for his bride, Eliza, and held high hopes for grand entertaining in the large double parlors. Peter and Eliza were married more than a decade before construction began on Rosalie.

Eliza became very religious, so in 1852, Peter donated the land for the members of the Methodist Church to build a parsonage for their minister on the estate. The parsonage is still on the property today.

By 1858, the Wilson family purchased

Rosalie

Rosalie from the Little estate, and Rosalie became well known as a real "Southern mansion."

The Wilsons could not know that the glory days of Southern splendor were about to come to a cannonball's halt. A few short years before their home became a command post for the Union forces that occupied Natchez, the Wilsons purchased a beautiful twenty-piece John Henry Belter parlor set. This suite of furniture has become so famous that other Belter furniture with the same pattern of carving is said to be of the "Rosalie pattern." Amazingly, the "Rosalie pattern" is still in the parlor today, along with rare Sevrès porcelain, Reed & Barton silver, a piano, and a harp.

Visitors today hear the story of the silver and gold-leaf pier mirrors and other valuables that were wrapped and buried when the cry rang out, "The Yankees are coming!" As it happened, according to a biography that Matilda Gresham wrote about her husband, General Walter Gresham, some of the Yankee officers were considerate enough to remove and store the curtains.

Union general Ulysses S. Grant once slept in the four-poster bed in an upstairs bedroom during his stay in the river city. During the summer of 1864, as many as five thousand Union soldiers were in Natchez, though the number lessened considerably when generals Grant and Sherman began their marches through Georgia and Tennessee.

Union general Gresham and his wife also lived at Rosalie during the war. They became such good friends with the Wilsons that they came back to visit long after the war ended.

The interior of Rosalie is grand and colorful, with its white walls, red damask drapes and upholstery, and a patterned, reproduction Brussels carpet in red and gold. The white-marble mantels, stained by roaring fires enjoyed by Yankee soldiers, still maintain a look of proud elegance. There is a gift shop on the premises.

Open daily for tours; an admission is charged.

Stanton Hall

LOCATION: 401 HIGH STREET, NATCHEZ, MS 39120

TELEPHONE: (601) 442-6282 OR 1-800-647-6742

FAX: (601) 446-8687

WEBSITE: www.natchezpilgrimage.com

Stanton Hall

Located within walking distance of downtown Natchez, Stanton Hall is among the grandest of the grand old Southern mansions. From its perch atop a slight incline, the house and grounds cover a city block. Protected from the elements by towering oak trees, Stanton Hall is as resplendent today as it was when it was completed.

From a distance, the house looks like a giant, ornate dollhouse. It has tall Corinthian columns across the front, and delicate, lacy, cast-iron railings adorn the front and side galleries. A cupola, or widow's walk, completes the fantasy-like appearance.

Although the exact date when construction started is not known, it is believed that planter and cotton broker Frederick Stanton began this magnificent Greek Revival-style mansion sometime in the 1850s. At the height of his wealth and influence, the Belfast, Ireland, native owned more than fifteen-thousand acres on six plantations in and around Adams County.

His city home, originally called Belfast, was to be his showplace, and he funneled much of his money into it.

Although Stanton hired Natchez architect Thomas Rose and a crew of local artisans to construct his residence, he ordered many building materials and decorative elements from Europe. Still intact today are silver doorknobs and hinges from England, and huge, ornate pier mirrors from France. Mantels, which were crafted from Carrera marble, were sculpted in New York, and the gas-burning chandeliers were made in Philadelphia.

Unfortunately, Frederick Stanton had little time to enjoy his masterpiece, because he died a few months after its completion. The house remained privately owned until 1894, when it became the Stanton College for Women. When the college closed in 1901, Stanton Hall became a private residence until 1938. At that time, the Pilgrimage Garden Club purchased the home, and it now serves as the club's headquarters. Club members manage the house, conduct tours, and operate a gift shop on the premises.

Visitors who enter the front doors of Stanton Hall are enveloped in the central hallway that extends seventy-two feet. Here, they take in the grandeur of the triple parlors, with their amazing, lavish plasterwork. The plasterwork becomes even more astonishing when one realizes that it was created by hand.

Period furnishing are used throughout, and many original pieces have been donated and returned to the house. The Louis XV rosewood parlor set is a source of pride for those who maintain the marvelous old structure.

Attached to a building that dates to the 1890s is a new building, which houses a wonderful Southern restaurant. The Carriage House Restaurant, which serves lunch, is well known for its consistently good regional cuisine. During the Pilgrimage, dinner is also served.

Open daily for tours; an admission is charged.

Vicksburg

Much of Vicksburg's rich and varied history is associated with the Civil War. From the hallowed hills of the Vicksburg National Cemetery, where nearly seventeen thousand Union soldiers were laid to rest, to the Vicksburg City Cemetery, where Confederate soldiers were interred, history is everywhere. This "Gibraltar of the Confederacy" was finally captured by Union troops in 1863 after a forty-seven-day siege. During the siege, townspeople moved into caves to avoid Union gunfire and cannonballs. It was lucky that they did, for some of the grand old homes were hit.

Although the homes survived the siege, cannonballs are still lodged in a few old walls. The houses stand elegant and proud, confirming that grace and stability can survive hard times and the horrors of war.

But there's more to Vicksburg than history. Today something new and glitzy casts a colorful glow on the mighty Mississippi River. It is casino gaming on big land-locked vessels, complete with Las Vegas-style bright lights. History buffs who are accustomed to the more sedate side of the city on the bluff have had to adjust.

For information, call the Vicksburg Convention & Visitors Bureau at (601) 636-9421 or 1-800-221-3536. The center is located near the Vicksburg National Military Park at the corner of Clay Street and Old Hwy. 27.

Anchuca

LOCATION: 1010 FIRST EAST STREET,
VICKSBURG, MS 39183
TELEPHONE: (601) 661-0111 OR 1-888-686-0111
FAX: (601) 661-0420
WEBSITE: N/A

Anchuca
COURTESY OF VICKSBURG CONVENTION AND VISITORS BUREAU

Whether its architectural style is Southern Colonial or Greek Revival, Anchuca is a place you'd love to call home. Built in 1830 by local politician J.W. Mauldin, the house was named Anchuca, which meant "happy home" in the language of a local tribe of Native Americans.

Anchuca sits on land which the Reverend Newitt Vick, the founder of Vicksburg, purchased for two dollars an acre. A later owner was Joseph Davis, brother of CSA president Jefferson Davis. After Jefferson Davis's release from serving a prison term for "subversive activities," he visited his brother at Anchuca. From Anchuca's balcony over the front entrance, he made a speech to supporters.

Anchuca's imposing exterior gives way to a more delicate, feminine interior, furnished with fine antiques and pieces of decorative art, representing the period from the late 1700s to the mid-1800s. There are some Victorian pieces, but Empire furnishings are abundant. Owner Loveta Byrne has a good eye for antiques and art, which you find obvious once you enter Anchuca. She has also owned and furnished historic homes in Natchez and New Orleans.

The former slave quarters, which were also built around 1830, are now luxurious bed-and-breakfast accommodations. There are also limited overnight accommodations available in the main house. Those who stay at Anchuca are invited to get away from it all, to experience the real Old South, with no phones, faxes, or e-mail. A gift shop is on the premises.

Open Wednesday through Saturday for tours of six or more (reservations requested); an admission is charged.

$\mathcal{B}$alfour House

LOCATION: (P.O. BOX 781, VICKSBURG, MS
39181) 1002 CRAWFORD STREET,
VICKSBURG, MS 39183
TELEPHONE: (601) 638-7113 OR 1-800-
294-7113
FAX: (601) 638-8484
WEBSITE: www.balfourhouse.com

Balfour House

Although Balfour House is a red-brick, Greek Revival house with ornate white trim, it bears little resemblance to any other house in the region. Even with Corinthian columns and other classic elements, the house is unique.

Built in 1835, Balfour House is known as the "House of Generals" because several high-ranking military leaders were in residence during the course of the Civil War. However, the house is best known for two other things. First, it was the site of the famous Balfour Christmas Eve Ball, which was interrupted by news that the Union army had penetrated the blockade, and a massive force was heading toward Vicksburg. All the officers at the ball bade their ladies farewell and went off to battle.

Secondly, it was the residence of diarist Emma Balfour, who kept an important account of the Siege of Vicksburg. From the window of her house, she had a bird's-eye view of the war on both sides of the river.

Here's a sample of what she observed:

"As I sat at my window, I saw mortars from the west passing entirely over the house and the parrot shells from the east passing by—crossing each other and this terrible fire raging in the center. One or two persons who had passes to leave the city if they could returned last night, Grant saying that no one should leave the city until it surrendered. I have almost made up my mind not to think of retiring at all at night. I see we are to have no rest. They are evidently trying to harass our army into submission. All night they fired so that our poor soldiers have no rest as we have few reserves, it is very hard on them."

The three-story elliptical spiral staircase is an outstanding feature of Balfour House, and the furnishings are authentic to the style of the

1850s. One wonders how such massive furniture could be transported up such delicate-looking stairs, but indeed it was, for the house is beautifully furnished. Its 1982 restoration won the Award of Merit from the Mississippi State Historical Society. This designated Mississippi Landmark now operates as a bed-and-breakfast inn.

Open for daily tours; an admission is charged.

Cedar Grove

LOCATION: 2200 OAK STREET, VICKSBURG, MS 39180

TELEPHONE: (601) 636-1000 OR 1-800-862-1300

FAX: (601) 634-6126

WEBSITE: www.cedargroveinn.com

Perched on a terrace near the Mississippi River, this peach-colored mansion is one of the Vicksburg houses that has Union cannonballs embedded in its walls. Built by John A. Klein in 1840, this sturdy Greek Revival-style house features massive Doric columns. Placed across the front of the house, these columns also support the upstairs gallery. Thigh-high, embellished wrought-iron railing surrounds the first-

Cedar Grove

and second-story galleries. A curved bay window is a dramatic feature of the left wing.

Cedar Grove is one of the largest antebellum homes in the South, and it was obviously built for comfort and stylish entertaining. There's a grand ballroom, and the lovely parlors feature original marble mantels and crystal chandeliers.

The mansion's décor is opulent, with fine period antiques used throughout. On a quiet night, you can hear the river traffic from the nearby Mississippi River from the galleries. Cedar Grove is now a popular and busy bed-and-breakfast inn and restaurant.

Open for daily tours; an admission is charged.

Duff Green Mansion

LOCATION: 1114 FIRST EAST STREET,
VICKSBURG, MS 39180

TELEPHONE: (601) 636-6968 OR 1-800-
992-0037

FAX: (601) 634-1061

WEBSITE: N/A

This unusual three-story Vicksburg mansion is one of the finest examples of Palladian architecture in the country. The house is known for its elaborate cast-iron grillwork and fine interior design and decor.

Duff Green, a merchant, had the house built for his wife as a wedding gift in 1856. Her parents donated the property on which it was built. Seven years later during the Siege of Vicksburg, when Yankee gunboats shelled the city, many of the townspeople—among them the Greens—left their homes near the river to take up temporary residence in nearby caves.

While living in a cave, Mrs. Green gave birth to a baby, who was appropriately named Siege Green. Throughout the Civil War, the Duff Green mansion served as a hospital for both Confederate and Union soldiers. As part of the home tour, guides point out the spot where the owner attempted a repair after a cannonball entered the wall.

The Duff Green mansion is a private home,

Old Capitol Museum, Jackson

The Old Capitol, as Mississippians call the State Historical Museum, is said to be one of America's best examples of Greek Revival architecture. Indeed it is, since it was begun in 1833 at the time the style was coming into its own. The Old Capitol is truly an outstanding representation of the classic simplicity and strength of the Greek Revival style.

The Historical Museum in Jackson is located on Capitol Green, the original square designated as the site for "the capitol" on the 1822 map of the city. Though some records and documents were lost during the Civil War when Jackson was burned by Union troops—thus the nickname "Chimneyville"—the capitol survived.

This massive structure was the seat of government until 1903, when the New Capitol was completed. During its reign as the official temple of state government, the first law in the United States recognizing the property rights of married women was passed here in 1839. And it was here that the state legislature voted to secede from the Union in 1861.

Today, permanent exhibits and accompanying texts tell the Mississippi story in chronological order, from DeSoto's journey through the region in 1540, right up to the state's recent significant historical events. The nation's first civil rights exhibit is here, along with important documents on the lifestyles of early Mississippi women. For information, call (601) 359-6920.

Duff Green Mansion

with the owners living on the third floor, but it also operates as a bed-and-breakfast inn.

Open daily for tours; an admission is charged.

Meridian

In 1864, General William Tecumseh Sherman, wrote: "Meridian, with its depots, store houses, arsenal, hospitals, offices, hotels . . . no longer exists." When you consider that Sherman and his ten thousand men completely destroyed Meridian, it becomes even more significant to see today's thriving and prosperous city. Today, Meridian is a busy medical, industrial, and business center for central Mississippi.

One special attraction in Meridian is the rare Dentzel Carousel. Located in Highland Park, the carousel features twenty-eight hand-painted and hand-carved horses. Built around 1895, this carousel is one of only three two-row Dentzel Carousels known to exist. For information on the carousel and other Meridian sites, contact the Meridian-Lauderdale County Tourism Bureau at (601) 482-8001 or 1-888- 868-7720.

Merrehope

LOCATION: 905 MARTIN LUTHER KING
MEMORIAL DRIVE, MERIDIAN, MS 39301
TELEPHONE: (601) 483-8439
FAX: N/A
WEBSITE: N/A

This twenty-room mansion had humble beginnings. In 1859, the daughter of a town founder and her husband built a cottage that evolved into Merrehope. The original structure is still attached to the current house, which grew to its present size by 1904. The architectural style is not easily identified, though the overall result is interesting and imposing.

It seems that each owner contributed some semblance of a different style. The house is part Greek Revival, but not entirely. It has a bit of an Islamic look, but not too much, although the origin of the Islamic influence cannot be determined.

Nine Ionic columns support the roof and its extension over the second-level gallery. The gallery features a large, railed balcony. There is even a semi-octagonal portico over a two-story bay window on the right side.

Local women's clubs formed the Meridian Restoration Foundation, Inc., and purchased the house. The name Merrehope is a combination of "Mer" for Meridian, "re" for restoration, and "hope" for the dream that two hundred club women had that they could restore the home to its 1904 condition. After a much-needed restoration, the former apartment house is once again a grand showplace. The doorway features etched, ruby-colored glass around the sidelight and transom. Inside, you'll find plaster cornices, ceiling medallions, and other design elements. The ladies of the clubs have selected appropriate period furnishings for use throughout the house.

Merrehope is especially festive during the Christmas holidays, when the foundation holds its annual "Trees of Christmas" event.

Open Monday through Saturday for tours; an admission is charged.

Columbus

Located on the edge of the rolling hill country and the rich, prairie land of northeast Mississippi, Columbus is a woman's town. It is the home of the highly acclaimed Mississippi University for Women, which was established in 1884 as the nation's first state-supported college for women, though it now admits men. To further emphasize the historical role of the women of Columbus, we must call attention to the fact that it was a few Columbus women who created the Confederate Decoration Day back in 1866. This holiday evolved into the nation's Memorial Day. These ladies had a generous nature and also decorated the graves of Union soldiers, who in the not-too-distant past had been the sworn enemies of their husbands, fathers, sons, and brothers.

Situated on a bluff overlooking the Tombigbee River, this city of thirty-thousand people is also a town filled with about one hundred magnificent antebellum mansions. A revitalized downtown, with antique and specialty shops, historic sites, and a residential high school for gifted students, join with a United States Air Force pilot-training facility nearby to keep things interesting. There's also an annual springtime Columbus Pilgrimage tour of historic homes and a big fall antiques show and forum.

The best place to get information about Columbus and its offerings is at the Welcome Center at 300 Main Street, which is also the first home of Pulitzer Prize-winning playwright Tennessee Williams. You can also call the Convention & Visitors Bureau at (662) 329-1191 or 1-800-327-2686.

Rosewood Manor

Rosewood Manor

LOCATION: 719 SEVENTH STREET NORTH,
COLUMBUS, MS 39701
TELEPHONE: (662) 328-7313
FAX: N/A
WEBSITE: N/A

It is most unusual to find four and one-half acres of beautifully landscaped grounds within a few blocks of downtown, but at Rosewood Manor, that's what you'll find. An added attraction is the narrow, winding, brick drive, which is laid out in a herringbone pattern. It leads up to the 1835 white-brick mansion. The white-and-glass gazebo, perfectly positioned on the grounds, stands as a focal point for the gardens. The setting is a perfect place for afternoon tea or coffee.

The Greek Revival/Federal-style house with its two-story portico is perched in a position to overlook a ravine, which has a story of its own. Cotton planter Richard Sykes built the house for his new fiancée, who happened to be a Yankee girl who didn't know Southern ways. Upon arrival, she took one look at the ravine and headed back up north, for she feared that vapors rising from the ravine would cause sickness. Sykes later married a Southern girl who held no such superstitions.

One interesting feature of the house is that the walls are three bricks thick; the bricks are handmade and obviously made to last. Four rooms—a four over four—open off a central hall on both floors. A wing has been added on one side, and the house boasts a full basement. The original heart-pine floor is still intact. Current owners Dewitt and Grayce Hicks bought the house in 1978, and have since added fine American and Continental antiques to their family pieces.

Also on the grounds is a small, restored chapel, complete with beautiful stained glass windows and original woodwork.

Rosewood Manor has been featured in many magazines and on television. It is a popular attraction whose owners believe that sharing their historic home is important to the community's tourism efforts. For more than twenty years, it was a Pilgrimage tour home.

Open each Wednesday, during special events, or by appointment. Tickets are available for a fee at the Welcome Center on 300 Main Street.

Temple Heights

LOCATION: 515 NINTH STREET NORTH,
  COLUMBUS, MS 39701
TELEPHONE: (662) 328-0599
FAX: N/A
WEBSITE: N/A

Temple Heights

This home is aptly named, for it resembles a Grecian temple with Doric columns on three sides. Built on a hill in 1837 by General Richard T. Brownrigg, who earned the rank of general with the North Carolina Militia, the style is primarily a Greek Revival exterior, with a Federal interior. Brownrigg came to Mississippi from the area near Edenton, North Carolina, where he owned a shipping line that ran between Edenton, Jamaica, and Belfast. He also owned fisheries, a plantation named Wingfield, and a home at Nags Head. By the early 1830s, eastern North Carolina was changing. Brownrigg also realized his businesses were not doing well, so he decided to relocate.

An entrepreneur and a man known to appreciate opportunities, Brownrigg heard that good land was selling for low prices on the rich prairie of northeast Mississippi, so he bought twenty-four-thousand dollars worth of prime land. In October 1835, he began transporting family members and about one hundred slaves from North Carolina to Mississippi. When they

arrived in December, Brownrigg was already well on his way to becoming a successful cotton planter and factor, with offices on the west bank of the river in what was then called West Port.

Brownrigg bought a twelve-room log house from Choctaw chief John Pitchlynn. Letters of the day indicate that his wife felt "stuck in the mud" so far from town, so Brownrigg built Temple Heights in Columbus. Research by Temple Heights' current owners and historians Carl and Dixie Butler suggest that the house was patterned after Mrs. Brownrigg's family home, Mulberry Hill, which overlooked the Albemarle Sound in North Carolina. Certain similarities can be seen in photographs of Mulberry Hill.

Temple Heights itself reflects elements of more than one style. The facade of the four-storied house is Federal and the porticoes are Greek, while the scale of the interior spaces and the decorative millwork are Federal. The result is that this comfortable home has warmth, but also has a certain sophistication, perhaps because it aptly combines a bit of East Coast culture with the Mississippi frontier.

After suffering from financial hardships caused by flood damage, Brownrigg died on Christmas Day in 1846. Thomas Harris bought Temple Heights in 1847 for only $3,600. At that time, columns were added, which enhanced the classic look. Updates continued until 1849. Mrs. Harris, who was from a Georgia political family, added servant's stairs, as well. The house was sold to the Fontaines, and then to the Kinnebrews, who owned it from 1887 to 1965.

Today, Temple Heights is recognized by experts for its authenticity. The Butlers, who bought the house in 1967, have made every effort to maintain the architectural integrity of the house, for they believe that a restored property should be a complete entity. The interior must be compatible with the exterior. When the Butlers began restoration, they used what was already in place to make authentic replacements. By matching existing cabinetry, by scraping and matching paint, and by duplicating existing woodwork with woodgraining, they succeeded in maintaining authenticity.

Restoration efforts focused on the period of Brownrigg ownership. Over the years, the Butlers have collected pieces appropriate to that time and the style of the house. Concentrating on decorative arts from the 1837 to 1847, they've acquired a major collection of Parian porcelain. Now one of the most significant Parian collections in the South, the Butler collection was recently exhibited at the New Orleans Museum of Art. The Butlers also have an important collection of Old Paris porcelain.

The original outdoor kitchen has been restored to the way it was in the late 1830s, complete with an open fireplace. During the Pilgrimage tour, you may even see a pot of greens cooking on the fire.

Each year, architectural students from Auburn University come to Columbus to sketch significant historic houses. The two houses they consistently choose to draw are Temple Heights and Waverley. Temple Heights is the only house in Columbus that is a Mississippi Landmark. It is also on the Historic American Building Survey, on the National Register of Historic Places, and is a part of the Columbus Pilgrimage spring tour.

Open for tours on Tuesday, Thursday, and Saturday. Tickets are available for a fee at the Welcome Center on 300 Main Street.

$\mathcal{W}$averley Plantation

LOCATION: WAVERLEY ROAD, ROUTE 2, BOX
234, WEST POINT, MS 39773
Waverly is located off Ms. Hwy. 50, be-
tween Columbus and West Point. Follow signs.
TELEPHONE: (662) 494-1399
FAX: N/A
WEBSITE: N/A

Waverley Plantation

If a location scout for a film was looking for a structure to represent the Old South, Waverley Plantation would be a good site. Located between Columbus and West Point, Mississippi, it is more than a mansion; it's a reflection of the region's history. Waverley was built for a Columbia University-educated lawyer who came to Mississippi with the U.S. Land Commission. The commission was ordered to dispose of land ceded to the government by the Chickasaw Indians in 1839.

Colonel George Hampton Young did his job for the Land Commission and, in the process, found a prime parcel of land, which he bought for himself. The verdant land, a few thousand acres near the Tombigbee River, was perfect for growing cotton. He left the government, gave up the practice of law, and devoted his time and energies to becoming a successful cotton planter. He also continued to buy land for cotton crops.

It is believed that the design of Waverley

may have been influenced by Orson Fowler's 1848 book, *A Home for All,* though Young was known to build according to his preference and needs. By 1849, Young's plans were in place, and construction began in 1850. He imported a few gifted craftsmen to build his home while he oversaw the planting of the cotton fields and the growth of the plantation. The plantation eventually included orchards, sawmills, gristmills, a kiln, a leather tannery, warehouses, a store, a kennel for hunting dogs, and even a brick swimming pool, which was fed by an artesian well. The house was finished in 1852.

Peeking quietly around one of the Magnolia State's biggest magnolia trees, you see Waverley, with its Ionic columns fronting a two-story recessed gallery. Small Doric columns stand guard beside the front door, which is surrounded by red Venetian glass transom and sidelights with a lyre motif. The house is built of cypress boards, which are painted white.

Atop the house on a hipped roof is a crown-like cupola, which has an octagonal design that boasts sixteen windows and a three-foot-high octagonal finial. More than ornamentation, the windows provide ventilation, as heat rises up from the central hall and the balconies to the cupola, and then out the sixteen windows.

Step inside, and look up to see the rotunda, rising about fifty-five feet over the entrance hall/ballroom. You will be surprised at the curving staircases that begin on the ground floor and wind around three octagonal balconies. From here, it's apparent that Waverley has four floors rather than three.

Waverley's geometric design is indeed amazing. What a place it must have been in its heyday, when grand soirées were lit by candles placed along the stairs, the balconies, and the "wedding alcove" in the parlor.

The plantation stood vacant for fifty years before Young's heirs sold it in 1962 to the Robert Snow family, who owns it today. The Snows began a major twenty-five-year restoration, which they primarily did themselves. While working on the restoration, they collected fine period antiques for their home and the antiques shop next to the main house.

Chippendale chairs and an 1850 English mahogany table grace the dining room; a Louis XVI settee and chairs are at home in the parlor; the library boasts a walnut French breakfront and a Federal sofa, adorned in deep red Scalamandre silk. Bedrooms feature important American and Continental pieces, including pieces by John Henry Belter and Chippendale, and a most impressive master suite attributed to the shop of nineteenth-century New Orleans cabinetmaker, Prudent Mallard.

Architecture, furnishings, and a country setting are enough to make Waverley a must-see for anyone who loves historic homes, but the Snow family and their graciousness make it even more special.

Waverley, a private residence, is a National Historic Landmark and a National Restoration Award winner. In addition to gracing the covers of national and international magazines, Waverley is also a Columbus Pilgrimage tour home. It has also been featured on the Arts and Entertainment's television series, "American Castles—Houses of the Confederacy."

Open daily for tours; an admission is charged.

Oxford

There's no mistaking that Oxford is a literary town. It just has that feel to it, perhaps because it's general knowledge that the town has

Florewood River Plantation, Greenwood

Florewood River Plantation is the most authentic antebellum experience you're likely to find in the South, and that is what it's meant to be. From the smell of the rich earth being turned by a mule-pulled plow—if you visit in the spring—to the fragrant aroma of cedar and pine on winter visits, you'll know it is the way plantations used to be: self-contained, clean and green, pretty and serene.

Sitting on one hundred acres of fertile land near the Yazoo River in the Mississippi Delta, Florewood—one of Mississippi's most exciting and unique state parks—is about two miles from Greenwood, Mississippi, the cotton capital of the world.

The plantation is self-contained with twenty-six buildings in the complex, including a schoolhouse/church, a smokehouse, barns, pottery and candlemaking shops, a loom room, a sewing room, a wash house, a blacksmith shop, and more. Everything is authentically documented and explained in detail, for Florewood River Plantation is a living-history museum of an 1850s plantation.

Let your first stop be the cotton museum at the Visitors Center. The museum is free, and once you've taken the self-guided tour, you will better understand the importance of cotton. There is also a great gift shop here where Mississippi souvenirs and specialty items are plentiful.

Next, take the tram to the Greek Revival planter's home, where you're greeted by the mistress of the manor. The two-story home is elegant in its simplicity and thoroughly dressed in fine antiques of the period. Costumed interpreters tell the story of the home and its contents, and explain such things as the wig dresser and the mirrored petticoat table. The table had a mirror placed so ladies could see if their ankles were appropriately hidden under hoop skirts.

Indeed, the special touches added by the interpreters are the real treats here, and these accounts of life on the plantation are historically accurate. The interpreters don't glorify nor do they condemn; rather, they inform, with a certain amount of flair and fun.

Florewood River Plantation is administered by the Mississippi Division of Parks.

Open Tuesday through Sunday; an admission is charged.

Florewood River Plantation is located two miles west of Greenwood, just off U.S. 82. For information, call (662) 455-3821.

Fax: (662) 453-2459

WEBSITE: N/A

---

groomed so many fine writers—from the esteemed William Faulkner to the currently popular John Grisham, who lived here until recently.

Oxford is also home to the state's beloved Ole Miss. But other than the obvious, it is a wonderfully Southern small town built around the Courthouse Square, which has Neilson's, the state's oldest department store on one side, and the great bookstore, Square Books, on the other.

Fans of William Faulkner may see some of the fictional Yoknapatawpha County in the scenes in and around Oxford today. It's a town in which to spend time to savor its special qualities. For information about Oxford, contact the

Tourism Council at (662) 234-4680 or 1-800-758-9177.

Rowan Oak

LOCATION: C/O OXFORD TOURISM COUNCIL,
P.O. BOX 965, OXFORD, MS 38677

Rowan Oak is located on Old Taylor Road in Oxford

TELEPHONE: (662) 234-3284 OR 1-800-758-9177

FAX: N/A

WEBSITE: www/olemiss.edu (go to "departments," then "museums.")

Rowan Oak
COURTESY OF UNIVERSITY OF MISSISSIPPI PUBLICATIONS DEPARTMENT

Rowan Oak is not a grand mansion on the scale of some of the homes in Natchez or Columbus. Built in 1844, it is actually a planter's home, built more for utility than grandeur. Regardless of its architectural importance, Rowan Oak, which is surrounded by cedars and oaks, is one of the state's most historically significant structures because of its former owner.

Novelist William Faulkner bought the "Old Baily Place" in 1930 and renamed it Rowan Oak. It became his private world, and from here he did his best work, some of which may be viewed during a tour of the house. He wrote the plot outline of *A Fable*, which later won a Pulitzer Prize for fiction, on the office wall.

The house is simply furnished in a casual, no-nonsense way. It's comfortable, but not elegant. The interest lies in the fact that Rowan Oak was the home of one of the most recognized writers in the world.

Ten years after Faulkner's death in 1962, his daughter Jill sold Rowan Oak to the University of Mississippi. The University Museums now run it as a house museum.

Open daily for tours except Monday; an admission is charged.

Holly Springs

This town comes right out of the 1830s, and it is indeed a lovely look at the past. Holly Springs was established as a planned community for the younger sons of wealthy planters from Virginia and the Carolinas. The original families purchased the land and set up plantations, complete with new homes. After the homes were ready for occupancy, the new owners moved to Mississippi.

During the Civil War, Union general Ulysses S. Grant made Holly Springs his supply base while he attempted to capture Vicksburg. The base was here until Confederate general Earl Van Dorn captured the Union supplies. Raids between the two forces continued in the area, and the capture of Vicksburg was delayed. Although control of Holly Springs changed many times during the Civil War, the town remained surprisingly intact.

General Grant's wife, Julia, lived at Walter Place during much of the war. On at least one occasion, she was known to have intervened on behalf of the friends she'd made in Holly Springs when the town was threatened. According to rumor, when the Confederate troops once retook the town and captured Mrs. Grant's residence, the soldiers remained Southern gentlemen and would not search her bedroom. Had they not been so chivalrous, they would have found important papers pertaining to Union troop movement.

The Marshall County Historical Society Museum displays Civil War artifacts and history, as well as a collection of antique clothing, costumes, farm tools, and Indian artifacts. Many lovely antebellum homes remain in Holly Springs, though few are open for tours except during the annual spring Pilgrimage. Holly Springs is about thirty minutes east of Memphis. For information, contact the Chamber of Commerce at (662) 252-2943.

Walter Place

LOCATION: 330 WEST CHULAHOMA AVENUE, HOLLY SPRINGS, MS 38635
TELEPHONE: (662) 252-2943 (THE CHAMBER OF COMMERCE)
FAX: (662) 252-2934
WEBSITE: N/A

This architecturally hybrid house was built in the late 1850s, at a time when Greek Revival had run its course, yet Gothic was not fully embraced. So the strong-minded, self-assured Colonel Harvey Washington Walter, a local lawyer and businessman, decided to use both styles in the home he was building for his large family. The front is classical, with its towering Corinthian columns and fanlighted pediment, but at each end of the house, two massive twin bays topped with octagonal battlement towers look almost medieval, adding a Gothic Revival flavor.

Whatever the predominant style, the Walter Place is one of the most interesting houses in Mississippi. The great red-brick, white-trimmed façade, complete with battlements offering protection from intruders, makes one think of a place of safety.

Marvelous Old Mansions

Walter Place
PHOTO BY JOE HIGGINBOTHAM

Perhaps it was a safe house, for it became the temporary home of Julia Dent Grant, wife of Union general Ulysses S. Grant, during the Civil War. She wanted to be near her husband, but safe from shelling, so he chose Holly Springs for her.

After the war, as things were about to return to normal, a yellow fever epidemic hit Holly Springs, and the Walter family turned their home into a hospital. At her husband's urging, Mrs. Walter left with the younger children for Huntsville, Alabama, far away from the sickness. Her husband and three grown sons were left to tend the sick. Sadly, all four men died within a week of each other, and weeks later Mrs. Walter received the heartbreaking news that she had lost her husband and her sons to yellow fever.

A Walter son-in-law oversaw the affairs of the house and family. Upon reaching adult-

hood, the children went their separate ways. One of the girls became a writer; the other, a doctor, long before many women were practicing medicine. Anne Walter left Holly Springs in the early 1890s for the Women's Medical College of Pennsylvania. Upon her return, she was not welcomed as a physician. She wrote about watching a woman nearly die from childbirth: "I was forced to sit idly by while a friend nearly died from a dangerous delivery, attended by doctors far older than I, but far less skilled in obstetrics."

Dr. Anne Walter Fearn later moved to Shanghai, where she remained most of her life. Her early social training in Holly Springs paid off, however, for she was a gifted hostess who once entertained Eleanor Roosevelt when she was in China. Irene Walter Johnson married Oscar Johnson, who founded the Johnson Shoe Company. This company would eventually become the International Shoe Company that manufactured Buster Brown shoes. Irene sold the home and the new owners ran into financial difficulties that forced them to rent out the rooms. When the house was sold as part of bankruptcy proceedings, Mrs. Johnson bought the house back.

With its colorful history, Walter Place is a Mississippi treasure. Owners Mike and Jorja Lynn, of Minneapolis and Holly Springs, are committed to the restoration of the property.

It is furnished with several pieces that are original to the house. The Walter Place is open for the annual Pilgrimage tour of homes.

Open by appointment (inquire through the Chamber of Commerce or the Marshall County Historical Museum); an admission is charged.

North Carolina

North Carolina is one of the few states in America that boasts two premier travel destinations: the beach and the mountains. In between, the state is clean and green, with small towns full of history and surprising treasures. Add a few big towns such as Charlotte, Raleigh, Winston-Salem, and Greensboro, which all have big-city amenities, and it is easy to see why more than seven million people are proud to call North Carolina home.

In 1585, aspiring colonists attempted to establish a settlement on North Carolina's Roanoke Island. This attempt and two others did not last. The third settlement attempt became known as the "Lost Colony."

Major colonization of the coastal plain began in 1663, when King Charles II deeded much of this land to eight Lords Proprietors—loyal monarchists and shrewd businessmen. As settlers were attracted by generous offers of land and personal-property rights, the population grew. In 1729, the Lords Proprietors sold their land shares back to the Crown, and Carolina became a Royal colony.

Over 130 years later, the Civil War brought eventual secession from the Union, and a tremendous loss of life and property. North Carolina contributed more men and supplies to the war effort than any other Southern state. North Carolina also has fewer antebellum mansions left standing than neighboring states. Most that have survived are privately owned and not open for tours.

This resilient state recovered and prospered again, and that prosperity continues today. For statewide tourism information, call (919) 733-8372 or 1-800-VISIT NC or visit their website at www.visitnc.com.

Wilmington and the Cape Fear Coast

The Cape Fear Coast is an amazing place. It boasts a subtropical climate and four distinct seasons. Water is almost everywhere, and outdoor sports are popular, but cultural opportunities flourish, too. There are both grand old mansions and plain, old-fashioned charm in Wilmington, the region's biggest town.

Perhaps that's why Hollywood came calling on the Cape Fear Coast. Dino De Laurentiis discovered its charms back in 1983. Since that time, various production companies have made several hundred feature films, television projects, music videos, and commercials here. Among the best known of the films are *Crimes of the Heart* and *Sleeping with the Enemy*.

The Cape Fear Coast is made up of Wilmington and the island communities of Wrightsville Beach, Carolina Beach, and Kure Beach. Author John Villani called Wilmington "One of the 100 Best Small Towns in America." Wilmington was founded in 1740 and was North Carolina's largest city by 1780, though inland growth soon caught up. Its population is around seventy-five thousand today.

The Cape Fear Coast offers a list of attractions to please every taste. An annual event that draws much attention is the North Carolina Azalea Festival, held each April. For more information, contact the Cape Fear Coast Convention and Visitors Bureau at 800-222-4757 or 910-341-4030.

The Bellamy Mansion

LOCATION: 503 MARKET STREET, WILMINGTON, NC 28401

TELEPHONE: (910) 251-3700

FAX: (910) 763-8154

WEBSITE: www.bellamymansionmuseum.org

Designed and built by James F. Post and completed just before the Civil War, the mansion was the city residence of Dr. John D. Bellamy. The Bellamy family left their new home on the eve of the Civil War, fearing a raging yellow fever epidemic and the threat of invasion by Union military forces. Following the surrender of Wilmington in 1865, Union General Hawley occupied the house. The

The Bellamy Mansion

Bellamys reclaimed the house later that year, and occupied it until 1946, when Ellen Bellamy, the last surviving daughter, died. Much of the fine carpentry work is the product of slave carpenters and free black artisans. Some of these individuals were supposedly freed on the mansion's steps after the end of the war.

This three-story mansion includes a raised basement and belvedere (or cupola). The antebellum masterpiece has twenty-two rooms and is an interesting blend of Greek Revival and Italianate designs. It has the appearance of a small, romantic castle, thanks to its ornate, pedimented entrance, its Palladian windows, its fourteen Corinthian columns stretching across the front and sides, and its small balconies under the two round-headed upstairs windows.

The grand old place stood vacant for many years. In 1972, a fire set by an arsonist wreaked havoc on the interior. Luckily, the house was saved. Now, as a stewardship property of Preservation North Carolina, it has been beautifully restored to its former grandeur.

Today, the Bellamy Mansion is a house museum featuring decorative arts, traveling exhibits, and elegant gardens. Tour guides tell of the house's construction, history, and restoration, which remains a work in progress.

Open for tours Wednesday through Sunday; an admission fee is charged.

The Burgwin-Wright House

LOCATION: 224 MARKET STREET, WILMINGTON, NC 28401
TELEPHONE: (910) 762-0570
FAX: (910) 762-8650
WEBSITE: www.cape-fear.nc.us; www.geocities.com/picketfence/garden/4354

John Burgwin was an Englishman who came to Wilmington via Charleston in 1750. By the early 1760s, he had made a name for himself in Wilmington as a planter, the owner of five ships, and a colonial official. His official positions included being private secretary to the governor, clerk of the Superior Court in New Hanover County, and the colony's treasurer.

In 1771, he built a Georgian-style house at the corner of Third and Market Streets. The house used existing stone walls from the first floor and cellar of an old jail as its new foundation. The design that Burgwin chose for his house showed that he was a man of good taste. The Palladian frontispiece is as elegant today as it was when it was new.

The original house featured simple fluted columns supporting the two-tiered porch.

The Burgwin-Wright House

These had been replaced with Ionic columns in the 1850s, but in 1991, these too were replaced by columns of the same simple design as the originals. Among the house's interesting features are the fresh-air areas, which allow ventilation; closets, rarely found in houses of this era; and a separate three-story kitchen building.

When John Burgwin moved back to his plantation, Joshua Wright, the stepson of Burgwin's business partner, bought the house. Thus, the house is now called the Burgwin-Wright House.

In 1781, the British commander, Lord Cornwallis, and his staff briefly occupied the house as the general's headquarters before they went on to defeat at Yorktown, Virginia. The house was subsequently called "the Cornwallis House." During the British occupation, the cellar was supposedly used as a dungeon for prisoners, though many escaped through an underground tunnel to the river.

The National Society of The Colonial Dames of America in the State of North Carolina bought the house in 1937. Today, thanks to efforts of the Colonial Dames, the third oldest house extant in Wilmington is beautifully restored and furnished with fine antiques. The elaborate paneling upstairs is a work of art. Docents tell the interesting history of the house, and guests are encouraged to view the kitchen and craft room behind the main house.

The Burgwin-Wright House's eighteenth-century-style gardens feature a parterre garden, a terraced garden, and an orchard.

Open Tuesday through Saturday; an admission is charged.

The Latimer House

LOCATION: 126 SOUTH THIRD STREET,
   WILMINGTON, NC 28401
TELEPHONE: (910) 762-0492
FAX: (910) 763-5869
WEBSITE: www.latimer.wilmington.org

From the time it was built in 1852 until 1963, three generations of Latimers have lived in this fine, four-story Italianate mansion. The lengthy family ownership and the house's current status as headquarters and house museum

Orton Plantation Gardens

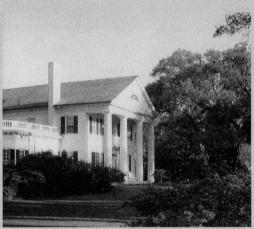

Located eighteen miles south of Wilmington on N.C. 133, these gardens were planted in 1910 by the Sprunt family. The gardens bloom from March through August, though the exact blooming dates of the azaleas, camellias, magnolias, and various annuals depend on the weather. The gardens are located on a former rice plantation, where beautiful, ancient live oaks arch over the paths. The antebellum Orton home isn't open to the public, but you can go inside a small white chapel nearby.

The gardens are open daily from March to November; call for seasonal hours; an admission is charged.

> *Location: From Wilmington, take U.S. 17 South to the Southport/Oak Island Exit. Take N.C. Hwy. 133 south. Take a left at the stoplight and follow the signs.*
> *Telephone: (910) 371-6851.*
> *Fax: (910) 371-6871*
> *WEBSITE: www.ortongarden.com*

Orton Plantation
COURTESY OF N.C. TRAVEL AND TOURISM DIVISION

Information for this section was taken from *North Carolina Traveler* with the permission of John F. Blair, Publisher.

---

for the Lower Cape Fear Historical Society guarantee that many of the furnishings and the décor, if not original to the house, will at least be authentic to the period. In fact, guests at the house museum say it has such a "lived-in" feeling that one expects the Latimer family to walk in and greet them.

Zebulon Latimer, who built the house for his bride, the local belle Elizabeth Savage, was a prosperous dry-goods merchant who came to the area from Connecticut. He hired the builder/architect James F. Post to design his showplace, which was the first home in town to have electricity. Ornate window cornices are exterior features of particular architectural interest. The exterior of the house has a sturdiness about it that seems indestructible. A lovely piazza with a canopied roof leads to an appealing Victorian garden, the site of exclusive garden parties even today.

Inside, decorative wallpaper, window treatments, oriental rugs, Empire and Victorian furniture, and old family portraits make this tour a popular one. The tour includes double par-

The Latimer House
COURTESY OF THE LOWER CAPE FEAR HISTORICAL SOCIETY, INC.

lors, the dining room, and kitchen on the main floor, and the bedrooms on the upper floors. The unrestored fourth floor has recently opened to the public so visitors can see how the mansion looked prior to restoration.

Open for daily tours; an admission is charged.

Poplar Grove Plantation

LOCATION: 10200 U.S. 17 NORTH, WILMINGTON, NC 28411

Poplar Grove is located nine miles north of Wilmington on U.S. 17 North.

TELEPHONE: (910) 686-9518, EXTENSION 26
FAX: (910) 686-4309
WEBSITE: www.poplargrove.com

This historic property is as good as it gets if you want authenticity. The 1850 manor house and the outbuildings have all been preserved and restored to reflect the time of construction. You can view the smokehouse, a tenant house, an outdoor kitchen, and an herb cellar. Monday through Friday, two resident craftspeople are on site, demonstrating weaving, basketmaking, and other handicrafts of the period. On Saturday and Sunday there is only one craftsperson on the site.

The style of the 4,284-square-foot plantation house is Greek Revival. Four Doric columns support the railed front porch on the main floor. Two stories sit over a full raised brick basement. The four-over-four frame structure is sided with weatherboard. The house was built of heart pine, which was cut on the land and planed at the plantation sawmill. Twelve fireplaces kept the place warm in cold winter months.

Wooden gutters and downspouts, concealed inside columns, transport rainwater to cisterns on the north side of the house. The rainwater was used for bathing and laundry, while drinking water came from a nearby well.

James Foy, Jr., purchased the 628-acre, self-supporting agricultural community in 1795. It supported the Foy family and sixty-four slaves. While living on this plantation, the Foys became important pioneers in the peanut industry, as well as influential participants in local government.

Centered in a grove of poplar trees on nearby Futch Creek, the original manor house

Poplar Grove Plantation

burned in 1849. Joseph Mumford Foy built the new house on its present site in 1850. After the Civil War, the plantation suffered hard times. With perseverance, sound management, and the use of peanuts as the cash crop, Poplar Grove once again flourished. Poplar Grove Plantation remained in the Foy family until 1971.

The house and grounds are now managed by the nonprofit Poplar Grove Foundation, whose mission is to educate, research, preserve, and present the nineteenth-century lifestyle of southern coastal North Carolina. To fulfill its mission, each room is impeccably furnished as it would have been in the 1850s. The furniture in the back parlor is American Empire and Rococo style. Elsewhere in the house, "cottage style" and Victorian pieces are used.

Some furnishings on display include an 1860 pie safe used by the Foys, a flax wheel, a plantation loom, and a scrub board and ringer. Each room has its own interesting story in this well-

preserved and lovingly maintained part of North Carolina history.

A very good gift shop and small restaurant are located on the premises.

Open daily; an admission is charged.

New Bern

Nestled comfortably on the mighty Neuse River, New Bern has its own special quality. Some of that special quality comes from being first settled by an expedition of Swiss Palatines in 1710. Located thirty miles inland from the Atlantic Ocean, New Bern is the state's second oldest town. The Swiss settlers named their new town for Berne, Switzerland.

This is a place where you'll want to stay a few days, for New Bern is quaint enough to be interesting and cosmopolitan enough to offer unique shopping opportunities in the fifty-six-block historic downtown area.

New Bern—locals pronounce it as "NU-bern," all one word with emphasis on the NU—is a town of firsts. Pepsi Cola was first concocted here, the state's first public school and first bank were opened here, and the first meeting of the North Carolina legislature was held here.

Other than the attractiveness of the town, the big attraction is Tryon Palace. The state's last and largest eighteenth-century brick plantation house, Bellair, is a few miles outside New Bern. Unfortunately, Bellair has been closed until further notice because of the disastrous 1999 floods.

For more information, contact the New Bern/Craven County Convention & Visitors Bureau at 1-800-948-1099 or (252) 457-9248 or the New Bern Chamber of Commerce at (252) 637-3111.

Attmore-Oliver House

LOCATION: 510 POLLOCK STREET, NEW BERN, NC 28562

TELEPHONE: (252) 638-8558

FAX: (252) 638-5773

WEBSITE: N/A

Built by New Bernian Samuel Chapman, this 1790 townhouse is actually located at 511 Broad Street, but the entrance is located at the back of the house at 510 Pollock. The house was enlarged to its present size in 1834, and Greek Revival elements were added to the unpretentious, two-story white frame house.

Across the back, double-tiered porches, which overlook a manicured lawn, run the width of the house. On the inside, floor cloths cover the heart-pine floors. Period antiques, which decorate each room, include a fine Chip-

Attmore-Oliver House

pendale drop-leaf dining table that belonged to Governor Josiah Martin when he lived in Tryon Palace. Among the parlor furniture is an Empire sofa and a pianoforte. The antique quilts are superb works of art. A doll collection and cradle in the children's bedroom is of interest, as is an old tin bathtub.

The Attmore-Oliver is not a showplace Southern mansion. It is however an educational house museum, with its exhibits of Civil War documents, weapons, and artifacts. The house was purchased in 1953 by the New Bern Historical Society, at which time restoration and efforts to find appropriate period furnishings began. Today, the house serves as the headquarters of the historical society.

Open for tours Tuesday through Saturday; there is no admission fee.

Tryon Palace

Tryon Palace

LOCATION: 610 POLLOCK STREET, NEW BERN,
NC 28563

TELEPHONE: (252) 514-4900 OR 1-800-
767-1560

FAX: (252) 514-4876

WEBSITE: www.tryonpalace.org

When the illustrious Tryon Palace, which was designed by John Hawks, was built in 1770, the British had high hopes for the colonies. The red-brick Georgian palace was the fortified home of British governor William Tryon. The palace also served as the capitol of the colony of North Carolina. Today it is still palatial in its setting amid fourteen acres of lush and lovely gardens.

At the time of its construction, Tryon Palace was one of the most elegant and impressive public buildings outside of England—and one of the safest. The palace is fortified with brick walls that measure three feet in thickness.

Governor Tryon faced colonial opposition at almost every turn, as "no taxation without representation" became a rallying call. The governor left North Carolina in 1771 to become the royal governor of New York. His replacement was Josiah Martin. Martin was also in constant conflict with the colonists. After a skirmish between the North Carolina militia and the British army, the Martin family, fearing insurrection, fled the palace.

After the Revolutionary War, the palace became the state capitol from 1777 until 1794. When it was vacated after the capital was moved to Raleigh, deterioration occurred. In 1798, a disastrous fire burned most of the grand palace.

After 150 years, the North Carolina legislature authorized the Tryon Palace Commission to supervise reconstruction and management of the old governor's palace. After years of researching and studying original plans, work began. A restoration trust fund was established by Mrs. Maude Moore Latham. Mrs. Latham died in 1951, before any substantial work had been done on the project; it was completed by a state commission headed by her daughter, Mrs. John Kellenberger. The palace began welcoming guests in 1959.

As you approach the palace, you walk through an allée of giant oaks. A colonnade joins the main building with the reconstructed east wing and the original west wing, the only part of the palace complex that survived the 1798 fire. The west wing serves as a stable, granary, and carriage house.

As you tour the palace, costumed guides describe each room's specific décor as well as the important English and American antiques located there. The library is filled with four hundred books known to have been owned by the Tryons. The parlor features a walnut spinet made in the 1720s by Thomas Hitchcock. The tables in the council chamber are still equipped with beeswax candles and quill pens. Margaret Tryon's bedroom includes doll furniture, which duplicate the full-scale furnishings.

One of the palace's highlights is the floor of the entrance hall, which is white Italian and black Belgian marble. Another feature is the staircase of mahogany and pegged walnut, which is illuminated by a skylight.

In the servants' quarters, people in period dress reenact typical daily activities of the palace, such as cooking, spinning, weaving, and laundering. You can also visit the palace gardens, which include a "green garden" with small trees and crepe myrtles; a wilderness garden; a kitchen garden; and two other colorful gardens.

The palace complex, which is now under the supervision of the North Carolina Department of Cultural Resources, covers fourteen acres and includes the palace and outbuildings, the gardens, the John Wright Stanly House, the Dixon-Stevenson House, and the New Bern Academy Museum. One of the outbuildings serves as a crafts and garden shop, where visitors can purchase plants grown on the grounds and other garden-related items, such as herbal vinegar. There is also a museum shop on the corner of Eden and Pollock Streets. A visitors center, where tickets are purchased, offers an orientation film.

Open for tours daily; an admission is charged.

Somerset Place

LOCATION: 2572 LAKE SHORE ROAD,
 CRESWELL, NC 27928
Somerset is located about seven miles south of Creswell, off U.S. 64.
TELEPHONE: (252) 797-4560
FAX: (252) 797-4171
WEBSITE: www.ah.dcr.state.nc.us/hs/
 someset/someset.htm

The historic Somerset Place, once a major coastal plantation, was named for the home county of its original owner, Englishman Josiah Collins. The plantation began around 1788, but

Somerset Place
COURTESY OF N.C. TRAVEL AND TOURISM DIVISION

it was about 1830 when Collins's grandson built the Collins mansion.

From the time it was built until the Civil War, Somerset Place was a gathering place for social events on the southern shore of the Albemarle Sound. During the plantation's heyday—from about 1800 until the early 1860s—the one hundred thousand or so acres produced massive crops of rice, corn, wheat, and some cotton. Somerset Place was home to more than three hundred slaves, most of whom came directly from their native West Africa in 1786. These industrious people became expert at rice cultivation. They also developed and dug a system of irrigation and transportation canals.

In fact, a carriage drive lined by huge cypress trees leads to the front entrance of the mansion alongside one of these canals. The three-story, fourteen-room Greek Revival-style frame house features wide railed porches on the first and second story.

Also part of the plantation compound were a sawmill, grist mills, numerous farm and work buildings, and houses for the slave community. With the Civil War and the end of slavery, the plantation system could not survive without workers. Like other plantations throughout the South, Somerset Place revamped its operations and turned to sharecropping.

The Collins family members sold the plantation to a relative in 1872. This relative's family farmed it on a smaller scale until the state of North Carolina bought it in 1939. Since the state purchased the property, important documents have been found, which shed light on how the plantation's early inhabitants, both black and white, lived.

Today, the Collins House is restored and beautifully furnished in the decor and style of the antebellum period. A few original pieces from the Collins family are still included. On the tour, you can also view the outdoor kitchen—where implements and utensils of the 1800s are exhibited—the smokehouse, and the icehouse.

A North Carolina Historic Site, Somerset Place and the lovely Lake Phelps are located near Pettigrew State Park. It is maintained by the North Carolina Division of Archives and History, Department of Cultural Resources, which works in conjunction with the Somerset Place Foundation.

Open for tours daily; free admission.

Hope Plantation
COURTESY OF HISTORIC HOPE FOUNDATION, INC.

Hope Plantation

LOCATION: 132 HOPE HOUSE ROAD,
   WINDSOR, NC 27983
The plantation is located four miles west of the town of Windsor, on N.C. Hwy. 308.
TELEPHONE: (252) 794-3140
FAX: (252) 794-5583
WEBSITE: www.albemarle-nc.com/hope/

Hope Plantation's long and illustrious place in the history of North Carolina began in 1723. It was then that the Lords Proprietors granted land in the Carolina colony to the Hobson family of Hope Village in Derbyshire, England. After Francis Hobson's death, his widow, Elizabeth, married Zedekiah Stone of New England. It was their son, David Stone, who inherited the land and built Hope Plantation between 1800 and 1803.

By age thirty-three, David Stone had been an attorney, a Superior Court judge, a member of both houses of the North Carolina General Assembly, and a member of the board of trustees for the University of North Carolina. He had also been elected to both the United States House of Representatives and Senate. In

1808, Stone was elected North Carolina governor. He served two terms before returning to the Senate.

A Princeton graduate, Stone was interested in architecture, although he did not obtain a degree in the field. Among Stone's architectural books was Abraham Swann's *The British Architect,* which he used to design Hope Plantation. Stone's basic Palladian design featured neo-classical elements and showed his preference for the Georgian Colonial style.

The house, with its two-story portico and widow's walk, or cupola, on top, is constructed of pine and cypress that was cut on the property. It has a full, above-ground basement that holds a "winter" kitchen and storage. The completed house is a three-story structure with a pedimented central pavilion and hipped roof.

The first floor features a wide central hall with rooms on either side. The hallway features authentic floor cloths. On the sides of

Historic Edenton

The Albemarle Sound area was the first area in North Carolina to be permanently settled and is often called the "Cradle of the Colony." In 1663, King Charles II granted huge tracts of land in the colonies to eight Lords Proprietors. Although growth under the direction of these men was slow, by the early 1700s large plantations were thriving in the region.

In 1712, the colonial assembly authorized the laying out of a town, which was eventually designated as the Port of Roanoke. The town grew politically important because so many wealthy landowners from the Albemarle region dominated the colonial assembly. In 1718, Governor Charles Eden built his home outside the village. After Eden's unexpected death in 1722, the town was renamed Edenton in his honor. From 1722 until 1740, Edenton was unofficially the capital of the colony.

In 1775, dissatisfaction with English rule increased. A group of illustrious men met in August 1774 and passed a number of resolutions. On October 25, 1774, a group of fifty-one women of Edenton, at the invitation of Penelope Barker, held a "tea party" at which each lady signed a pledge to support the resolves. This was the first known action of a strictly political nature by a body of women taken anywhere in the colonies.

When the home of James Iredell went on the market in 1948, the newly formed Edenton Tea Party Chapter of the Daughters of the American Revolution purchased the house and formed the James Iredell Association. Iredell became the state's attorney general at age twenty-eight and held the position throughout the Revolution. After the war, President Washington appointed Iredell to serve as an associate justice on the first United States Supreme Court, a position he held until his death in 1799.

Barker House in Historic Edenton
COURTESY OF N.C. TRAVEL AND TOURISM DIVISION

By the 1960s, five different groups were acting independently of each other to preserve and restore historic sites in Edenton. By 1967, the groups agreed to join efforts under the auspices of a supervisory agency called Historic Edenton. Today, the umbrella organization is the Edenton Historic Commission, which supervises several state-owned sites.

Visitors can tour seven different sites on one of two tours. The longer tour includes St. Paul's Church, which was begun in 1736, but not completed for thirty years. It is the second oldest house of worship in North Carolina.

The tour also includes the Cupola House, a Jacobean house built around 1725; the Barker House, which was the home of Penelope Barker of tea-party fame; and a small schoolhouse that was moved from Bandon Plantation. Novelist Inglis Fletcher used this schoolhouse as an office when she wrote her twelve historical novels about the years from Raleigh's first colony to the constitutional convention of 1789.

continued

the hall are the dining room and the family parlor. The parlor, which is decorated in a rich gray color, contains several chairs and other period furnishings. The second floor holds the handsomely decorated formal drawing room and a library with floor-to-ceiling bookcases where fourteen hundred volumes are displayed.

One of two plantations owned by Stone, Hope was part of the eight thousand acres that Stone owned. The self-contained plantation had a grist mill, a sawmill, a blacksmith shop, and houses for spinning and weaving. In addition to raising cattle, Hope Plantation produced cotton, corn, and wheat.

Thanks to the work of ardent preservationists who acquired the mansion and eighteen acres in 1966, the plantation is now owned and maintained by the Historic Hope Foundation. Visitors begin their tour at the site's Heritage Center in the Hope Forest. A gift shop is located on the premises.

Open daily for tours; an admission is charged.

Raleigh

It is apparent that the more than 284,000 people who live in Raleigh love their state capital. Founded in 1792 and named for Sir Walter Raleigh, today Raleigh is a town of museums and parks. It's a place where the arts thrive. Locals say it is the city that pulls the state together—where the mountains and the beaches have a meeting of the minds. Raleigh and the neighboring cities of Durham and Chapel Hill are home to the prestigious Research Triangle Park, where Nobel Prize-winning scientists work in high-tech and biotech industries.

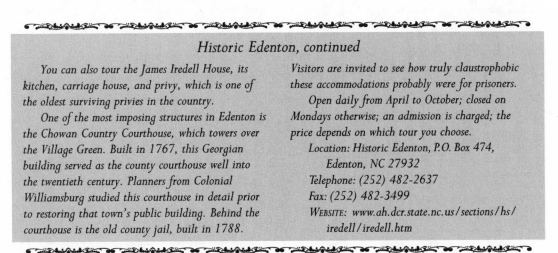

Historic Edenton, continued

You can also tour the James Iredell House, its kitchen, carriage house, and privy, which is one of the oldest surviving privies in the country.

One of the most imposing structures in Edenton is the Chowan Country Courthouse, which towers over the Village Green. Built in 1767, this Georgian building served as the county courthouse well into the twentieth century. Planners from Colonial Williamsburg studied this courthouse in detail prior to restoring that town's public building. Behind the courthouse is the old county jail, built in 1788.

Visitors are invited to see how truly claustrophobic these accommodations probably were for prisoners.

Open daily from April to October; closed on Mondays otherwise; an admission is charged; the price depends on which tour you choose.

Location: Historic Edenton, P.O. Box 474, Edenton, NC 27932
Telephone: (252) 482-2637
Fax: (252) 482-3499
WEBSITE: www.ah.dcr.state.nc.us/sections/hs/iredell/iredell.htm

Raleigh has earned the designation of being the country's first "Green Survival City" for its commitment to conserving the city's natural beauty. The J.C. Raulston Arboretum at North Carolina State University has an eight-acre garden and the nation's most effective plant-introduction program. The Martha Frank Fragrance Garden at the Governor Morehead School for the Blind is another new and wonderful experience for garden lovers. This garden provides a welcome sensory experience that employs scent, sound, and touch as ways for those who cannot see to enjoy the garden.

The North Carolina Museum of History is a great place to begin a sojourn around the state. Exhibits range from pre-colonial artifacts to the present. Since the state claims the title "first in flight," it is a treat to see a replica of Orville and Wilbur Wright's famous airplane.

For additional information, call the Greater Raleigh Convention & Visitors Bureau at 1-800-849-8499 or (919) 834-5900 or the Capital Area Visitor Center at (919) 733-3456.

The North Carolina Executive Mansion

LOCATION: 200 NORTH BLOUNT STREET, RALEIGH, NC 27601
TELEPHONE: (919) 733-3456
FAX: N/A
WEBSITE: www.ah.dcr.state.nc.us

The North Carolina Executive Mansion
COURTESY OF N.C. TRAVEL AND TOURISM DIVISION

Although this book does not include many Victorian mansions because there are enough to fill a separate volume, we decided to include this site because it is so unique. This grand home was built in 1891 as the fourth official residence for North Carolina's governors and their families. It is one of only twelve executive mansions specifically built and continuously used as the official residence for the governor.

The house has 34,806 square feet and sits on a five-acre site in downtown Raleigh. Five gardens grace the mansion and provide outdoor areas for entertaining.

Inside, the first floor offers six spacious public rooms connected by a large central hall. The second floor serves as the private residence for the first family. The third floor and basement are used for offices, laundry, and storage.

The highlight of the grand hallway is the crimson and gold hand-hooked rug that features all the governors' names and administration dates. The hallway's elegant Corinthian columns, its sixteen-foot ceilings, glittering cut crystal chandeliers, and a grand staircase crafted of native heart pine all set the tone for the rest of the tour.

The two front rooms are formal parlors, which were originally used when the sexes separated after dinner. The ballroom, originally called the music room, is decorated with French mirrors, a pair of Sheffield chandeliers, gilded walls, French gilded furniture, and a suite of mahogany Victorian parlor furniture.

The library has heart-of-pine woodwork that was returned to its original splendor in 1983, when sixty years of paint was removed. The dining room features an eighteen-foot table that seats twenty-four guests. The nineteenth-century chandelier, which was brought from Germany, was a gift to the mansion. A collection of china, crystal, and silver used throughout the one-hundred-plus years is displayed in the breakfront.

Tour hours vary, so call the Capital Area Visitor Center at (919) 733-3456 for hours of operation and reservations.

Limited tours are offered throughout the year; tours are by appointment only and last a half hour; admission is free.

Haywood Hall

LOCATION: 211 NEW BERN PLACE, RALEIGH, NC 27601

TELEPHONE: (919) 832-8357

FAX: N/A

WEBSITE: N/A

As a strong proponent of education, John Haywood would be pleased to know that his home is now a source of learning about the past. After all, Haywood, the first elected treasurer for the state of North Carolina, educated all twelve of his own children and nine of his friends' children. Now operating as a house museum, Haywood Hall continues the tradition of education.

When Haywood's Federal-style house was started in 1799, it became the first house within the original city limits of Raleigh that was on its original site. Haywood's requirement was that the house be large enough for entertaining and housing a big family.

The two large rooms on either side of the spacious downstairs hall could easily accommodate a major legislative function. Perhaps the spaciousness of the white clapboard house was one reason it became an unofficial meeting place for legislators and dignitaries visiting Raleigh. The cordial and hospitable Haywood not only served as state treasurer for forty years, but he was also elected as Raleigh's first

Haywood Hall

mayor. Today, the two-story portico with its slender, fluted columns continues to welcome guests.

Amazingly, Haywood Hall remained the residence of Haywood family members from 1799 to 1977. After the last descendant to live in the house died, the house was willed to the National Society of the Colonial Dames of America in the State of North Carolina. The Colonial Dames have undertaken the ongoing restoration of the grand old home. The Dames have taken their work quite seriously, from having small chips of old paint examined by the North Carolina Division of Archives and History to determine exact colors and textures, to having faux marble and woodwork perfectly duplicated by fine North Carolina craftsmen. The work of the Colonial Dames is supported financially by the Friends of Haywood Hall, Inc.

Not much has changed at Haywood Hall, which is one reason it remains such a treasure. From a distance, the exterior strongly resembles the Mordecai House in Raleigh, which was built a few years earlier.

Tours are available every Thursday from 10:30 a.m. until 1:30 p.m., except during January and February, when the house is closed for refurbishing; admission on Thursday is free, though donations are appreciated. Group tours may be booked in advance for tours other than on Thursday, but they must pay to do so.

*M*ordecai House

LOCATION: ONE MIMOSA STREET, RALEIGH,
 NC 27604
TELEPHONE: (919) 834-4844
FAX: (919) 834-7314
WEBSITE: www.capitalareapreservation.org

Joel Lane, the father of Raleigh, built the plantation house now known as the Mordecai House for his son and daughter-in-law. The

Mordecai House

younger Lane's daughter, Margaret, married attorney Moses Mordecai, thus giving the house its current name. The Mordecais were prominent in the development of Raleigh.

When the house was built in 1785, it sat in the middle of thousands of acres of cultivated fields. It was the largest plantation in the region at that time. The house still has many of the original furnishings and family portraits, for it was home to the same family from its construction until 1963. The heirlooms still intact are of particular importance because of their authenticity. The city of Raleigh purchased the Mordecai House in 1969.

Around 1825, Nancy Mordecai had builder William Nichols, who was known for building public buildings including the State Capitol, add new rooms and a two-tiered portico on the front. The Ionic columns supporting the portico gave the rambling house a Greek Revival look. An outdoor kitchen was added in 1842. Today, the kitchen garden has been faithfully restored.

Now part of the Mordecai Historic Park, the plantation tour includes a chapel built by slave carpenters in 1847, the one-room law office of two United States senators, and other nineteenth-century buildings moved to the plantation site. Also located at the park is the structure in which President Andrew Johnson was born. The building served as a kitchen for the tavern where Johnson's parents worked. Johnson was born in the loft above the kitchen. Guests are often amazed that an American president came from such humble surroundings.

The park's "village" lets us see what life was like in early Raleigh. The site is managed by Capital Area Preservation (CAP) in cooperation with the Raleigh Department of Parks and Recreation. CAP is a nonprofit historic preservation organization whose goal is to preserve historic buildings and cultural landscapes.

Open daily except Tuesday; an admission is charged.

House in the Horseshoe
COURTESY OF N.C. DEPARTMENT OF CULTURAL RESOURCES

House in the Horseshoe

LOCATION: The house is located ten miles
  north of Carthage on S.R.1621.
TELEPHONE: (910) 947-2051
FAX: (910) 947-2051
WEBSITE: www.ah.dcr.state.nc.us/sec-
  tions/hs/horsesho/horsesho.htm

Built by Philip Alston in 1772, this house
was one of the first "big houses" built on North
Carolina's frontier. It claimed a page in the history books during the American Revolution
when it became the site of a confrontation between feuding Whigs and Tories.

In the summer of 1781, David Fanning, a
guerrilla fighter whose tactics were a constant
thorn in the Patriots' side, was leading a group
of prisoners to Wilmington for confinement.

Alston, a colonel in the local militia, was in
hot pursuit. When Alston and his militia caught
up with one lone member of Fanning's brigade,
they beat the man to death.

Seeking revenge, Fanning and his men surrounded Alston's home on July 29, 1781. Shots
were exchanged for hours, until Mrs. Alston
waved a white flag and arranged for a ceasefire.
After the war, Alston was charged in the
murder of a political opponent, but never con-
victed because no one would testify against
him. He moved to Georgia, where he was fa-
tally shot while sleeping.

Before leaving North Carolina in 1790,
Alston sold his home to a man named Perkins,
who then sold it to retiring North Carolina
governor Benjamin Williams in 1798. Members of the Williams family lived in the house
until 1853. In 1954, the Moore County Historical Association purchased the property. The
house, which opened to the public in 1957, is
now a designated state historic site.

The site, which received its name because
of its location atop a hill in a bend of the Deep
River, now offers guided tours of the house.
In the downstairs dining room, docents tell
about the events of August 5, 1781, and even
point out the brick fireplace, where Mrs. Alston
huddled her children to protect them from the
gunfire. With a portrait of Governor Williams
hanging in the background over the mantle,

guides tell about the governor's accomplishments as you tour the parlor.

The upstairs bedrooms display furniture of the period, allowing guides to talk about life on the colonial frontier. Visitors can also view the nearby loom house, corncrib, and well.

Open every day from April through October; closed on Mondays from November to March; admission is free.

Greensboro

Along with Winston-Salem and High Point, Greensboro is one of the cities that makes up the Piedmont Triad. For years the region has been a good place to call home. You may even recognize some of the people who hail from Greensboro: William S. Porter, who used the pen name O. Henry, and Dolley Madison, the outspoken wife of President James Madison. You can learn more about these two—and many more—at the Greensboro Historical Museum. Consisting of ten galleries and two restored houses, the museum presents national history with a local slant. There is also a woodworking shop and a blacksmith shop on the premises.

The 185,000 people who live in Greensboro appreciate the city's many amenities. The Cultural Center at Festival Park is an architectural showplace that houses about twenty-five arts organizations, with an emphasis on the performing arts, and five galleries that feature visual arts.

And speaking of visual arts, fans of French artist Henri Matisse will want to visit the Weatherspoon Art Gallery on the campus of the University of North Carolina at Greensboro. Nationally recognized, this contemporary art museum displays some of Matisse's work as part of the museum's permanent collection.

The Old Greensborough Historic District offers antique shops and the Tannenbaum Historic Park is where you'll find the Hoskins Farmstead Colonial Heritage Center. The British started their attack at the battle of Guilford Courthouse in 1781 from the edge of Joseph Hoskins' fields. At the Colonial Heritage Center, visitors can learn about their cultural and ethnic heritage by seeing, touching, smelling, and even tasting the realities of eighteenth-century North Carolina. There is also a diorama of the Revolutionary War battle at Guilford Courthouse. For more information about Greensboro, contact the Convention & Visitors Bureau at 1-800-344-2282 or (336) 274-2282.

$\mathcal{B}$landwood Mansion

LOCATION: 447 WEST WASHINGTON STREET,
GREENSBORO, NC 27401
TELEPHONE: (336) 272-5003
FAX: (336) 271-8049
WEBSITE: www.blandwood.org

Preservation Greensboro, Inc., magnanimously saved and restored this architectural treasure, which was the home of John Motley Morehead, North Carolina's popular governor from 1841 to 1845.

When Blandwood was first built in 1790, the mansion was only a two-story, four-room clapboard farmhouse. In the 1820s, it was enlarged and spiffed up a bit. In 1844, Governor Morehead hired architect Alexander Jackson Davis to renovate the farmhouse into an Italianate villa—a style that was becoming a popular alternative to Greek Revival.

Davis stuccoed the house and constructed a tall, projecting tower in the center. The tower is topped by a flat-topped cupola. An arched doorway was inset at the front, and arcades with arches were added on each side. The arcades connected the kitchen on one end to the governor's law office on the other end. Davis also added large twin parlors and a grand entrance hall. The exterior additions included pocket windows and shutters, and a low-pitched, tin hip roof.

Blandwood Mansion
COURTESY OF BLANDWOOD

It was an appropriate showplace for a governor, and it remained in the Morehead family until 1897. In its second life, Blandwood housed the Keeley Institute for Drug and Alcohol Rehabilitation.

By 1964, the institute was gone and the once illustrious Blandwood was in danger of demolition. At this point Preservation Greensboro, Inc., came to the rescue. Today, the house is restored to reflect the days of the governor's occupation, with many original Morehead furnishings returned to the home. This early Italianate house and its period furnishings are an important part of the history of North Carolina.

Old Salem, Winston-Salem

The Moravians are creative, industrious people whose astute attention to detail is evidenced in the living-history town of Old Salem. Members of the early Protestant sect called the Unity of Brethren, the Moravians derived their name from their homeland, Moravia, now part of the Czech Republic. Persecuted for centuries in their own land, the Moravians emigrated to Bethlehem, Pennsylvania, in 1740. Thirteen years later, they bought a one-hundred-thousand-acre tract in the Carolina wilderness and named it Wachovia, after the ancestral home of their patron. Salem, founded in 1766, became Wachovia's principal town.

While most eighteenth-century back-country settlers were struggling in isolation to raise food for their children, Salem's residents worked together to create the South's first public waterworks.

Salem was a "congregation town," meaning that the church governed the economy and social structure of the community, in addition to being its spiritual center. The church owned all the land and controlled business operations. Marriages had to be approved by the church elders, and strict dress codes were enforced. From the age of fourteen, single men lived together; they shared in the preparation of meals, kept a communal garden, and worshipped together daily. Single women lived together in their own house across the town square. Even in the cemetery, God's Acre, the dead were segregated according to gender and marital status.

Tours of Old Salem usually begin at the Single Brothers House, a large, half-timbered structure built in 1769. Here, costumed craftsmen—including a joiner, a weaver, a cooper, a potter, and a tinsmith—use traditional tools and methods to reproduce Salem wares.

You can also visit Salem's first privately owned home, the Miksch House, which was built in 1771;

Old Salem

the Vierling House, built in 1802, which was the home of Salem's most prominent early physician; Salem Tavern; the Boys School; the Market-Fire House; the Shultz Shoemaker Shop; and the beautiful gardens that grow only period plants. Don't forget to visit the popular Winkler Bakery, where you can purchase bread, cookies, and distinctive Moravian sugar cakes. The Tavern Annex, built in 1816, now houses the Old Salem Tavern Dining Room.

Stop at the Visitor Center for information on all there is to see and do at Old Salem. Expect to pay around fifteen dollars for adult admission; eight dollars for children ages five to sixteen. Old Salem is open all week, year-round.

Also of interest is The Museum of Early Southern

continued

Decorative Arts (MESDA), which is operated by Old Salem, Inc. The museum houses twenty-four period rooms of beautifully crafted furniture, textiles, ceramics, silver, paintings, and other work produced by Southern craftsmen between 1640 and 1820. For information about Old Salem and all its offerings, call 1-888-OLD SALEM or (336) 721-7350; their website is www.oldsalem.org.

Information for this section was taken from North Carolina Traveler with the permission of John F. Blair, Publisher.

Situated on four acres of lovely grounds and gardens, Blandwood is a National Historic Landmark.

Open for tours Tuesday through Sunday; an admission is charged.

The Hezekiah Alexander Homesite

LOCATION: 3500 SHAMROCK DRIVE,
  CHARLOTTE, NC 28215
TELEPHONE: (704) 568-1774
FAX: (704) 566-1817
WEBSITE: www.charlottemuseum.org

The oldest existing home in Mecklenburg County has stood on its current site since 1774. The centerpiece of this six-hundred-acre plantation was a "Rock House." The architectural style of the home was reminiscent of houses seen in Maryland and Pennsylvania at the time.

The exterior walls are completely built of stone. Some of the walls are twenty-eight inches thick at the base but taper off to a fourteen-inch thickness at the roofline.

This structure was home to Hezekiah Alexander, his wife, and their ten children. A blacksmith-turned-planter, Alexander became a wealthy and influential member of the Charlotte, North Carolina, community. When Charlotteans heard of the British attack on the Massachusetts colonists in 1775, they were quick to record their dissatisfaction with the British by writing the Mecklenburg Declaration of Independence. Alexander was one of the twenty-seven men who attached their signatures to this revolutionary document. Because no actual copy of this document still exists, some historians dispute Charlotteans' claim that they announced their declaration of independence months before action was taken in Philadelphia. But, it doesn't stop Charlotte's citizens from proudly making the claim.

In the 1950s, six chapters of the Daughters of the American Revolution joined together to save the home from destruction. Today, the homesite, which is listed on the National Register of Historic Places, is run by the Daughters

Biltmore Estate, Asheville

Built for George W. Vanderbilt, Biltmore was modeled after the elaborate sixteenth-century chateaus of France's Loire Valley. Surrounded by rolling forestland and enhanced by a lagoon, a conservatory, and numerous formal and informal gardens, Biltmore is one of North Carolina's most frequently visited tourist attractions.

Ever since it opened as a private home in 1895, Biltmore has excited interest for the balance and beauty of its design and the luxury of its amenities. Not only did it have the unheard-of luxuries of central heating, indoor plumbing, electric lights, and mechanical refrigeration, but guests could also enjoy a bowling alley, a gymnasium, and an indoor pool—astonishing features at the time.

The grandson of industrialist Cornelius Vanderbilt, George Vanderbilt decided to build his country home in Asheville because the mountain views and climate pleased him. He purchased 125,000 acres of forestland and hired two of America's foremost designers to plan the estate.

Architect Richard Morris Hunt oversaw construction of the 250-room mansion, which took one thousand workers six years to complete. Landscape architect Frederick Law Olmsted, who designed New York's Central Park, laid out the gardens and the park area surrounding the house, including the approach road from the main gate. The formal flower gardens adjacent to the house were based on those at the Vaux le Vicomte chateau near Paris.

Although Biltmore Estate is still owned by Vanderbilt's descendants, today only eight thousand acres of the original property remain; the rest was sold to the federal government and became part of either the Blue Ridge Parkway or Pisgah National Forest.

Admission prices vary for adults and youth;

Biltmore Estate
USED WITH PERMISSION FROM BILTMORE ESTATE, ASHEVILLE, NORTH CAROLINA.

children ages nine and under are admitted free when accompanying a paying adult. You should expect to pay a great deal more than the average fee for the other houses in this book, but you should also expect to spend a whole day at the estate. A three-mile approach road winds through century-old trees toward the house and parking area. You first see the French Renaissance house across a long lawn with a reflecting pool in the center. This scene may be familiar from the movies, Being There, Richie Rich, and The Swan.

Each room has a distinctive tone. The medieval-style Banquet Hall has a seventy-foot ceiling arching over a table that seats sixty-four. Flemish tapestries and a dozen elk and moose heads hang on the walls, and a carved mantel spans three fireplaces. The two-story Baroque-style Library has elaborately carved walnut paneling, a marble mantel, and an

continued

eighteenth-century ceiling painting imported from a Venetian palace.

The self-guided tour lasts about two hours, taking you through major rooms on the main floor, and family areas and guest rooms on the second and third floors. The tour then leads downstairs to the service area, where you can also see the recreational areas. You may also roam the gardens, which are especially beautiful in the spring, and visit the Biltmore Estate Winery. Another good time to visit is during the Christmas season, when the entire house is lavishly adorned in holiday finery. There are also gift shops and restaurants on the estate.

For more information, call 1-800-543-2961.

Information for this section was taken from *North Carolina Traveler* with the permission of John F. Blair, Publisher.

of the American Revolution and the Hezekiah Alexander Foundation.

The home, situated on a lovely park-like setting just three and one-half miles from downtown Charlotte, is furnished with pieces that date from the 1750s-1800s. The collection is one of the largest assortments of Southern Piedmont furnishings in the area. Costumed staff members conduct tours that include an adjoining kitchen, a barn, and a nearby springhouse that still runs natural spring water. There are gardens that produce materials used in the demonstrations on the site. The herb garden supplies herbs for the kitchen, while the garden that grows cotton, flax, and bed straw produces materials for weaving demonstrations.

Open Tuesday through Sunday; an admission is charged.

South Carolina

South Carolina has been an integral part of American history since the British founded Charles Towne on the Ashley River in 1670. As the colony prospered, disenchantment with British rule became a way of life. Battles ensued, and South Carolina finally won its independence.

In the early years, Charleston was a city of great wealth—primarily made from the production of cotton, tobacco, rice, and indigo. It was also a seaport and urban center for young America. It's no wonder that so many of South Carolina's grand old mansions are located in and around Charleston.

In the mid-1830s, many planters went westward in search of more fertile soil, so there was a noticeable decline in the construction of grand homes throughout South Carolina.

In the 1840s, when the issue of states' rights became a serious concern, South Carolina was a leader in the movement to lessen Washington's control. Secession was the rallying cry, and South Carolina was the first state to secede from the Union. In fact, the first shot of the Civil War was fired on Fort Sumter in the Charleston harbor. Later in the war, General William T. Sherman literally blazed a trail through the state, practically burning Columbia to the ground.

In the years since, South Carolina's historic sites, beaches, mountains, and many festivals have made this state a favorite vacation spot. For more information, contact the South Carolina Department of Parks, Recreation and Tourism at (803) 734-1700.

Historic Beaufort

Thanks to the lack of extensive damage during the Civil War and the efforts of local preservationists, Beaufort (pronounced "Bew-fert" with the accent on the first syllable) teems with nineteenth-century homes. Although most are privately owned and not open for public viewing, you can take a wonderful walking tour of the downtown area. You can find maps and information about the walking tour at the visitors center near the downtown marina (843-524-3163).

Although evidence indicates that Native Americans lived in this area, at least seasonally, as early as 4,000 B.C., written history began five hundred years ago when Spanish captain Pedro de Salaza discovered the area in 1514. This makes Beaufort County only second to St. Augustine as the site of a landing on the North American continent by Europeans.

In 1562, French explorers led by Jean Ribaut settled near Port Royal. When Ribaut returned to France for reinforcements, the soldiers that he left behind revolted, built their own ship, and sailed back to France.

In 1566, the Spaniards built Fort San Felipe on present-day Parris Island. In 1587 Queen Elizabeth I sent Sir Francis Drake to drive the Spanish from Florida. Deciding to concentrate on St. Augustine, the Spanish withdrew from what is now South Carolina.

By March 1663, King Charles II granted this area to the Lords Proprietors, and the territory became part of the Carolina colony. In 1679, an English colonization party landed at Port Royal, but took the advice of the local Native Americans and ventured north to found what came to be Charleston.

The area around Port Royal continued to stave off threats from both the Spaniards and the Native Americans until 1712, when successful expeditions against both lessened the threat of attack. It was that same year that the South Carolina colonial legislature laid out plans for the town of Beaufort.

Beginning around 1740, Beaufort gained its prosperity largely because of indigo. Because the British paid a sizeable bounty for the crop, the citizens of Beaufort tended to be against the patriot cause during the Revolutionary War. After the war, prosperity returned around 1790 with the rise of Sea Island cotton, which brought fabulous wealth to the area. Great plantations sprang up and the planters built summer residences in Beaufort to take advantage of the cool river breezes. When the Civil War broke out, the citizens of Beaufort were definitely on the side of the secessionists. Beaufort was captured by Union forces in November 1861 and remained under Union control for the rest of the war. Prosperity returned again with the establishment of Parris Island Marine Base during World War II. Today, controlled development has insured that the town's historic character is carefully preserved.

One of the highlights of the walking tour is the John Mark Verdier House, on 801 Bay Street. Verdier, who was a local merchant and planter, made his first fortune with indigo. As indigo markets declined, so did Verdier's fortunes. After a short stay in debtor's prison, Verdier returned to catch the next wave of prosperity with Sea Island cotton. He built this home around 1801.

In 1825, the Marquis de Lafayette was scheduled to attend a grand reception in Beaufort. Unfortunately, his ship was delayed, so he did not arrive until well into the night. He did not have time for a long stop, but refused to disappoint the multitude that had gathered to cheer him. He delivered a speech from the

continued

Charleston

The prevailing attitude in lovely old Charleston seems to be, "What is the use of hurrying when one is where one wants to be?" Indeed, native Charlestonians love their city, and well they should. Except for the traffic, it is a step back in time—with old brick streets winding by massive, often colorful, townhouses. It's a city where the clip-clop of horses' hooves make the old-world charm even more pronounced. Throughout the day, tourist-filled horse-drawn carriages transport visitors from Broad Street to the Battery, and back again.

Charleston is a town of piazzas rather than porticoes; of cobblestone streets and the sweet sounds of the Gullah dialect, if you're lucky enough to hear it. Whether you're riding in a carriage or walking and gawking, you will see a variety of fascinating architectural gems. As rice and cotton flourished, planters built grand homes on their plantations, but also built townhouses in Charleston. These townhouses were strongly influenced by the architecture in

Historic Beaufort, continued

balcony of this house, thus insuring it would always be called the "Lafayette House."

When rumors started that the house would be torn down in 1946, a group of concerned citizens formed the Committee to Save the Lafayette Building. The committee rehabilitated the house and gave it to its successor organization, the Historic Beaufort Foundation, in 1967. The foundation restored the house in 1976 and operates it as a headquarters and an interpretive center, illustrating the architectural heritage of Beaufort.

You can also see the Secession House at 1113 Craven Street where Edmund Rhett, one of the leading advocates of secession, held many impassioned meetings. Tradition claims that the Beaufort delegates to the Secession Convention went directly from this house to a boat, which took them to the convention where they voted, to a man, for secession.

The Joseph Johnson House, otherwise known as "the Castle," is located at 411 Craven Street. Built

in 1850, this Italian Renaissance house is an interesting site because the house's exterior color changes with the light. Sometimes it appears gray, sometimes tan, and on rare occasions it even seems pink.

Other houses of interest are the James Robert Verdier House at 501 Pinckney Street, which is nicknamed "Marshlands," and Tidalholm, where the movies The Big Chill *and* The Great Santini *were filmed. Another striking structure is "The Anchorage" at 1103 Bay Street.*

If you are interested in staying in a bed-and-breakfast inn housed in one of the historic homes, you can choose from the Rhett House Inn, the Bay Street Inn, and the Beaufort Inn. You can also dine at the Beaufort Inn .

For more information about Beaufort, contact the Beaufort Chamber of Commerce at 1-800-638-3525. Their fax number is (843) 986-5405; their website is www.beaufortsc.org.

Barbados. Although they were built close together, the townhouses were staggered, so each one could catch the sea breeze.

By the time the Revolution rolled around, Charleston was known in some circles as "Little London."

During the Civil War, Charleston was a bastion of Confederate sentiment. The town is still seeped in rich history, which can be experienced almost any time of the year. In addition to the grand homes, you can visit the area's colorful gardens. Places like Cypress Gardens near Moncks Corner and Magnolia Gardens near Charleston are little pieces of paradise, especially in the spring.

For information, contact the Charleston Area Convention & Visitors Bureau at (843) 853-8000 or 1-800-868-8118.

$\mathcal{D}$rayton Hall

LOCATION: 3380 ASHLEY RIVER ROAD,
CHARLESTON, SC 29414

Drayton Hall is located nine miles northwest of Charleston, on S.C. Hwy. 61.

TELEPHONE: (843) 769-2600 OR 1-888-
349-0588

FAX: (843) 766-0878

WEBSITE: www.draytonhall.org

By the time young English colonist John Drayton began construction on this Georgian-

Drayton Hall
COURTESY OF DRAYTON HALL, NATIONAL TRUST FOR HISTORIC PRESERVATION

Palladian mansion overlooking the Ashley River near Charleston, he had already inherited twenty plantations. The house was begun in 1738, and European and African-American craftsmen took four years to complete it. Today, Drayton Hall is said to be the first true Palladian house in America.

John Drayton managed the growing of indigo and rice from this plantation that someone once called "Mr. Drayton's Palace." Legend has it that the house was left unscathed during the Civil War because a slave was sent to greet advancing Union troops with news that the people at the house had smallpox. According to the legend, the Yankees chose not to approach the property for fear of the deadly disease. Other sources say that a Drayton cousin, who was a Union officer, intervened.

Despite wars, numerous hurricanes, and earthquakes, this great old house remains in pristine condition, relatively unchanged since its construction. Drayton Hall is so authentic that the Drayton family, who kept the home for seven generations, never even altered the original structure to add plumbing or electricity.

The red-brick mansion has two floors plus a full raised basement. Andrea Palladio supposedly inspired the double portico of Doric and Ionic columns on the front. Though it is uncertain if an architect designed Drayton Hall, it is evident that patterns—some from William Kent's *Designs of Inigo Jones*—were used in its construction.

When you tour this National Trust site today, the house contains no furniture. Without the distraction of furniture, the amazing architectural details are even more pronounced. The basement's central hall, with four large rooms at the corners, features a huge fireplace once used for cooking.

The representation of classical design at Drayton Hall is most impressive. The great hall features Doric pilasters, a small parlor has Ionic pilasters, and the Great Hall on the second floor features Corinthian pilasters. Nothing is more impressive than the wall panels with decorative leaf motif or the tobacco-leaf designs in the ceiling plaster. The drawing room's pilasters have Ionic capitals that were carved into the wet plaster. Other outstanding decorative features are the carved wooden cornices and the handsomely carved fireplaces and overmantels. The most unusual mahogany double stairway is joined by a landing with a beautifully carved wooden panel that also displays a leaf motif.

There is a gift shop on the site.

Open daily; an admission is charged.

Aiken-Rhett House

LOCATION: 48 ELIZABETH STREET, CHARLESTON, SC 29401
TELEPHONE: (843) 723-1159
FAX: (843) 722-4176
WEBSITE: www.historiccharleston.org

Built in 1818 by merchant John Robinson, this late Federal-style house was transformed into a Greek Revival home when William Aiken, Jr., inherited the house from his father in 1833. The young Aiken and his wife, Harriet Lowndes Aiken, spent three years in Europe collecting furnishings for their home. Some of these pieces still remain in the house today.

When the Civil War started, William Aiken, Jr., was a rich, successful businessman, rice planter, and politician. He served in the state legislature from 1838 to 1844, was elected governor two times, and served in the U.S. House of Representatives from 1851 to 1857.

Aiken was opposed to secession, though he supported it monetarily. A twist of irony is that the Aikens' daughter married the son of her father's political adversary, who was an ardent secessionist. The story of the Aiken-Rhett

Middleton Place, Charleston

For lovers of the Low Country and those who appreciate natural beauty manicured to perfection, Middleton Place may be the place of your heart. The oldest landscaped garden in America, Middleton Place was begun in 1741, when Henry Middleton imported a landscape architect from England to design a sanctuary of beauty on the Ashley River. Indications are that it took one hundred slaves ten years to create the elaborate terraces, paths, and ponds. All of this effort seems appropriate since Henry Middleton was, after all, the president of the First Continental Congress. His son Arthur was one of the signers of the Declaration of Independence.

Middleton Place, Charleston, S.C.
Courtesy of Middleton Place Foundation

Today, sixty acres of formal eighteenth-century gardens make this a favorite place to visit on the east coast. Azaleas and magnolias are resplendent in the spring, with the myriad blooms of kalmia, crepe myrtle, and roses following suit in the summer. The flowers create a blaze of color under the centuries-old, moss-laden oak trees, no matter what the season.

You can also see the Middleton Place House as part of a guided tour that interprets the Middletons' vital role in history. And what an impressive house it is! Built in 1755 in a Tudor-Gothic Revival style, the reddish-brown brick house was once the gentleman's guest wing. After the main house was burned during the Civil War, the guest wing became the family residence. Today it includes collections of art and furniture important to the history of America.

Also on the site, you can view a blacksmith, a potter, a carpenter, and a weaver recreating the activities of a self-sustaining plantation. Agricultural displays and live animals add to the authenticity. There is a restaurant and museum shop on the premises. Tour-ticket proceeds support the work of the nonprofit Middleton Place Foundation.

Open daily; an admission fee is charged; prices vary depending on whether you just tour the gardens or tour the house as well.

Location: 4300 Ashley River Road, Charleston, SC 29414

Middleton Place is located fourteen miles northwest of Charleston, on scenic S.C. Hwy. 61.

Telephone: (843) 556-6020

Fax: (843) 556-6020

Website: www.middletonplace.org

wedding is recorded in Mary Boykin Chestnut's book, *A Diary from Dixie*.

In 1857-58, the house was remodeled a second time, employing Victorian elements. It has remained virtually unaltered since because the Aiken family lived here until 1975. Over the years, as their numbers and needs diminished, the family members simply sealed off various rooms, thus protecting and preserving the house.

Since 1995, the house has been a property of the Historic Charleston Foundation, a group known for important work in the conservation of Charleston's historic properties. The group chose to leave the paint, wallpaper, floor coverings, and light fixtures from the 1850s period as they found them. Instead of restoring the house, the Aiken-Rhett House has been carefully preserved. The result is a fascinating and authentic look at the nineteenth century.

Of particular interest on the tour of the house are the ballroom and double parlors where Governor and Mrs. Aiken entertained dignitaries such as Jefferson Davis. The cast-iron railing in the entrance hall provides an outstanding look at the craftsmanship of the era. The art gallery exhibits the remnants of more than thirty-five sculptures and paintings that the Aikens brought back from Europe in the 1830s.

This house offers one of the country's most

Edmondston-Alston House

important and best documented examples of the lifestyle of a planter/politician in the antebellum South. A gift shop is located on the premises.

Open daily; an admission is charged.

Edmondston-Alston House

LOCATION: 21 EAST BATTERY, CHARLESTON, SC 29401

TELEPHONE: (843) 722-7171

FAX: (843) 722-4176

WEBSITE: www.middleton.org

The stately Edmonston-Alston House on Charleston's High Battery is one of the city's most splendid dwellings, a gracious example of early nineteenth-century commitment to elegance, style, and comfort.

When Charles Edmonston of Scotland built his residence in 1825, he was at the height of his success as a Charleston merchant. His late Federal-style house was one of the earliest constructed in the developing waterfront location. The site was a comfortable distance from the noise and confusion, a few blocks to the north, of mercantile wharves and warehouses—including his own. From his piazza he could monitor the arrival and departures of ships carrying his cargoes.

Economic reversals during "The Panic of 1837" forced the sale of Edmonston's house. Charles Alston, a member of a well-established Low Country rice-planting dynasty, bought it in 1838. Alston modified the appearance of the house in a fashionable Greek Revival style by adding a third-floor piazza with Corinthian columns, a second-floor iron balcony on the east facade, and a parapet across the front on which he proudly displayed the family coat of arms. These additions are evident when looking at the 1831 streetscape, *View Along East Battery*, on loan from Yale University's Art Gallery, on display in the morning room.

The house would be the Alstons' city residence for more than eight decades and is still in the family; today the first two floors are open to the public with tours conducted by the staff of the Middleton Place Foundation, a nonprofit educational trust.

Alston family furniture, silver, books, and paintings remain in place in the high-ceilinged rooms, much as they have been for over a century and a half. A popular room in the house is the library, with a collection of over two thousand books on display. Water-cooled breezes funnel in from the piazzas, with their unlimited vistas across Charleston Harbor. In the 1860s, these piazzas provided a front-row vantage point to history as General P.G.T. Beauregard joined others at the Alstons' to watch the bombardment of Fort Sumter. Robert E. Lee must have also appreciated the harbor view the night he took refuge here from a widespreading fire that threatened his hotel further uptown.

The Edmonston-Alston House has been featured on a segment of "America's Castles," a popular television series presented by the Arts & Entertainment network.

Open daily for tours; an admission is charged.

$\mathcal{H}$eyward-Washington House

LOCATION: 87 CHURCH STREET, CHARLESTON, SC 29401

TELEPHONE: (843) 722-0354

FAX: (843) 722-1784

WEBSITE: www.charlestonmuseum.com

From the outside, the Heyward-Washington House looks as though it may be austere. The three-story brick façade, with no frills, appears to be utilitarian. Built in 1772 by a rich, rice planter named Daniel Heyward, it is not exactly Georgian and a bit too early to be Federal. Daniel left the house to his son Thomas. Thomas was a London-educated lawyer and planter who become a patriot leader, served in the Continental Congress, and was a signer of the Declaration of Independence. When the British occupied Charleston in 1780, Thomas was arrested and sent to prison in St. Augustine, Florida. His family remained in their home, where his wife Elizabeth refused to pay homage to the British. She later died in childbirth. Of the six children she bore, only one lived.

Washington became part of the house's name after a visit by President George Washington in 1791. When Washington stayed in the house for a week, he wrote that he'd gone to a concert where there were four hundred ladies, "the number and appearance of which exceeded anything I had ever seen." But the Heyward family was not at home during Washington's visit. They retreated to their country house for the duration of his stay.

Heyward sold the house in 1794 to John Grimké, whose two daughters Sarah and Angelina, abhorred slavery and became active in the abolitionist movement after they moved to New Jersey. They also helped found the feminist movement in America. The Grimké sisters fought to show that blacks and women were not mentally inferior. In the 1840s, the Charleston police were instructed to arrest the Grimké sisters should they ever return to Charleston. When they did not return, the house became a boardinghouse and later a bakery.

The interior reflects the taste and style of the builder. Of particular interest is the fretwork over the mantel in the drawing room, which was made by Charleston craftsman Thomas Elfe. Elfe, who came to Charleston from England in 1747, was one of the most prolific cabinetmakers of the era. It is thought that he created more than two thousand pieces of fine cabinetwork in and around Charleston.

Now owned by the Charleston Museum, this National Historic Landmark also houses other important Charleston-made pieces from the eighteenth century. Noteworthy is the 1775 Holmes library bookcase and an exquisitely carved mahogany bed.

Original outbuildings remain on site at the Heyward-Washington House, making it even more important to the history of Charleston. The two-story kitchen exhibits a huge hearth, a beehive oven, and cooking utensils of the day.

Open for tours daily; an admission is charged. (Tickets may be purchased at the Charleston Museum.)

Joseph Manigault House

Joseph Manigault House

LOCATION: 350 MEETING STREET,
CHARLESTON, SC 29403
TELEPHONE: (843) 723-2926
FAX: (843) 722-1784
WEBSITE: www.charlestonmuseum.com

Joseph Manigault's brother Gabriel, a lawyer and talented amateur architect, designed this house around 1800. Even though Gabriel was considered a "gentleman architect," thanks to his efforts this house was the first house in Charleston designed by an architect. The house is also one of the most important neo-classical houses in the United States.

The Manigault House is one of the most distinguished in Charleston. It is a living example of the rich and lavish lifestyle of rice planters. The Manigaults, who were educated in Europe, were known to have sophisticated tastes. The two brothers were descendants of the elder Gabriel Manigault, who became one of the wealthiest men in young America. From the time the Huguenot family arrived in South Carolina in 1765, they began to take their place in history.

Today, the graceful, elegant lines of their home reflect their tastes. An archway in the entrance hall serves as a perfect frame for the curving, cantilever central staircase. Period furnishings are displayed throughout the house, some of it the work of early Charleston craftsmen. The impeccable furniture also includes fine period pieces from France and England.

This house was not always the showplace it is today. It was almost destroyed in the name of progress in the 1920s. During World War II, it served as a U.S.O. canteen. Today, the Manigault House is a National Historic Landmark, owned and operated by the Charleston Museum.

Open daily; an admission is charged. (Tickets may be purchased at the Charleston Museum.)

Nathaniel Russell House

Nathaniel Russell House

LOCATION: 51 MEETING STREET,
　　CHARLESTON, SC 29403
TELEPHONE: (843) 724-8481
FAX:
WEBSITE: wwww.historiccharleston.org

Charleston reached the height of its prosperity between the Revolutionary War and the War of 1812. This prosperity attracted the attention of entrepreneurs—some of them from far north of the Mason-Dixon line. One such speculator was Nathaniel Russell, a Rhode Islander whose father was a chief justice and one of the state's most prominent men.

Nathaniel arrived in Charleston in 1765 at the age of twenty-seven. He built a wharf and a warehouse on East Bay street, and located his office in a building across the street. His residence was above his office. Because Russell was "in trade," the Low Country aristocracy composed of planters, doctors, lawyers, and clergy, did not embrace him socially. Nevertheless, Russell amassed a fortune and was known in some circles as the "King of the Yankees."

By 1800, the merchant prince had two daughters. Their mother, the former Sarah Hopton, was also descended from a rich merchant family. By 1808, Russell built his grand townhouse on Meeting Street as a showplace for his girls. His strategy must have worked for one daughter married a Middleton of the Middleton Place family, while the other married an Episcopal priest who later became the bishop of South Carolina. Through their daughters, the Russells finally achieved their place in Charleston society.

One of the daughters lived in the home until the 1850s, after which it became the home of Robert F.W. Alston, a planter and governor of South Carolina. After the Civil War, the women in the Alston family were forced to support themselves by opening a girls' boarding school.

Today, the Nathaniel Russell House is owned and maintained by the Historic Charleston Foundation. The most prominent feature in the house is the "flying" staircase, an unusual circular stair that looks as though it is soaring upward without support. The three-story mansion is not a typical Charleston "single house." With its Adamesque design reflecting the fashion of the day, the house is far grander than most single houses.

Inside, tall windows create perfect lighting. The house's graceful interiors, considered among the best in the country, include geometrically shaped rooms and elaborate plaster ornamentation. This house showcases the skill of Charleston craftsmen. The construction materials, furnishings, and art, all acknowledge the grand lifestyle of the merchant elite. The second-floor rooms, which have wrought-iron balconies extending over the garden, include a formal drawing room across the front and an oval music room. The music room's fluted pilasters frame window-like mirrors. A two-story dependency wing includes a kitchen, work area, and servants' quarters. There is a gift shop on the premises.

Open daily; an admission is charged.

Boone Hall Plantation

LOCATION: 1235 LONG POINT ROAD, MT.
    PLEASANT, SC 29465
Boone Hall Plantation is located off S.C. Hwy. 17 North, in Mount Pleasant.
TELEPHONE: (843) 884-4371
FAX: (843) 884-0475
WEBSITE: www.boonehallplantation.com

As you drive slowly through the three-

Boone Hall Plantation

quarter-mile-long, moss-draped avenue of live oaks to Boone Hall Plantation's massive main house, you realize that these oak trees have lived through the history of this country. Captain Thomas Boone planted these oaks in 1743. But it was earlier than that, in 1680, that Major John Boone—an English settler from the "First Fleet"—received a large land grant from the Lords Proprietor. He used the land to establish a cotton plantation and later owned parcels of land throughout the Charleston area that totalled more than seventeen thousand acres.

Over the years, the Boones of Boone Hall would figure prominently in South Carolina history. Major John Boone's daughter Sara married Andrew Rutledge. Two of her grandsons made a mark in the state's history. Edward Rutledge was a signer of the Declaration of Independence, and John Rutledge was the first governor of South Carolina.

Around 1750, the Boones built their

wooden frame house. The plantation had its own cotton gin, brick kiln, circular smokehouse, and slave quarters. The skilled craftspeople and house servants lived in the square brick houses near the "big house." After the original house burned, it was rebuilt in 1935, using bricks made on the plantation. Today, the avenue of oaks, the first floor of the plantation house, the smokehouse, gin house, and nine slave cabins may be seen on a tour of Boone Hall. The part of the main house that is available for touring is furnished in fine period antiques.

If Boone Hall looks familiar, perhaps you've seen it on television or in the movies. The ABC-TV miniseries *North and South* was filmed here, as was the film, *Sweet Bird of Youth*.

There is a restaurant and gift shop on the premises. Because the Boone Hall property is popular with bus tours, it is often crowded.

Open daily; an admission is charged.

Mepkin Abbey, Moncks Corner

In an earlier life, Mepkin Abbey was a prosperous plantation along the rich Cooper River. When it was first sold in 1681, the land was part of a three-thousand-acre tract belonging to Sir John Colleton, one of the original Lords Proprietors of the Carolinas. In 1762, a prosperous French Huguenot merchant named Henry Laurens purchased the property. Laurens would eventually become a prominent patriot during the Revolutionary War and the owner of several plantations, though Mepkin remained his favorite. The British burned the grand plantation during the Revolutionary War, and the Union army burned it again during the Civil War.

It is thought that the name "Mepkin" originates from the Native American word meaning "serene and lovely." It is certainly an appropriate moniker. Long known for its beauty, the place attracted the attention of others who also appreciated its solitude.

Two of the people who were attracted to Mepkin were publisher and philanthropist Henry Luce and his wife, Clare Boothe Luce, who acquired the land in 1936. They later donated a major portion of the property to the Trappist Monks of the Abbey of Gethsemane in Kentucky. But the Luces remained at Mepkin, for they are buried here.

In 1949, twenty-nine Kentucky monks began the formation of the Monastery of the Immaculate Heart of Mary, known as Our Lady of Mepkin. The monastic tradition thrives at Mepkin Abbey, where work allows the monks to share in the divine work of creation and restoration. The tradition also helps provide for their livelihood and establish a sense of solidarity and community.

Casual visitors and retreatants who wish to stay on the grounds for a few days are welcome at Mepkin Abbey, if space is available. The monastery remains a place of peace and beauty. The gardens and chapel are open daily. Contact the Guestmaster at Mepkin Abbey for more information.

Open daily; admission is free.

Location: 1098 Mepkin Abbey Road, Moncks Corner, SC 29461

Telephone: (843) 761-8509

Fax: (843) 761-6719

Website: N/A

Hampton Plantation

LOCATION: 1950 RUTLEDGE ROAD,
MCCLELLANVILLE, SC 29458

Hampton Plantation is located eight miles north of McClellanville, off U.S. 17.

TELEPHONE: (843) 546-9361

FAX: (843) 527-4995

WEBSITE: southcarolinaparks.com

Hampton Plantation
COURTESY OF SOUTH CAROLINA DEPARTMENT OF PARKS, RECREATION, AND TOURISM

Hampton Plantation State Historic Site, a National Historic Landmark built around 1750, was one of the largest Georgian-style mansions on the Santee River during its heyday. Between 1750 and 1785, Daniel Huger Horry enlarged the mansion to include a dining room, study, and a ballroom. In 1791, the mansion became even more impressive when Harriott Horry, daughter of Eliza Lucas Pinckney, added the Adamesque portico. Harriott's mother Eliza, who ended up living at Hampton Plantation in her later years, is credited with initiating indigo cultivation in South Carolina. Indigo production began one of the first economic booms in the state.

The house eventually passed into the Rutledge family when Harriott Horry, daughter of Daniel and Harriott Pinckney Horry, married Frederick Rutledge. Hampton remained in the Rutledge family for over 160 years. In 1971, Archibald Rutledge, the last Rutledge to live in the house, sold the prop-

erty to the state of South Carolina. Archibald, the first poet laureate of South Carolina, returned to his boyhood home in 1937, when he retired from teaching English at Mercersburg Academy in Mercersburg, Pennsylvania. For the next thirty-four years, he dedicated a large portion of his time to renovating the house and beautifying the grounds.

Today, Hampton Plantation, which is managed by the South Carolina State Park Service, offers a realistic look at the early days of a Low Country rice plantation—its riches, rewards, and eventual decline. The plantation stands on the banks of Hampton Creek, a tributary of the South Santee River, where the fertile ground was perfect for rice cultivation. Rice plantations prospered until the Civil War abolished slavery. After the war, many of the former slaves became sharecroppers and continued to work the fields.

The tour of Hampton focuses on its architecture, the area, and the history of the plantation's owners. The house has been purposefully left unfurnished to accentuate the architectural details. Guest are encouraged to also enjoy the 322-acre grounds to experience the best of the Low Country.

Open daily from Memorial Day to Labor Day; closed on Tuesday and Wednesday otherwise; an admission is charged.

Columbia

Prudent legislators wanted their state's capital city to be centrally located, so Columbia became the compromise location for Upstate farmers and Low-Country planters. The capital was moved from Charleston to Columbia in 1786. By 1787, the streets were laid out on a two-mile square plot, and the town's growth was off to a steady start.

From its austere beginnings late in the state's development, Columbia caught up quickly. The textile industry brought jobs and a tax base, which encouraged and funded education. This included the establishment of the University of South Carolina in 1801, which was called South Carolina College at the time.

When Union general William T. Sherman entered Columbia on February 17, 1865, three-fourths of the city was burned. Columbia became another casualty of the war, but not for long. These stalwart people rebuilt, and the city continues to thrive today.

The most interesting way to learn more about the history of the state is to visit the Columbia Duck Mill, which gets its name because the building that houses the South Carolina State Museum formerly housed a manufacturer of heavy cotton duck fabric. The renovated mill now holds four stories of significant South Carolina history and artifacts. For information about Columbia, contact the Columbia Metropolitan Convention & Visitors Bureau at (803) 254-0479 or 1-800-264-4884.

Hampton-Preston Mansion

LOCATION: 1615 BLANDING STREET,
   COLUMBIA, SC 29201
TELEPHONE: (803) 252-1770
FAX: (803) 929-7695 (HISTORIC COLUMBIA
   FOUNDATION)
WEBSITE: N/A

This mansion was originally owned by the merchant Ainsley Hall. In 1823, Wade Hampton I saw the house and approached Hall about purchasing the property. When Hall said the property was not for sale, Hampton persisted. Hall then asked thirty-five thousand dollars for

Hampton-Preston Mansion

the house—a sum equivalent to $450,000 in 1996. Hampton was not phased. In fact, he stated his family was prepared to move in that evening. When Hall claimed he couldn't move that quickly because of a lack of help, Hampton sent a contingency of slaves and wagons to expedite the process.

After the sale, Hall and his architect Robert Mills began construction on a house across the street, which is now known as the Robert Mills House.

Built in 1818, the Hampton-Preston mansion was initially a late-Federal style. When the red-brick house was updated to a Greek Revival style, the brick was stuccoed and a suite of rooms was added. The house, which features a full-width Doric portico and wrought-iron railing, is a two-and-one-half-story structure built over a full arcaded basement.

During the years, there have been four women who played an important part in the history of the house. The first was Mary Cantey Hampton. The house was actually bought for her, and she lived there for forty years.

Her daughter Caroline and Caroline's husband, John Smith Preston, lived for eight years at Houmas House, one of Wade's Louisiana plantations, before returning to Columbia in 1840. The Hampton-Preston Mansion was spared destruction during the Civil War, even though the son of Caroline Preston's half-brother was a Confederate army general.

When the Union army occupied Columbia, the house was used as the headquarters for Union general John A. Logan. When the Union troops were leaving, Sister Baptista Lynch, Mother Superior of the Ursuline Order of nuns, asked Logan to spare the house so it could be used as a shelter for the girls in her care, since the convent had burned. The Mother Superior remembered the house because the sisters once taught John and Carolina Preston's daughters. After staying four months, the nuns returned the home to the original owners.

In 1873, the Hampton-Preston family sold their homeplace to Emma Moses, wife of Governor Franklin Moses, so it became the governor's mansion. In 1890, it became the College for Women, which was later called Chicora College for Women. The college occupied the house for forty years.

The South Carolina Tricentennial Commission funded the restoration of the house in 1968. In 2000, Historic Columbia Foundation, with assistance from the Symphony League of the South Carolina Philharmonic, completed a new restoration of the house. The current interpretation shows the evolution of the house under its many owners.

Today, the restored mansion is furnished with period antiques, some of which are from the plantations of the Hampton and Preston families. It is an excellent example of the home and furnishings enjoyed by affluent South Carolinians before the Civil War. The drawing room's Rococo Revival furniture was a favorite of Caroline Hampton Preston.

The Hampton-Preston House is managed by the Historic Columbia Foundation. A gift shop is on site.

Open for tours Tuesday through Sunday; an admission is charged.

Robert Mills House
PHOTO BY BILL BARLEY / COURTESY OF THE HISTORIC COLUMBIA FOUNDATION

Robert Mills House

LOCATION: 1616 BLANDING STREET, COLUMBIA, SC 29201
TELEPHONE: (803) 252-1770
FAX: (803) 929-7695 (HISTORIC COLUMBIA FOUNDATION)
WEBSITE: N/A

Born in Charleston in 1781, Robert Mills was one of the first architects trained in America. He first learned the basics of architecture from his brother Thomas, a teacher of drawing. At the age of nineteen, Mills moved to Washington to work for the Irish architect James Hoban, who was commissioned to build the United States Capitol. In Washington, Mills met an amazing amateur architect named Thomas Jefferson.

Jefferson hired the young student of architecture to make drawings and introduced him to other architects, among whom was Benjamin Latrobe. Mills would go on to become Latrobe's protégé. He later created many designs using the "Jeffersonian" style, but his designs were primarily for government buildings, such as the U.S. Treasury Building. However, Mills is probably best known as the designer of the Washington Monument.

This Federal/Greek Revival house in Columbia was designed in 1823 for merchant Ainsley Hall, who died before its completion. Hall's wife sold the house to the Presbyterians who used it as a theological seminary. The Columbia Bible College occupied it later. In 1960, a group of preservationists, who later organized as the Historic Columbia Foundation, saved the house from demolition. Ironically, although the house is one of ten documented residences designed by Mills, the house was never used as a residence.

The beautiful structure now known as the Robert Mills House is a testament to Mills's preference for symmetry and simplicity. Noticeably Greek, with tall Ionic columns supporting a portico, the red-brick, two-story-over-basement house also has Venetian windows.

On the inside, curved walls, twin parlors, ceiling ornamentation, and silvered doorknobs further attest to Mills's style. During restoration in the 1960s, marble mantels and crystal chandeliers were installed on the main floor. Interior furnishings, which include American Federal, English Regency, and French Empire pieces and two fine Aubusson rugs, reflect the period of construction. The mansion's vibrant color scheme includes eggplant walls with cherry silk curtains in the dining room. The house represents the high-style glamour of the era.

Today, the Robert Mills House is managed by the stellar preservation group, the Historic Columbia Foundation. Tours begin at the gift shop.

Open Tuesday through Sunday; an admission is charged.

Rose Hill Plantation

LOCATION: 2677 SARDIS ROAD, UNION, SC 29379

Rose Hill is located eight miles south of Union, off U.S. 176.

TELEPHONE: (864) 427-5966

FAX: (864) 427-5966

WEBSITE: www.southcarolinaparks.com

This sprawling plantation was once owned by Governor William H. Gist. Known as the "Secession Governor" because he presided over South Carolina's secession from the Union, Gist found there was no governor's mansion

Rose Hill Plantation
COURTESY OF ROSE HILL PLANTATION

ready for occupancy when he was elected in 1858. As a result, he lived and worked at Rose Hill, which was known simply as the "Gist Mansion."

The stuccoed-brick home was built between 1828 and 1832 in the Federal style. Front and rear porches were added sometime prior to 1860, along with sidelights and fanlights at the front entrance. A delicate railing surrounds the first- and second-story front porches.

A spiral staircase sets off the period furnishings that include a wardrobe and four-poster bed that belonged to Governor Gist. An 1832 pianoforte and an eighty-one-key piano stand in the ballroom on the second floor. When the ballroom was not in use, a sliding partition divided it into two big rooms.

The forty-four surrounding acres are spacious and pretty enough to be part of the tour.

Today, this is a South Carolina Historic Site, where you can tour the plantation buildings, including the mansion and the kitchen house which are both original to the time Gist lived here.

Open on Monday, Thursday, Friday, Saturday, and Sunday for tours; other times by appointment; an admission is charged.

*F*ort Hill House

LOCATION: HISTORIC PROPERTIES, FORT HILL/
TRUSTEE HOUSE, BOX 345615 (103
TILLMAN HALL), CLEMSON UNIVERSITY,
CLEMSON, SC 29634
TELEPHONE: (864) 656-2475
FAX: (864) 656-7451
WEBSITE: www.clemson.edu/welcome/
history/forthill.htm

Although Dr. James McElhenny, the pastor of the Old Stone Church, built Fort Hill in 1803, it did not become a prominent house until 1825. From 1825 until 1850, it served as the residence of John Caldwell Calhoun. Calhoun served his state and country well as vice president, secretary of war, and a United States senator.

Calhoun's daughter, Anna Maria, married Thomas Green Clemson. The Clemsons inherited the estate and bequeathed it for the

Fort Hill House
COURTESY OF CLEMSON UNIVERSITY

establishment of Clemson Agricultural College, now Clemson University. As founder of the school, Clemson designated that the home be preserved and open for the inspection of visitors, since it was once the residence of "the illustrious man who spent his life in the public service of this country." The home is now a National Historic Landmark.

The imposing, white two-story mansion with the Doric columned portico and piazzas looks like the home of a distinguished statesman. Many of the fourteen rooms feature important Calhoun and Clemson family heirlooms and fine period antiques. Of particular note is a mahogany sideboard made of paneling taken from the frigate USS *Constitution*.

Also on the Clemson campus is Hanover House, which was built in 1716. It is a fine example of early French Colonial architecture. The Hanover House is open weekends except during university holidays.

Open daily for tours except during university holidays; an admission is charged.

Pendleton

For a town of fewer than five thousand people, Pendleton has performed quite a feat by having one of the country's largest historic districts in its midst. The area that is now the Pendleton Historic District was formed after the Cherokees ceded their territory to South Carolina in 1777, although the town per se was not established until 1790.

Situated in the foothills of the Blue Ridge Mountains in the northwest corner of South Carolina, the area attracted the families of Low Country gentry, who built summer retreats in the area. It is their homes that comprise the bulk of the historic district. Today, Pendleton honors its history with a big Spring Jubilee the first full weekend in April.

Information is available at the Hunter's Store (circa 1850), located at 125 East Queen Street. You can also call the Pendleton District Commission at 1-800-862-1795; their FAX number is (864) 646-2506.

Ashtabula Plantation

LOCATION: PENDLETON HISTORIC
  FOUNDATION, P.O. BOX 444, PENDLETON,
  SC 29670
Astabula Plantation is located on S.C. Hwy.
88, about three miles from Pendleton.
TELEPHONE: (864) 646-7249 OR 1-800-
  862-1795
FAX: (864) 646-2506
WEBSITE: www.pendleton-district.org

This Georgian-style house could be at home in the South Carolina Low Country. It is a two-story clapboard house with a porch on two sides. Built by native Charlestonian Lewis Ladson Gibbes between 1825 and 1828, it stands to reason that Ashtabula would have similarities to the Low Country because of all the connections to important families from that region. Gibbes' wife Maria Henrietta was a Drayton of Drayton Hall; Maria's mother was a Middleton of Middleton Place. Both Drayton Hall and Middleton Place remain architectural landmarks in the Charleston area.

When the Gibbeses advertised their home for sale in 1837, it was described as, "the most beautiful farm in the Up-country." Indeed it was. Dr. O.R. Broyles was attracted enough to it to purchase the property. Ashtabula was sold again in 1851 before being purchased by Robert Adger of Charleston in 1862. Adger,

his wife, and daughter Clarissa lived in the Upstate during the Civil War years. During this time, Clarissa Adger Bowen kept a diary, which has since been published.

Clarissa Bowen's diary tells of forty Union cavalry soldiers who came to seek retribution for Federal wagon trains burned by Confederates in Tennessee. They said the armistice in effect was broken, and commenced to help themselves to horses.

Before the second group of raiders arrived, Clarissa's husband and two former slaves hid the family silver chest behind the house, concealing it with an overturned leaf cart. The raiders missed the silver chest, but helped themselves to jewelry, firearms, clothing, and food.

Today, the silver chest is on display in Ashtabula's sitting room; the silver remains in the Bowen family. After later owner Frederick W. Symmes of Greenville died, Mead Corporation bought the plantation to use as a tree farm. Mead awarded the house and ten acres to the Pendleton Historic Foundation, which still manages the property today.

Decorative arts and authentic family pieces, which represent several periods, are now on display here. Next to the main house is the "annex," a two-story brick dwelling that holds the kitchen, plantation office, servant quarters, and a traveler's room.

Open Sunday afternoon from April through October; other times by appointment; an admission is charged.

Woodburn Plantation

LOCATION: 130 HISTORY LANE, PENDLETON, SC 29670

Woodburn Plantation is located on S.C. Hwy. 76, about two miles from Pendleton.

TELEPHONE: (864) 646-7249 OR 1-800-862-1795

FAX: (864) 646-2506

WEBSITE: www.pendleton-district.org

Woodburn Plantation
PHOTO BY KAREN DILLARD / COURTESY OF PENDLETON HISTORIC FOUNDATION

Perhaps it should be expected that anyone with a name like Charles Cotesworth Pinckney would be a leader among Southern men. Actually, they were—for more than one prominent South Carolinian answered to the name. The Cotesworth Pinckney who was born in 1789 was the son of Governor Thomas Pinckney and the builder of Woodburn. He was also the nephew of General Charles Cotesworth Pinckney, for whom he was named. General Pinckney was a member of the Constitutional Convention in 1787.

Cotesworth Pinckney of Woodburn was elected lieutenant governor of South Carolina in 1833. Though he was a graduate of Harvard Law School, he was a planter at heart, which is why he apparently loved Woodburn, the summer home he built in 1830. It seems that Low-Country planters developed a fondness for Upstate mansions.

The four-story Greek Revival house featured porticoes stretching across the length of the house on the first and second stories. The house was also where Cotesworth Pinckney and several other enlightened gentlemen planters began a program to educate the blacks who lived and worked on area plantations.

Pinckney sold the home to David Taylor in 1848. In 1852, Taylor sold it to Dr. John B. Adger, a Presbyterian minister and missionary. In 1859, Adger's brother Joseph bought Woodburn just in time for relatives from Charleston to seek refuge during the Civil War. In 1881, the Adger brothers' nephew, Major Augustine Smythe, who was a trustee of

Clemson College, took over the plantation and raised fine horses and cattle. He also developed it into one of the state's most productive farms. The Adger-Smythes owned the plantation for fifty years.

The owners prior to the Depression did not fare as well, so Woodburn became one of the properties bought by the government. The government in turn gave it to Clemson College. In 1966, Clemson deeded it to the Pendleton Historic Foundation, which still manages the ongoing restoration.

The foundation operates Woodburn as a house museum with eighteen furnished rooms on three levels open for viewing. The furniture in the house today includes items from descendants of families who lived at Woodburn.

Open Sunday afternoons from April through October; other times by appointment; an admission is charged.

The Burt Stark Mansion

LOCATION: 400 NORTH MAIN STREET, ABBEVILLE, SC 29620

The Burt Stark Mansion is located at the intersection of S.C. Hwy. 20 and S.C. Hwy. 28 in Abbeville.

TELEPHONE: (864) 459-4297 OR 459-4688

FAX: (864) 459-4068

WEBSITE: www.emeraldis.com/abbeville

This mansion is truly an architectural grande dame of the South. David Lesley, a lawyer, district judge, and planter, built this house in the 1830s. The style is pure Greek Revival, and the home is pure Old South, both on the exterior and interior. Lovely though it is, the home's historical importance comes from its role during the Civil War.

It was here at the Burt Stark Mansion that the War Between the States actually came to an end. On May 2, 1865, the last Confederate council of war met here. In attendance at this most important and poignant meeting were President Jefferson Davis, Secretary of State Judah P. Benjamin, cabinet members Mallory, Regan, Breckenridge, and five brigade commanders of the Confederate army. The generals and cabinet members convinced President Davis that the Southern resources—both men and money—were exhausted. Since General Robert E. Lee had already surrendered at Appomattox, the advisors cautioned that another campaign would only bring more misery.

President Davis sadly admitted, "All is indeed lost." The war council then formally disbanded the Confederate armies. Unbeknownst to the embattled Confederate president, on that same day, May 2, 1865, President Andrew Johnson offered a reward of $100,000 for his capture. This great man, who once had

The Burt Stark Mansion
PHOTO COURTESY OF MS. MARGARET F. BOWIE, ABBEVILLE
PRESERVATION COMMISSION

grandiose plans for his beloved South, was captured on May 10 near Irwinville, Georgia.

Today this National Historic Landmark offers a visit back to 1900, complete with fine antiques, silver, crystal, rugs, and art of the era. Mary Stark Davis, the last member of the family who bought the house in 1900, donated the grand old mansion and its historic contents to the Abbeville Historic Preservation Commission.

Open for tours on Friday and Saturday; other times by appointment; an admission is charged.

Redcliffe Plantation

LOCATION: 181 REDCLIFFE ROAD, BEECH
    ISLAND, SC 29842
Redcliffe State Historic Site is located near North Augusta, off U.S. 278.
TELEPHONE: (803) 827-1473
FAX: (803) 827-1473
WEBSITE: www.discovercarolina.com

Redcliffe was the home of South Carolina's politically prominent Hammond family for more than 116 years. The two-and-one-half story, sixteen-thousand-square-foot mansion was built in 1859 by James Henry Hammond. Hammond was a cotton planter, a governor of South Carolina, and a United States congressman and senator.

The place he called home was important to Hammond. He designed Redcliffe for entertaining and for showcasing his extensive art collection. It was also a cherished homeplace where the Hammond family gathered to weather the storms of war, politics, and finances.

In 1935, James Henry Hammond's great-grandson, magazine editor John Shaw Billings II, began restoring the mansion to its former grandeur. In 1973, Billings donated the estate and its collections to the state of South Carolina to ensure its preservation. Today, the

369 acres remaining with the estate comprise Redcliffe Plantation State Historic Site.

Now, the people of South Carolina and others who appreciate historic preservation may see this replica of another time, complete with family furnishings and documents, art, and artifacts from plantation life.

Open Thursday through Monday year-round; an admission is charged.

Tennessee

Tennessee is a state for all seasons, lifestyles, and sounds—a place where the sweet melody of a mountain dulcimer blends with the riveting, rollicking sounds of American country music. Nashville, the state capital, is also home to the Grand Ole Opry, the world's longest-running radio show. Although the Opry has moved to a new location, the restored Ryman Auditorium and Museum continues to tell the story of the state's early music makers and offers live musicals and special events.

If you're in Nashville and want something other than music, the city offers a number of historical sites and antebellum homes for touring. The Tennessee State Museum showcases the state's whole history and highlights such legendary figures as the Cherokee hero, Sequoyah, and President Andrew Jackson. From Nashville, you can travel to the land the Cherokees called "Shaconage," meaning "place of the blue smoke." It's no wonder so many settlers followed frontiersmen like Daniel Boone and David Crockett over the blue ridges to settle the valleys of the Great Smoky Mountains, Cumberland Gap, and the Cherokee National Forest.

You can travel from the brick sidewalks in Jonesborough, the state's oldest town, to the plateaus of the Cumberlands, for a superb view that will take your breath away. You can view the serenity of the town of Sewanee, home to the University of the South and the Episcopal seminary or shop the quaint downtowns of railroad stops like Bell Buckle and Wartrace. You can hear the riverboat's calliope on the Mississippi River at Memphis, or follow the scenic parkway system to discover Civil War battlefields, Amish crafts, and small-town hospitality. Whether you visit Nashville, Memphis, Chattanooga, Knoxville or points in between, there's a timelessness that lingers over this wonderful land.

For more information, contact the Tennessee Department of Tourist Development at 1-800-602-TENN, extension 847 or visit their website at www.tnvacation.com.

Memphis

Graceland is probably the best-known mansion in Memphis, but the twentieth-century former home of "the King" does not fit within this book's guidelines. It still remains the second most visited house in America, second only to the White House.

Memphis also calls itself the birthplace of the blues. In recent years, downtown Memphis has become a magnet for tourists. The Beale Street complex offers food and entertainment that focuses on Memphis's musical history and Southern traditions. You can hear the music of W.C. Handy and B.B. King performed by some of the best blues bands in the country.

To honor Memphis's place in the long struggle for equality, the city now proudly calls itself home to the National Civil Rights Museum.

For more information about Memphis, contact the Memphis Convention and Visitors Bureau, at 47 Union Avenue, Memphis, TN 38103. Their telephone number is 910-543-5300; their fax number is 901-543-5351.

The Mallory-Neely House

The Mallory-Neely House

LOCATION: 652 ADAMS AVENUE, MEMPHIS, TN 38105
TELEPHONE: (901) 523-1484
FAX: N/A
WEBSITE: N/A

In 1852, Isaac Kirtland, who made his money in banking and insurance, built this Italianate mansion for his wife and their eight children. The house's last occupant, Frances "Miss Daisy" Neely Mallory, lived in the house until her death in 1969. Her heirs deeded the house and its furnishings to the Shelby County chapter of the Daughters, Sons, and Children of the American Revolution. The D.A.R. opened the house as a museum in 1973 and deeded the house to the city of Memphis in 1985.

Today, you can tour the three-story,

twenty-five-room mansion. When the Memphis Museum System began their long and tedious process of restoration, they scraped, sponged and vacuumed away years of paint, soot, and grime. Their efforts revealed vibrant colors and wonderful wood grains in the doorways. You can now see stenciled and hand-painted ceilings, parquet floors, and stained-glass windows that were purchased at the 1893 Chicago World's Fair. The house still retains its original furnishings.

The renovated carriage house now serves as a gift shop that carries Victorian-styled items.

Open Tuesday through Sunday, except in January and February; guided tours begin on the hour and half-hour until 3:30 p.m.; an admission is charged.

The Hunt-Phelan Home

LOCATION: 533 BEALE STREET, MEMPHIS, TN
TELEPHONE: 1-800-350-9009
FAX: (901) 525-5042
WEBSITE: www.hunt-phelan.com

The Hunt-Phelan Home is one of the oldest houses in Memphis and the last of the Beale Street mansions. The same architect who designed the Washington Monument designed the house, and the artist who worked on the elaborate border design on the United States currency is the person who worked on the

The Hunt-Phelan Home
COURTESY OF MEMPHIS CONVENTION AND VISITORS BUREAU

decorative scrollwork found in the house. Built from 1828 to 1832 by William R. Hunt, the mansion played a significant role during the Civil War.

Prior to the war, the Hunt-Phelan Home played host to many influential people, including Jefferson Davis and his wife, Varina, and Andrew Jackson. Early in the war, General Leonidas Polk visited Hunt at his home. Soon after, Hunt found himself on a mission as a colonel in the Confederate Army. Polk sent Hunt to New Orleans to steal one-hundred-thousand dollars in gold bullion to help raise the Provisional Army of Tennessee. On this mission, Hunt was successful, but he couldn't prevent the Union army from confiscating his home.

When the city of Memphis surrendered to Union occupation in 1862, Colonel Hunt's wife, Sarah, loaded many of the family heirlooms onto a boxcar and fled the city. Because of her quick actions, Sarah saved many of these treasures for posterity.

Fortunately, General Ulysses S. Grant decided to make the Hunt-Phelan Home his headquarters while he was in Memphis. Supposedly, Grant insisted that his men remove their spurs upon entering the library in order to protect the inlaid floors. It was in the library that Grant and Sherman planned the first assault on Vicksburg. In 1863, Pemberton used Colonel Hunt's sword in the surrender of Vicksburg. That sword remains in the house today.

The home remained in Union hands and was used as a Federal hospital. A Freedman's school was built on the property in 1864. In 1865, Sarah Hunt returned home with a boxcar loaded with her possessions and reclaimed the house. In 1880, General Grant showed his respect for the home by paying a visit to Sarah Hunt.

Since Sarah's return, the house has remained in family hands, making the furniture original to the home. In the 1970s, the mansion was occupied by Stephen Phelan, a successful engineer, who never married and became a recluse in the last years of his life. Upon his death in 1993, Phelan left the home to his nephew, Bill Day. After Phelan's death, the family formed a board to restore the home, its contents, and the grounds. Today, you can see the furnishings, the artwork, and the thousands of books that one family collected over 160 years.

Even as early as the 1850s, this Georgian/Federal-style house was impressive. It had running water, a hot-air furnace with a duct system, and a swimming pool. Some of the furnishings on display today date back to the 1600s and were considered antiques even when the Hunts lived here.

When you tour the house today, you are given a tape recorder and headphones. Voices portraying various family members guide you through each room. Of particular interest is the library where you see Colonel Hunt's whisky decanter and glasses that were probably used by General Grant during his stay here. A map of Vicksburg is on display on the table— a reminder that plans for the first assault were made in this room.

When you cross the upstairs veranda, there is a room lined with glass cases. Here personal letters written by Jefferson Davis to Colonel Hunt; letters from Nathan Bedford Forrest when he worked for Colonel Hunt and the Memphis-Selma Railroad after the war; documents signed by Andrew Jackson; a letter from the colonel to Sarah during the war; and family photographs are all showcased.

In addition to being open for regular tours, the mansion is available for private parties.

Recently a guest suite has been made available for overnight stays. Future plans include the restoration of the Freedom's school and the addition of a hotel in the back of the ten-acre site.

Open daily from Memorial Day to Labor Day; the remainder of the year, the home is closed on Tuesday and Wednesday; an admission is charged.

Columbia

"What Wall Street will do if you don't know stock, Columbia will do if you don't know mules," the late Will Rogers supposedly said about Columbia's reputation in mule-trading circles. Today, Columbia continues to honor its mule-trading heritage with an annual Mule Day Festival, held the first weekend in April each year. The event draws a huge crowd of revelers who come to view decorated floats, race carts, and see many, many mules.

But there's a majestic feel to Columbia and Maury County that is more reminiscent of a thoroughbred than a mule. Marvelous antebellum homes join with pretty country to invite long, relaxing drives on which you will discover the treasures of the old homes and country stores.

Columbia is home to about thirty-three thousand people, many of whom can trace their roots back to the town's settlement in 1807. It was then that Columbia was established on the low, limestone bluffs of the Duck River, right in the middle of fertile farmland and gently rolling hills.

For information about Columbia and Maury County, contact the Convention and Visitors Bureau at 1-888-852-1860.

The Athenaeum

LOCATION: 808 ATHENAEUM STREET, COLUMBIA, TN 38401
TELEPHONE: (931) 381-4822
FAX: (931) 540-0745
WEBSITE: www.mtsu.edu/~histpres/ APTA

This is an architecturally eclectic mansion that is certainly atypical for the period. This exotic blend of Greek Revival, Gothic, Italianate, and Moorish styles was constructed in 1835 by master-builder Nathan Vaught as a residence for Samuel Polk Walker, the nephew of President James K. Polk. Walker never lived in the house, but it became the home of Reverend Franklin Gillette Smith. A Vermont native and Princeton graduate, Reverend Smith came to Columbia as rector of the Columbia Female Institute, a church-affiliated finishing school for young ladies. He became dissatisfied with the quality of education at the

The Athenaeum
COURTESY OF TENNESSEE TOURIST DEVELOPMENT

institute, so he founded a competing girls' school, The Athenaeum, in 1852. At this school, he offered young women the opportunity to study some of the same subjects as young men. Athenaeum means "seat of learning," so it was appropriate that these young women were exposed to such non-traditional subjects as physics and calculus.

The school occupied a twenty-two-acre campus and grew into one of the most prestigious schools in the South, housing as many as 125 boarding students at its peak. Today, the tradition of that school continues. During the first week of July each year, the Athenaeum conducts a school for young ladies where they come in full nineteenth-century dress and participate in the same courses of instruction and activities as did those in the original school.

The main house, which is the only surviving structure, served as the school's rectory—

the home of the head of the school. The school closed in 1903, but the house remained in the Smith family until 1973, when an heir deeded the property to the Association for the Preservation of Tennessee Antiquities, which owns and manages it today.

The interior of the house is decorated with period furniture, including a ten-piece Meeks parlor set, which belonged to Mrs. Smith's daughter, Sally. Other items of interest include the wood-carpeted floors and the original Italian-made chandelier.

Open Tuesday through Saturday, February through December; an admission is charged.

The James K. Polk Home

LOCATION: 301 WEST SEVENTH STREET,
   COLUMBIA 38401
TELEPHONE: (931) 388-2354
FAX: (931) 388-5471
WEBSITE: www.jameskpolk.com

Little did the parents of James Knox Polk know that the house they built in 1816 would be the ancestral home of an American president. Although Polk left this home to attend the University of North Carolina, he returned after college. He also began his legal and political careers while living in this house. Polk would go on to serve as a Tennessee legislator and governor. He served fourteen years in the

The James K. Polk Home
COURTESY OF TENNESSEE TOURIST DEVELOPMENT

United States House of Representatives, the last four as Speaker of the House. When he was elected the eleventh president of the United States, he became the first speaker to become president.

Although this house is not as grand as the neighboring Rattle & Snap, it is a spacious townhouse that is stylish in its simplicity. To begin a tour of the home, you enter through an off-center entrance. Once inside, the architecture takes second place to the story of Polk's life. The house is filled with Polk's personal items and artifacts of his presidency. You learn that during Polk's term as president, the United States annexed Texas and Oregon, acquired New Mexico and California from Mexico as a result of the Mexican War, and established the United States Naval Academy and the Smithsonian Institution.

Polk devoted his life to his work, leaving Washington on trips lasting more than one day only twice during his tenure as president. He died in 1849 at the age of fifty-three.

Today, the Polk Home is furnished in period pieces, many of which were used by the Polks in the White House or while they resided at Polk Place in Nashville. The Polk collection includes portraits, mirrors, glassware, silver, and the rosewood-and-crimson brocaded furniture in the parlor.

Next door, you can visit the Sister's House, which was built for Polk's sister. The exhibits here include Mrs. Polk's jewelry and her inaugural ball gown.

Open daily; an admission is charged.

Rattle & Snap

LOCATION: TENN. HWY. 243, COLUMBIA, TN 38401

Rattle & Snap is located between Columbia and Mount Pleasant.

TELEPHONE: (931) 379-5861 OR 1-800-258-3875

FAX: (931) 379-0892

WEBSITE: www.rattleandsnap.com

What a wonderful surprise to find an impeccably restored mansion tucked away in a quiet country corner of middle Tennessee! But this is not just any mansion. Rattle & Snap

Plantation is one of the finest examples of Greek Revival architecture in the South. A National Historic Landmark, it is also one of the most dramatically designed homes in the South.

In 1792, Colonel William Polk won about 5,468 acres of Tennessee land from the governor of North Carolina during a game of chance popular in colonial America called "Rattle & Snap." A hero of the Revolutionary War, Colonel Polk owned more than a hundred thousand acres of Tennessee territory but always referred to his favorite lands as his "Rattle & Snap tract."

Colonel Polk divided this tract of land between his oldest four sons by his second wife, Sarah Hawkins. His oldest son, Lucius Junius, and his second son, Leonidas, would both build grand mansions. His third son, Rufus K., would erect a frame home popular at the time. Hamilton Place, Lucius's home, stands across from Rattle & Snap today. Unfortunately, Leonidas's home, Ashwood, and Rufus's home, Westbrook, were both lost to fire. There remained for the fourth son, George Washington Polk, named for the general with whom his father had so long served, to build the grand mansion around 1845 and take the name of the tract of land for the name of his home.

The Polks, for the most part, were ardent Confederates. Son Leonidas, a graduate of

Rattle & Snap
Photo Courtesy Rattle & Snap

West Point, would become First Bishop of Louisiana's Episcopal church, then missionary Bishop to the Southwestern territory. He later gave his life serving as a lieutenant general during the battle of Pine Mountain. Colonel Polk's nephew, James K. Polk, would become the eleventh president of the United States.

In 1862, word reached the families that General Don Carlos Buell's Army of the Ohio was on the move to reinforce Grant at Shiloh, so the Polks knew to hide their valuables. Tradition says that one of the Polk sons was lowered into a hollow column, where he left a basket containing the family silver until the threat of Yankee pillaging had passed. Another story says that the house was not torched because a Union captain spotted a Masonic ring on George Polk's portrait hanging in the home and reported it to his superiors. Whether General William Nelson, spearheading for Buell, or General Buell, or the captain was a Mason is not known. But by this simple feat, the order to torch Rattle & Snap was rescinded.

After the war, George Polk's fortunes declined and forced him to sell Rattle & Snap. The mansion was even a derelict for a while. It was used as a storage house and barn for hay and feed. In 1952, new owners began a major stabilization and renovation project that perhaps saved Rattle & Snap from a senseless doom. In 1979, the current owner began a five-year adaptive restoration returning the grand mansion to its 1845 character. As a young man, the owner knew of the house when he attended Columbia Military Academy, a short distance down the Andrew Jackson Highway in Columbia. When he retired from the publishing business in Nashville, he began his labor of love on Rattle & Snap.

Ten Corinthian columns highlight the façade of this grand old lady. Researchers believe the capitols for the columns were cast in the foundries in Pittsburgh and Cincinnati and transported by river and oxen to the house site. The columns support a colonnade that stretches across the front of the house. Four of the columns, all thirty-one feet tall, are set forward under a pediment. Tall, narrow, arched side-light doors, found only at Rattle & Snap, frame the lower front doorway as well as the doorway to the balcony on the second floor above.

The floor plan is shaped in a reversed "L" to allow ample space for double parlors, double dining rooms, and a music room downstairs.

The restoration included using old chips of paint to produce authentic colors and finding wallpaper pieces under layers of wall coverings to restore the actual look of the house. Deep reds and golds in the Wilton carpets, woven in England, and the rich Scalamandre silks and satins of the furniture and draperies are enhanced by the reflections in the huge over-mantel gilt mirrors. Magnificent chandeliers of the period adorn each room.

Inside the house, you'll find a major collection of Victorian furniture as well as other important period pieces many of them original Polk family heirlooms. These pieces include a half-test bed, dresser and wardrobe attributed to New Orleans furniture maker Prudent Mallard. Many other Mallard pieces are in the collection as well as pieces by Antoine Quervelle, John and Joseph Meeks, Signourey, Phyfe and others.

In addition to the house, the tour includes re-created gardens, the carriage house/stable, the ice house, and the 1845 demonstration farm. You can also enjoy lunch at the plantation, but reservations are required. There is a gift shop on the premises as well.

Open daily, except closed Sundays between November 1 and April 1; an admission is charged.

Rippavilla Plantation

LOCATION: 5700 MAIN STREET, SPRING HILL,
    TN 37174
TELEPHONE: (931) 486-9037
FAX: (931) 486-9055
WEBSITE: N/A

Rippavilla Plantation
COURTESY OF RIPPAVILLA PLANTATION

The eleven hundred acres of rich farm land that surrounded this plantation home are still much the way they looked in the 1860s. The twelve-thousand-square-foot Greek Revival house was built between 1851 and 1855. Apparently, Nathaniel E. Cheairs, the mansion's builder, was a demanding taskmaster. He stopped construction three times to have the brick walls replaced because he did not think they were stable.

During the Civil War, Cheairs served as an officer in the Confederate army. He was imprisoned after it was his dubious honor to carry the white flag of surrender to Ulysses S. Grant at Fort Donelson. He was released and captured again while serving on the staff of General Nathan Bedford Forrest.

Cheairs' plantation also played a prominent role during the war. At various times, the home served as the headquarters for Forrest, Benjamin F. Cheatham, and John Bell Hood for the Confederacy, and Bull Nelson and James Wilson for the Union army. Important strat-

egy sessions were held here prior to the Battle of Franklin, and in November 1864, the Battle of Spring Hill was actually fought on Rippavilla's grounds.

Today the plantation is owned and managed by a public/private preservation partnership, which allows it to serve several purposes. Since its million-dollar restoration, the house serves as a representative of the grand style of antebellum plantations in Tennessee. It also houses a museum for documents and artifacts used by the Army of Tennessee during the Civil War. In addition, the house is the office for the Tennessee Antebellum Trail, a self-guided driving tour of nine antebellum mansions and sites along a ninety-mile loop in Middle Tennessee. As if that wasn't enough, it is the regional visitor center, where maps and information are available for tourists.

The interior of the house showcases some

of the original furnishings and some important items that were returned to Rippavilla. A sunroom, which was added in 1920, is furnished to reflect that decade.

A new addition to the plantation is a restored "freedman's school," which was established by the Freedman's Bureau shortly after the Civil War to educate the recently freed slaves. The schoolhouse was moved from another site and reconstructed here. Each log was numbered to insure its correct placement after the move. The school, which looks as it did in the 1860s, now contains desks and other classroom materials.

Open Tuesday through Sunday; an admission is charged.

$\mathcal{C}$arnton Plantation

LOCATION: 1345 CARNTON LANE, FRANKLIN, TN 37064

TELEPHONE: (615) 794-0903

FAX: (615) 794-6563

WEBSITE: www.carnton.org

Around 1826, former Nashville mayor Randal McGavock began construction of his two-story plantation home near Franklin, just south of Nashville. The house was located on land that was part of a North Carolina land grant. Randal's father came from County Antrim in Ireland in the 1750s. Carnton was

the name of his homeplace there. The word "carn" is Gaelic for "stones raised to honor a fallen chieftain." Little did they know how prophetic the name would be.

On November 30, 1864, one of the bloodiest battles of the Civil War was fought on and around this land. As the Federal troops attempted to cross the Harpeth River on their way to Nashville, Confederates commanded by General John Bell Hood attacked them just south of Franklin. Smarting from being outfoxed the night before at Spring Hill, Hood was looking for a fight. The Federal troops were dug in behind a good defensive position, while the Southerners threw themselves against the fortifications. After five hours of intense fighting, the loss of life was staggering. Of the twenty-three thousand Southern infantrymen engaged in the assault, seven thousand were reported killed, seriously wounded, or missing. One of the worst things for the Confederacy was the number of generals lost—six killed, five wounded, and one captured. The Union army only reported 2,326 men lost, including 189 killed.

Many of the Confederate wounded were taken to Carnton, where Randal McGavock's son, John, lived with his wife Carrie. The house was quickly transformed into a field hospital. Carrie labored with the others nursing the wounded. She used up her linens for bandages, then her husband's shirts, and finally her own undergarments. Amputated limbs were piled in the yard. It is said that, at one time, the bodies of four dead generals lay on Carnton's rear gallery.

The dead were hastily buried on the battlefield in groups according to their home states. In 1866, John McGavock set aside land for a cemetery, which became the final resting place for almost 1,500 Confederate soldiers. The McGavock Confederate Cemetery is the nation's largest private Confederate cemetery.

Today, Carnton is beautifully furnished and restored. The cemetery is maintained by the Franklin chapter of the United Daughters of the Confederacy.

The mansion's style is "new classical," a style popular just before Greek Revival became prominent. After John McGavock inherited the property, he added a Greek Revival two-story portico at the front and a massive two-story gallery at the rear. Seven square columns support the roof over the gallery, which extends past the end of the house to catch the prevailing summer breezes.

The home incorporates the finest examples of workmanship available in the area. The colorful interior is light and airy because of the number of tall windows throughout the house.

Open daily for tours; an admission is charged for the house tour; the cemetery is free.

Nashville

The vibrant city of Nashville is the capital of Tennessee and the country-music capital of the world. You only need to take a gander at the music-related activities and opportunities in Music City, USA, to confirm this.

There's the Grand Ole Opry, Opryland Hotel, The Country Music Hall of Fame and Museum, Music Row, Ryman Auditorium, riverboats where music shows are performed, and the many private museums paying homage to individual stars.

Though Nashville's 2.5-billion-dollar music industry keeps the town on top, there is much more to this exciting city than rhinestone cowboys. Nashville boasts sixteen colleges and universities, the great Cumberland Science Museum, the Parthenon, the Tennessee State Museum, art galleries, world-class restaurants, and superb shopping. The place that more than a half-million people call home is also the headquarters for the Southern Baptist Convention and the United Methodist Publishing House. Some people even call it Vatican city South— for Protestants.

For more information, contact the Nashville Convention & Visitors Bureau at (615) 249-4700.

Belle Meade Plantation

LOCATION: 5025 HARDING ROAD, NASHVILLE,
TN 37205

Belle Meade is located seven miles west of downtown; 3.5 miles west of I-440.

TELEPHONE: (615) 356-0501 OR 1-800-
270-3991

FAX: (615) 356-2336

WEBSITE: www.bellemeadeplantation.com

Belle Meade Plantation
PHOTO COURTESY TENNESSEE TOURIST DEVELOPMENT

Called the "Queen of Tennessee Plantations," Belle Meade was world-renowned in the nineteenth century as a thoroughbred-horse farm. Since the early 1800s, Belle Meade produced some of the top thoroughbred bloodlines in the country. Several Kentucky Derby winners, including Secretariat, can trace their lineage directly to Belle Meade. The plantation's most famous horse was Iroquois. In 1881, he became the only American-bred horse to win the prestigious English Derby.

The plantation began in 1807 when settler John Harding purchased a small tract of land. Over the years, he and his son William built their land into a 5,400-acre plantation. With the completion of a Greek Revival mansion, Belle Meade soon became a center for social events. Among the frequent guests there were presidents Grover Cleveland, Teddy Roosevelt, and William Howard Taft.

After a fire in 1853, the fourteen-room mansion was remodeled and enlarged to incorporate a Greek Revival style. Today, the brick-and-limestone house features massive, twenty-six-foot-high columns, which support the portico roof. Perhaps because of the national reputation of the Hardings and their thoroughbreds, the plantation was spared the destruction so prevalent during the Civil War, although there was a skirmish on the lawn.

As the Harding family died, so did the fortunes of Belle Meade. The surrounding acreage was sold, but the mansion and thirty acres remain as a symbol of more glorious days. Furnishings in the mansion leave little doubt about how wealthy the Hardings were. Trophies and paintings of celebrated horses fill the central hall. A large portion of the furnishings in the house now are original, with the rest being appropriate to the mid- to late-nineteenth century.

Now owned by the Association for the Preservation of Tennessee Antiquities, the property is open for tours, conducted by guides dressed in period attire. Visitors can explore a carriage house and stable filled with antique carriages and an authentic log cabin, dating from 1790. There is also a reconstructed 1830s "saddle bag style" slave cabin. This cabin was moved from Cleveland Hall in Hermitage, Tennessee. The visitors center, which is in a separate building, has been fully restored to display the 1880s kitchen. It features a café and unique museum shop.

Open for tours daily; an admission fee is charged.

Belmont Mansion

LOCATION: 1900 BELMONT BOULEVARD, NASHVILLE, TN 37212

The house is located on the campus of Belmont University.

TELEPHONE: (615) 460-5459

FAX: (615) 460-5688

WEBSITE: www.belmontmansion.com

Belmont is a mansion that was home to a Southern belle whose life and loves would have rivaled Scarlett O'Hara. Born in 1817, Adelicia Hayes was widowed at the age of twenty-eight.

Her first husband left her a fortune in plantation lands and cattle ranches in Tennessee, Louisiana, and Texas.

She married Joseph Acklen in 1849. It was Acklen who tripled his wife's wealth with sound investments. Belmont was built before Acklen died during the Civil War. Despite the loss of her husband, Adelicia made the most of the opportunities offered by the war. She came to New Orleans and negotiated contracts for her cotton with both the Confederate and Union armies. She then arranged to ship the cotton abroad despite the embargo, and made another million dollars or so by selling the cotton from her Louisiana plantations to the Rothchild family in Europe.

The Belmont Mansion survived Union occupation during the war with little or no damage, although the rest of the estate did not fare so well. After the war, the mansion regained its status as a site for social gatherings. The ballroom is still considered one of the grandest private rooms in Tennessee.

During her lifetime, Adelicia socialized with such worldly people as Napoleon III, Emperor of Spain, and Queen Victoria. But her life wasn't without tragedy. In addition to the early deaths of her first two husbands, only four of her ten children survived past infancy. In 1867, Adelicia married her third husband, Dr. William Cheatham. A society newspaper reporter,

Belmont Mansion

The Acklens' collection of marble statues, which Adelicia purchased during her Grand Tour of Europe, are impressive. A collection of nineteenth-century cast-iron garden ornaments is said to be the largest in the United States. There is also a gift shop on the premises.

Open for tours during June, July, and August seven days a week; from September through May, tours are available on Tuesday through Sunday; an admission is charged.

The Hermitage

LOCATION: 4580 RACHEL'S LANE,
  HERMITAGE, TN 37076
TELEPHONE: (615) 889-2941
FAX: (615) 889-9909
WEBSITE: www.thehermitage.com

The Hermitage, the Tennessee home of Andrew Jackson, was considered a showplace when it was built in 1819. Affectionately known as "Old Hickory," Jackson was the nation's seventh president, and the first president to hail from Tennessee. He was well known as a rugged frontiersman, an Indian fighter, and the hero of the War of 1812. Jackson was also a man of fierce pride and a fiery temper. Although he could be rough around the edges, he could also be polished when necessary. The Hermitage reflects his refined taste in architecture and furnishings.

who was one of the two thousand wedding guests, wrote that you could not see the bride for the brilliance of her diamonds.

After Adelicia made plans to move to Washington, D.C., she sold Belmont in January 1887. She died that same year, at the age of seventy, while on a shopping trip in New York City.

The land developers who bought Belmont in 1887 sold it to two ladies who started Belmont College for Women. The house is now owned by Belmont University and managed by the Belmont Mansion Association.

On the exterior of this ornate Italian villa, you will see a recessed entry behind tall Corinthian columns. Simpler columns beside downstairs windows support the balconies. Inside, the house reflects the wealth and position of its owner. Many of the superb furnishings and artwork are original to the house.

When Jackson bought the land in 1804 where the Hermitage now stands, he lived in a log cabin for seventeen years, until the house was completed in 1821. The main house was originally a simple, rectangular, Federal-style brick building, though Jackson remodeled it extensively in 1831. With the help of architect David Morison, Jackson added two wings and a one-story Grecian portico.

While Jackson was serving his second term as president, the house was heavily damaged by fire in 1834. With the help of two master builders, Jackson rebuilt the house using the original walls and foundation, adding more Greek Revival elements to the new structure.

A popular place in the mid-1800s, the remodeled house featured tall white columns and wide porticoes across the front on the first and

The Hermitage
Courtesy The Hermitage

second stories. The house's tall ceilings and spacious rooms were perfect for Andrew, his son, Andrew, Jr., and his daughter-in-law Sarah, who loved to entertain family and friends.

Guests were greeted in the entrance hall, where the walls were adorned with French wallpaper designed by the Dufour Company. The double parlor was furnished with Empire pieces.

Another striking feature in the dining room is the "eighth of January" mantel. Although there is not historic documentation, a story is told that a soldier who fought under Old Hickory at the Battle of New Orleans worked on this mantel only on the anniversary of the battle (January 8th) for twenty-four years. When the hickory mantel was completed, Jackson supposedly installed it himself.

Today, this National Historic Landmark is maintained as it appeared during Jackson's presidency and the eight years that followed. Even the table remains set as if expecting the president and guests for dinner. There is also a cafe and gift shop on the site.

Open daily for tours, except the third week of January; an admission is charged.

Cragfont

LOCATION: 200 CRAGFONT ROAD, CASTALIAN SPRINGS, TN 37031

Cragfont is located five miles east of Gallatin.

TELEPHONE: (615) 452-7070

FAX: N/A

WEBSITE: www.srlab.net/cragfont

General James Winchester was a brave man who came to a wilderness and carved a niche for himself. From his arrival in Tennessee in 1785 until his death in 1826, the Maryland native was a major force in just about every phase of life in Middle Tennessee—the military, politics, commerce, and education. He was captured by the British three times in two wars. He served as Tennessee's first speaker of the senate, and he was a successful miller, merchant, and planter. He also counted men such as Andrew Jackson and Sam Houston as close friends.

The area where he decided to settle was still so much of a frontier that it was only four years

Historic Rugby

Nestled in the clean and green Cumberland Plateau, this restored nineteenth-century Victorian English village is a rare treat. At the dedication of the Rugby Colony in 1880, British author and social reformer Thomas Hughes said, "We are about to open a town here in this strangely beautiful solitude . . . a centre in which a healthy, reverent life shall grow."

Hughes, who had studied law at Oxford, practiced law in London, and served as a member of Parliament, had a dream of creating a utopia in the Tennessee wilderness. He obtained one hundred thousand acres of Tennessee land from a Boston capitalist. His concept was to provide a place for the younger sons of English gentry to thrive in a cooperative society. Because of primogeniture, the eldest son inherited everything, thus leaving the younger sons without estates or titles. Hughes named this grand experiment "Rugby," after the English school he had attended which had also been the setting for his book, Tom Brown's School Days.

At its peak, the town drew hundreds of young English gentry and other settlers to Hughes's self-proclaimed "New Jerusalem." But apparently the gentility of some of these settlers was not a good match for the Cumberland Mountains' rugged terrain. Cruel winters, a typhoid epidemic, and financial troubles took their toll. Today, you can still see about twenty of the original Victorian buildings. The Thomas Hughes Public Library has more than seven thousand volumes, making it one of the most extensive collections of Victorian literature in the country. The Christ Episcopal Church, which was built in 1887, still holds services each Sunday.

The village is listed on the National Register of

Home built in 1884 for Rugby founder Thomas Hughes
COURTESY OF TENNESSEE TOURIST DEVELOPMENT

Historic Places and is a Tennessee Historic Site. Although many of the surviving buildings are privately owned, seven are open for daily tours and three are open for visitor lodging. Some of the private homes are open to the public during the Annual Rugby Pilgrimage held the first weekend in August.

Some historic buildings open daily; winter hours vary; an admission is charged.

Location: (P.O. Box 8) 5517 Rugby Highway, Rugby, TN 37733

Rugby is located about 125 miles northeast of Nashville; 70 miles northwest of Knoxville; and 35 miles from both I-75 and I-40, on Tenn. Hwy. 52.

Telephone: (423) 628-2441

Fax: (423) 628-2266

Website: www.historicrugby.org

Cragfont
COURTESY OF TENNESSEE TOURIST DEVELOPMENT

after his brother's death by marauding Indians when Winchester decided to build Cragfont in 1798. Here, he and his wife Susan raised their fourteen children. One of his sons, Marcus, became the first mayor of Memphis.

Winchester chose to situate his new home on a rocky bluff above a big spring, hence the name Cragfont. Because there were not many craftsmen on the frontier, Winchester brought stone masons and carpenters from Maryland to build his mansion. In a time when most frontier homes were log cabins, Cragfont was grand indeed. The three-story structure was built in a T-shape, using Tennessee limestone that was quarried nearby. When first looking at the exterior, one notices seven iron stars across the front. These stars are not simply ornamentation; they serve as anchors for iron supporting rods.

Completed in 1802, the house even had a

ballroom upstairs, something unbelievable for the frontier. From either side of the ballroom, porches looked out over gardens and the distant hills. Today, the house is beautifully restored and furnished with many items that once belonged to the Winchester family. Several descendants have returned items that were original to the old homeplace. Pieces that are not original to the home are carefully selected American Federal antiques.

General Winchester died in 1826, but his family stayed at Cragfont until the mid-1860s. Some who have lived at Cragfont over the years report that occasionally Winchester family members seem to appear as "apparitions." The state of Tennessee purchased this historic property in 1956. Today it is managed by the Sumner County chapter of the Association for the Preservation of Tennessee Antiquities.

Open Tuesday through Sunday, from April 15 through November 1; an admission is charged.

Oaklands

LOCATION: 900 NORTH MANEY AVENUE, MURFREESBORO, TN 37133
TELEPHONE: (615) 893-0022
FAX: N/A
WEBSITE: www.rutherfordcounty.org

From its modest beginnings as a plain, one-

and-one-half-story, two-room house, Oaklands evolved into an impressive Italianate mansion. The house was begun in 1815 by Sally Hardy Murfree, daughter of the man for whom Murfreesboro is named, and her husband, Dr. James Maney. The house was also home to the Maneys eight children.

When historians were researching the restoration of the house, there were no documents to verify exactly who added what at what time. We do, however, know that an addition with a Federal look was added in the 1820s. We also know that one of Dr. Maney's sons, Major Lew Maney and his wife, Rachel Adaline, who was the daughter of Tennessee governor Newton Cannon, built the last addition in 1858. This addition created the Italianate façade that you see today. It contained a spacious hallway and four new rooms, making it one of Tennessee's most elegant homes

During the Civil War, there was a great deal of activity in and around Oaklands. At different times during the war's four years, both Union and Confederate armies camped on the fifteen hundred acres. In June 1862, the house was the headquarters for Union troops.

While the Union officers were staying at Oaklands, Confederate cavalry officer Nathan Bedford Forrest made a surprise attack. The Union general surrendered in one of the rooms at the mansion. One story says that this particular general had dined with the Maney family the night before and was quite ill on the day of the attack. Some theorize that this illness was not solely coincidental, but staunch Southerners believe that Forrest was such a superior soldier that he did not need to rely on food poisoning to force an opponent to surrender.

Later that same year, President Jefferson Davis and his aide, Colonel George Lee, the son of Robert E. Lee, stayed at the mansion while visiting Confederate troops.

Today the house has been restored to reflect the lifestyle of the 1850s. The house could be called a house of arches, for it boasts a series of curved arches and delicate columns across the front portico. The front entrance has an arched door and slender, arched sidelights.

Once inside the house, an arched doorway leads to a spectacular free-standing, curved staircase. In the dining room and parlor, heavy draperies cover some of the windows and patterned carpet features gold medallions in bold red blocks. Rachel Maney chose all of these colors when the Italianate style was in fashion.

About thirty percent of the furniture in the house is original to the Maney family. The other pieces are period antiques.

Open for tours Tuesday through Sunday; an admission is charged.

Virginia

The grand architectural styles of early America—Colonial, Federal, Greek Revival, and Gothic Revival—are more prevalent in Virginia than any place else in the South. While Virginia has scores of Greek Revival houses (the style most people acquaint with the style of a Southern mansion), the Commonwealth is more famous for its eighteenth-century dwellings, which can be seen nowhere else in the South in such numbers.

Virginia's solid, grand homes are among the oldest in the country. Most of these houses were designed by architects from elsewhere, or copied from "pattern books," originating far north of the Mason-Dixon line. Even the building crews and craftsmen were often imported from northern cities. In the mid-1700s, the English styles were still preferred. The styles were reflected in the sturdy, compact brick construction, the high-hipped roof, the arched windows, and the no-frill approach to refined design details. Between 1780 and 1820, Italian architect Andrea Palladio was an influence on Virginia architecture, as was the self-taught architect, Thomas Jefferson.

Rather than being concentrated in towns, Virginia's marvelous old homes are scattered across the rich farmlands. What a pleasure to see the great colonial mansions of the beautiful state of Virginia, but you can also visit other outdoor paradises such as the Blue Ridge Mountains, the Shenandoah Valley, and the Norfolk Botanical Gardens, a WPA project built in 1936. Today, the botanical gardens are seasoned to perfection. They boast more than two hundred thousand azaleas, an exquisite rose collection, and a "fragrance garden" for the visually impaired.

For additional travel information, contact the Virginia Tourism Corporation at 1-800-932-5827 or (804) 786-4484.

Bacon's Castle

LOCATION: 465 BACON'S CASTLE TRAIL,
SURRY, VA 23888

Bacon's Castle is located seven miles east of Surry, on State Road 10.

TELEPHONE: (757) 357-5976

FAX: (804) 775-0802 (APVA)

WEBSITE: www.apva.org (see the Bacon's Castle site listing)

Bacon's Castle
COURTESY OF VIRGINIA TOURISM CORPORATION

The history surrounding what is thought to be the oldest brick house in America is most intriguing. The intrigue begins with Arthur Allen, the man who built the home. He was an immigrant with money who patented the land for this estate on March 14, 1650. But where he came from, why he came to Virginia, and how he acquired his vast wealth remains a mystery. After building his grand home, he became a merchant and planter.

In 1665, Allen built the brick Jacobean-style, two-and-one-half-story house using a cruciform (the shape of a cross) design. Apparently influenced by the architecture seen in English manors, this house would be at home in the English countryside. The castle-like structure features triple chimneys clustered at either end of the house. The chimneys are turned at an angle. The Flemish gables add a medieval feel to the place.

Four years after the house was built, Allen died, leaving the estate to his son Major Arthur Allen II. In September 1676, an aggressive, young, Cambridge-educated planter named Nathaniel Bacon organized a revolt to protest Virginia governor William Berkeley's refusal to protect the frontier against Indian attack. Major Allen was a firm supporter of Governor Berkeley and was with him when the rebellion broke out.

About seventy of Bacon's men commandeered Allen's mansion in his absence. They used the house as a stronghold during the three-month rebellion, which became known as Bacon's Rebellion. Bacon, who was himself a gentleman planter, was never at the house and did not condone his men's activities there. Some made a mess of the house and gardens and stole whatever they could carry. Shortly after the rebellion was quashed, Bacon died of dysentery.

After the British arrived to end the rebellion, Major Allen returned to his home to begin repairs. Allen later sued and received money to compensate for the damage Bacon's men caused at the house and for the loss of cattle, wine, and other supplies. After Major Allen's death, his son, Arthur Allen III, inherited the property. Arthur's wife Elizabeth was the mistress of the manor for about sixty-three years, and it was during this time that renovations were made. By the time Elizabeth's grandson, Allan Cocke, inherited the property, it was widely known as "Bacon's Castle."

The Cocke family sold the homeplace in 1843. A year later, it was auctioned to John Henry Hankins, a plasterer who made more alterations to the house, and also made the plantation profitable again. After the Civil War, when all the Southern plantations faced tremendous hardships, Bacon's Castle was sold several more times. It finally ended up in the hands of Walker Pegram Warren and his wife. After the death of the Warrens, the Association for the Preservation of Virginia Antiquities (APVA) purchased Bacon's Castle in 1973.

Since the APVA took it over, important restoration and archaeological excavations have taken place. This National Historic Landmark, which now offers interpretive tours and artifacts that reflect three centuries of remarkable American history, is one of Virginia's best showplaces.

Open Tuesday through Saturday, from April through October; an admission is charged.

Carter's Grove

LOCATION: 8797 POCAHONTAS TRAIL, WILLIAMSBURG, VA 23187

Carter's Grove is located eight miles east of Williamsburg, on U.S. 60 E. From Williamsburg, Carter's Grove is accessible by the South England Street entry to Carter's Grove County Road.

TELEPHONE: 1-800-HISTORY OR (757) 229-1000

FAX: (757) 220-7173

WEBSITE: www.history.org

Beginning with John Carter, who came to the area in 1649, the Carter family of Virginia would become some of the greatest proponents of colonial architecture. John's son, Robert "King" Carter, amassed more than three hundred thousand acres of rich Virginia farmland, as well as the slaves necessary to work the land. A planter, merchant, fur trader, and agent for Lord Fairfax, King Carter showcased his vast wealth by his lavish lifestyle and the construction of homes and other structures, including Christ Episcopal Church in 1732.

Carter's Grove
COURTESY OF VIRGINIA TOURISM CORPORATION

Carter Burwell, King Carter's grandson, began work on this stately, two-hundred-foot long Georgian mansion on the James River in 1749. Known as Carter's Grove, this massive, elegantly styled brick house was restored and renovated in the late 1920s.

One memorable feature inside is the stair hall. Of special note is the wide elliptical arch that spans the area. The elaborate ornamentation and Ionic columns on each side accent the space. While the stairs meander upward to the left, a short hall on the right leads to doors that go to other parts of the house. The house gets rave reviews for the outstanding woodwork done by a master carver and his assistants, who worked from 1752 to 1755 to complete the elaborately paneled interior.

Carter Burwell died just after the completion of Carter's Grove, though five generations of Carters owned the plantation until 1838. The house has had several owners and "updates" over the years. In 1928, the Archibald M. McCrea family hired Richmond architect, W. Duncan Lee, to renovate and enlarge the house. With the addition of hyphens to connect the three detached buildings, the grand mansion now has five connected sections. It is now about 128 feet longer than its original 72 feet.

In 1963, the property was purchased by the Sealantic Fund, Inc., which in turn gave the house to the Colonial Williamsburg Foundation, which still owns and manages the property. Colonial Williamsburg doubled the acreage and undertook archaeological research, which netted an amazing discovery—the site of Wolstenholme Towne, a settlement destroyed by Indians in 1622. The Winthrop Rockefeller Archaeology Museum and the partially reconstructed Wolstenholme Towne is a must-see.

Today Carter's Grove is beautifully furnished with antiques and art. It remains one of America's loveliest homes.

Open daily from mid-March through October; an admission is charged.

Colonial Williamsburg

This is the area where America began. A visit to remarkable Colonial Williamsburg leaves no doubt about the way things were from 1699 to 1780, when Williamsburg was still the capital city of colonial Virginia.

Today, Williamsburg is a genteel but busy town near the James River that has become America's most famous colonial restoration. And it is not just a meticulous restoration. It is one so cleverly done visitors feel as though they've been transported back in time. You might listen in on a conversation with Martha Washington and friend in a quiet garden, or hear Thomas Jefferson speaking about his love of architecture.

You can go to the local tavern, where Patrick Henry and his entourage are bemoaning the fact that their Virginia is still part of the British empire. You can hear rumors on the street about plans for a war against England. And, you can watch eighteenth-century craftsmen and shopkeepers at work.

Colonial Williamsburg is history coupled with art. It's an American museum village that attracts about one million visitors a year to the more than five hundred public buildings, private homes, stores and taverns, tradesmen practicing historic trades, interpreters, and ninety acres of gardens. Eighty-eight original eighteenth-century buildings survive, with many more carefully reconstructed on their original foundations.

The concept of Williamsburg began in 1926, when the Reverend Dr. W.A.R. Goodwin, rector of the Bruton Parish Church, had an idea for the restoration of the colonial capital. He discussed his idea with John D. Rockefeller, Jr., who shared his interest in historic preservation. For the next thirty years, Rockefeller gave the restoration of Williamsburg his personal attention. He also set up an

The Governor's Palace at Williamsburg
COURTESY OF VIRGINIA TOURISM CORPORATION

endowment to help provide for the restoration and its educational programs.

Rockefeller once said, "As the work has progressed, I have come to feel that perhaps an even greater value is the lesson that it teaches of the patriotism, high purpose, and unselfish devotion of our forefathers to the common good."

Today, this National Historic Landmark is managed by the Colonial Williamsburg Foundation, a nonprofit educational organization deriving its financial support primarily from admission fees, sales of authorized reproductions, books, and crafts, gifts and donations, and income from the management of resort properties. There are restaurants and shops throughout the village.

Open daily; an admission is charged.

Williamsburg is located in southeastern Virginia, between Richmond and Norfolk.

Telephone: 1-800-HISTORY or (757) 229-1000

Fax: (757) 565-8965

WEBSITE: www.colonialwilliamsburg.org

James River Plantations

Strategically located between the James and Chickahominy Rivers and close to the colonial capitals of Williamsburg and Jamestown, Charles City County offers treasures from four centuries. First established in 1616, the county is now known for the gracious manor houses known as the James River Plantations. In this book, you will find descriptions of three houses along VA. 5 where you can take tours of these National Historic Register properties. If you are visiting this area, you might also wish to visit Evelynton and Westover Plantation. Evelynton is not included in this guide because the original manor house was destroyed by fire during the Civil War. The present mansion, which is open to the public, was built in 1937. The manor house at Westover is not open to the public, but its impressive gardens are.

Ironically, there is no Charles City in Charles City County, but you can see the 250-year-old courthouse in the heart of the community. Through the years, the county has been home to presidents Benjamin Harrison, William Henry Harrison, John Tyler, as well as Robert E. Lee. It was home to Edmund Ruffin, who fired the first shot of the Civil War, and Lott Cary, the first black American missionary to Africa and the founding father of Liberia. It was the site of one of the first free black communities in America and the third oldest organized free black church.

For information about the James River Plantations, call 1-800-704-5423.

Sherwood Forest Plantation

LOCATION: 14501 JOHN TYLER HIGHWAY, CHARLES CITY, VA 23030
TELEPHONE: (804) 829-5377
FAX: (804) 829-2947
WEBSITE: www.sherwoodforest.org

Remember hearing "Tippecanoe and Tyler, too" in early history classes? Well, Sherwood Forest is the home of John Tyler, who was the vice-presidential candidate represented in that campaign slogan. The slogan must have worked, because William Henry Harrison, the "Tippecanoe" part of the phrase, was elected. When Harrison died shortly after his inauguration, Tyler became president of the United States. He served from 1841 to 1845. Prior to becoming president, Tyler had been a two-term governor of Virginia and had served in both the United States House of Representatives and the Senate.

In an interesting twist for a former president, Tyler, who was an avid supporter of states' rights, re-entered the public arena in 1861 as a member of the Confederate Congress. Although John Tyler died in 1862,

Sherwood Forest Plantation
COURTESY OF SHERWOOD FOREST

Sherwood Forest is still a working plantation, owned by the grandson of President Tyler.

The name "Sherwood Forest" supposedly came from Tyler's political adversary, Henry Clay. When President Tyler decided not to run for re-election to the nation's highest office, Henry Clay was relieved. Because of their disagreement about where the Whig Party should go, Clay considered Tyler a political outlaw. Clay said he was delighted that "Robin Hood" Tyler was retiring to his "Sherwood Forest." President Tyler liked the comment so much, he changed the name of his plantation from Walnut Grove to Sherwood Forest.

Although Tyler bought Sherwood Forest and its sixteen hundred acres in 1842, the house was built around 1730. The house originally exhibited an architectural style sometimes called "Virginia Tidewater," but Tyler added hyphens that attached dependencies. The hy-phen on the western end houses a sixty-eight-foot ballroom. The ballroom, coupled with the other additions, made Sherwood Forest three hundred feet long across the façade. This led to the claim that Sherwood Forest was the longest historic home in the state. According to legend, the long, narrow ballroom was designed specifically for guests to dance the Virginia Reel.

During the house's final renovation in 1845, Julia Gardiner Tyler had a preference for the popular Greek Revival style. This resulted in the addition of porches, pilasters, cornices, and ornate medallions. The Greek Revival elements are still seen in the doorways and formal rooms. Minard LeFevre's book, *The Beauties of American Architecture*, published in 1842, probably influenced the design of the doors.

The eighteenth-century furniture, art, and artifacts seen in this National Historic Landmark today belonged either to the Tylers or to the wife of the house's current owner, who grew up on a prominent South Carolina plantation. You can see china used at the White House, as well as family furniture that President Tyler used during his stay at the White House. Historians are particularly impressed with the only remaining copy of America's first book of law drawn up by Virginia's House of Burgesses. There is also a gift shop on the premises, where light refreshments are available.

Open daily; an admission is charged.

Shirley Plantation

LOCATION: 501 SHIRLEY PLANTATION ROAD,
CHARLES CITY, VA 23030
TELEPHONE: (800) 232-1613
FAX: (804) 829-6322
WEBSITE: www.shirleyplantation.com

Shirley Plantation
COURTESY OF VIRGINIA TOURISM CORPORATION

Six years after English colonists arrived in Jamestown in 1607, Shirley Plantation was founded. By 1638, Edward Hill I had established ownership of Shirley, and today members of the tenth and eleventh generations of the Hill-Carter family continue to live here. It is the oldest family-owned business in North America. Edward Hill III, who was a member of the Virginia House of Burgesses, began the present mansion for his daughter Elizabeth, who married John Carter, the eldest son of King Carter. The house was finally completed in 1738.

One of the interesting interior adornments is the wide use of the pineapple, which was the colonial symbol for hospitality. You can see pineapples in the hand-carved woodwork throughout the house. It is also used as a three-foot finial on the peak of the roof. It seems only appropriate to use this symbol because the Hills and later the Carters entertained lavishly. Guests included their neighbors the Byrds and Harrisons as well as other prominent Virginians.

During the Revolutionary War, Shirley served as a supply center for the Continental Army. Twice, it was a listening post for both sides in the no-man's land between the British at City Point, which is now Hopewell, and Lafayette's troops at Malvern Hill.

Later, Ann Hill Carter was born at Shirley. She was the wife of Henry "Light Horse Harry" Lee and the mother of Confederate general Robert E. Lee. Robert received some of his schooling in the converted laundry house at Shirley.

Today, the home is still largely in its original state. The famous carved walnut staircase that rises three stories without visible means of support is the only one of its kind in America. The superb paneling and elegant woodcarving are fine examples of the work of eighteenth-century artisans.

Shirley is still an 800-acre working plantation operated by the descendants of Hills and Carters. You can also tour a number of brick outbuildings built in 1723. A large two-story kitchen, a laundry house, and two barns, including one with an ice cellar beneath it, form a unique Queen Anne forecourt. Other original structures include the stable, smokehouse, and dovecote.

Open daily except major holidays; an admission is charged.

Berkeley Plantation

LOCATION: 12602 HARRISON LANDING ROAD, CHARLES CITY, VA 23030

Berkeley Plantation is located eighteen miles west of Williamsburg and thirty-five miles east of Richmond on Va. Hwy. 5. The plantation is three miles east of the Charles City County courthouse.

TELEPHONE: (804) 829-6018

FAX: (804) 829-6757

WEBSITE: www.jamesriverplantations.org

Good Housekeeping magazine once suggested, "If you only have time for one plantation, Berkeley should be at the top of your list." The manor house was built in 1726 by Benjamin Harrison IV. His son, Benjamin V, who was the plantation's second owner, was a signer of the Declaration of Independence and a three-term governor of Virginia. Benjamin's third

Berkeley Plantation
COURTESY OF VIRGINIA TOURISM CORPORATION

son, William Henry Harrison, was born at Berkeley. William would go on to become famous as an Indian fighter. His exploits earned him the nickname "Tippecanoe," which became part of the slogan "Tippecanoe and Tyler, too" when William ran for president. In 1841, William became the ninth president of the United States. His grandson, Benjamin, became the twenty-third president.

The original mansion was built of brick that was fired on the plantation. The early Georgian home is said to be the oldest three-story brick house in Virginia and the first house with a pediment roof. The handsome Adam woodwork and the double arches of the Great Rooms were installed by Benjamin Harrison VI in 1790 under the direction of Thomas Jefferson. The rooms are furnished with eighteenth-century antiques.

Occupying a beautifully landscaped hilltop

overlooking the James River, Berkeley also offers ten acres of formal terraced boxwood gardens. The lawn extends a quarter-mile from the front door to the James River. Inside the house, you can dine at the Coach House Tavern in the same room where George Washington and the succeeding nine presidents of the United States also dined.

Open daily; an admission is charged

Richmond

Richmond is by far one of the most historically significant state capitals. In 1609, Captain John Smith and Chief Powhatan traded for a tract of land where the English could establish a settlement. Located near present-day Richmond, the settlement was called "None Such." Actually founded in the 1730s, Richmond was designated the capital of Virginia in 1779.

In 1861, Richmond became the capital of the Confederate States of America and the stronghold of Confederate military power. Many Union generals failed in their attempts to capture Richmond until General Ulysses S. Grant finally found a way to cripple the city by attacking nearby Mechanicsville and Petersburg.

When the Confederacy collapsed and Richmond was evacuated, Confederate troops burned the Confederate government's warehouse in a fire that spread to nearby buildings.

Despite the fire, there are still many interesting historic structures to see in Richmond. Today, the city, which is rich in history, offers a great place to tour. Although space did not allow the coverage of all the historic buildings in this city, there are a few worth mentioning briefly.

Built in 1813, the oldest continuously used Governor's Mansion housed three Virginia governors who became United States presidents: Thomas Jefferson, James Monroe, and John Tyler. President William Henry Harrison also lived in the mansion when his father was governor.

Agecroft Hall was built in England in the fifteenth century, dismantled in 1920, and shipped to its present James River site. Today, house and garden tours are available Tuesday through Sunday; an admission is charged. Maymont is a Victorian country estate, which was given to the city by Major James Dooley. Formal gardens, a nature center, a farm for children, and Virginia wildlife habitats are available for daily tours.

The poignant and proud Museum of the Confederacy is known for its extensive collections. The White House of the Confederacy, which is covered in this book, is located next door.

The old and elegant capitol, which was designed by Thomas Jefferson, is open for daily tours. To learn more about the history of this fascinating city, see The Valentine: The Museum of the Life and History of Richmond and the Virginia Historical Society and Museum, both of which are open daily. For information on all these attractions and more, call the Richmond Convention & Visitors Bureau at 1-888-RICHMOND.

*W*ilton House Museum

LOCATION: 215 SOUTH WILTON ROAD,
    RICHMOND, VA 23226
TELEPHONE: (804) 282-5936
FAX: (804) 288-9805
WEBSITE: www.wiltonhousemuseum.org

Whether Wilton is simply elegant or elegantly simple, it is a marvelous old Georgian mansion. Built between 1750 and 1753, Wilton enjoys a place of prominence overlooking the James River. It was first the home of aristocratic colonial Virginia planter, William Randolph III. The proud Randolph family can claim Jeb Stuart, Thomas Jefferson, Chief Justice John Marshall, Robert E. Lee, and Lady Astor among its descendants. By the end of the eighteenth century, the Randolph family holdings included sixty-two thousand acres of land.

Wilton played host to numerous luminaries over the years. Among the guests at Wilton were George Washington, who was in Rich-

Wilton House Museum
COURTESY OF THE NATIONAL SOCIETY OF THE COLONIAL DAMES OF AMERICA OF THE COMMONWEALTH OF VIRGINIA

mond for the 1755 Virginia Convention when Patrick Henry made his "Give me liberty or give me death" speech. Cousin Thomas Jefferson was also a frequent guest. During the Revolutionary War, the Marquis de Lafayette and nine hundred soldiers stayed here from May 10–20, 1781.

The planter society reigned supreme from the Revolutionary War until the Civil War. The Randolph family slowly lost its assets over the years, and by the time Robert Randolph died in 1859, his daughter Kate had to sell the house for debts.

After it changed ownership four times between 1860 and 1932, the once-grand and historically significant house was deserted and neglected. The huge estate was zoned for industry. The bank that owned Wilton planned to demolish the house, though they agreed to salvage the beautiful paneling for resale.

White House Of The Confederacy

Some Southerners still refer to this house as "the other White House." Today, this house that served as the executive mansion of the Confederate States of America reflects the life and times of Confederate president Jefferson Davis.

For a brief time, the official residence was located in the first capital of the Confederacy, Montgomery, Alabama. Once Virginia seceded from the Union, however, the capital was transferred to Richmond.

The city of Richmond purchased the Greek Revival mansion from its last private owner, a wealthy merchant, and rented it to the Confederate government for the use of the young Davis family from late August 1861 until March 1865.

After Richmond fell in April 1865, the Federal officers used the White House as their headquarters in the state during the years of Reconstruction. When Richmond reacquired the house in 1870, city authorities had the house inventoried and the contents auctioned away.

For twenty years, the old house served as a public school. In 1889, the house was facing demolition when some of the leading ladies of Richmond formed the Confederate Memorial Literary Society to save it. The society opened the house as the Confederate Museum in February 1896, and visitors poured in from around the South, the nation, and the world. Original furnishings began to return, along with manuscripts, uniforms, flags, and all manner of artifacts associated with the war years. In 1976, a new building went up on the property to house these treasures, and a twelve-year, $4.5 million-dollar restoration began on the house.

Visitors touring the White House today can see richly colored, ornate antebellum rooms restored to their wartime luster. Sixty percent of the furnishings and fixtures are original to the house. Of special note

White House of the Confederacy
COURTESY OF VIRGINIA TOURISM CORPORATION

is the portrait of Jefferson Davis featured in one of the parlors, a portrait painted in the house during the war.

You can hear the story of Jefferson Davis's two-year imprisonment for treason, his release and return to private life, and his posthumous pardon by President Carter in 1978. The Museum and White House of the Confederacy remain Virginia's premier Civil War attractions.

Open daily; an admission is charged.
Location: 1201 East Clay Street, Richmond, VA 23219
Telephone: (804) 649-1861
Fax: (804) 644-7150
WEBSITE: www.moc.org

The National Society of the Colonial Dames of America heard of Wilton's plight, and even in the midst of the Depression, they raised the $38,500 to buy the house and a new location for the house. The house was dismantled and moved to its new, safer site. Since the society became the owners of Wilton in 1933, the house has been carefully restored to its more affluent early days.

Through their energy and funding, the Colonial Dames have collected period furniture and decorative arts comparable to those of the Randolphs. And even the extraordinary paneling that was almost sold separately is still used in each room throughout the house. The rooms are colorfully painted and beautifully decorated in period antiques. There is also a gift shop on the premises. Today, the golden age of Virginia is once again alive at Wilton.

Open for tours Tuesday through Sunday; an admission is charged.

Fredericksburg

Fredericksburg has been a home to presidents, and it didn't do too badly in shaping the nation's history, either. Once called home to George Washington and James Monroe, Fredericksburg played an important role in colonial times as well as the Civil War. Located equidistant between Washington, D.C.,

and Richmond, Fredericksburg offered easy access to the two capitals. In the early days when transportation was via horseback, location was a major factor in a town's prosperity.

Founded in 1728, Fredericksburg fared well from its perch on the Rappahannock River until the Civil War brought hate and havoc to the tranquil town. Fredericksburg was the site of a major battle between 143,000 Union and 92,000 Confederates troops in December 1862.

Today, the town of approximately twenty thousand people takes full advantage of its history by offering tours, festivals, museums, antiques, and historic-house tours. And then there is the Fredericksburg and Spotsylvania County Battlefields Memorial National Military Park, which encompasses about 7,800 acres and four Civil War battlefields.

For additional information, contact the City of Fredericksburg Visitor Center at 1-800-678-4748 or (540) 373-1776.

Chatham Manor

LOCATION: 120 CHATHAM LANE,
    FREDERICKSBURG, VA 22405
TELEPHONE: (540) 371-0802
FAX: (540) 371-1907
WEBSITE: www.nps.gov/frsp

From Chatham's terraced garden on a wooded bluff above the Rappahannock River, you can view both the town of Fredericksburg and the river below. Because of its history, Chatham has earned the tranquility of this peaceful setting.

Built between 1768 and 1771 by William Fitzhugh, Chatham is situated on land originally scouted by Captain John Smith in 1608. When the Fitzhugh family acquired the property, they developed it into one of the most prosperous plantations in the Old Dominion. The twelve-thousand-square-foot red-brick Georgian mansion was named for William Pitt, the Earl of Chatham.

After the Revolutionary War, Fitzhugh, who had supported the war financially, found that his comfortable home and hospitality attracted many national leaders, including George Washington. The strain of playing host to a never-ending stream of visitors prompted

Fitzhugh to sell Chatham and remove himself to the relative tranquility of Alexandria.

When J. Horace Lacy owned the home during the Civil War, it was called the Lacy House. When Major Lacy joined the Confederate cause, his family left for the safety of other Virginia locations. Though the house vacated by the Lacys became the headquarters for Union army generals, and even hosted a visit from President Abraham Lincoln in 1862, the house was still vandalized by Union troops. They burned the fine paneling for firewood, wrote graffiti on the plaster, and broke windows.

Twice during the war, Chatham was a hospital for nearby battlefields. Clara Barton and Walt Whitman were among those caring for the wounded. Another person who helped to heal the wounded at Chatham was Dr. Mary Walker, the only woman from the Civil War to win a Congressional Medal of Honor.

Chatham Manor suffered the same fate as many Southern plantations, but it slowly regained its former grandeur. Chatham's last private owner was John Lee Pratt, an industrialist who owned it from 1931 until his death in 1975. Upon his death, he willed it to the National Park Service for preservation.

Today, about half the rooms are open to the public. The formal garden, which is one of the loveliest in the area, is a favorite of tourists visiting Fredericksburg. The house is also the

Chatham Manor
COURTESY OF VIRGINIA TOURISM CORPORATION

headquarters for Fredericksburg and Spotsylvania County Battlefields Memorial National Military Park.

Open daily for tours; a nominal admission fee is charged.

Kenmore

LOCATION: 1201 WASHINGTON AVENUE,
FREDERICKSBURG, VA 22401
TELEPHONE: (540) 373-3381
FAX: (504) 371-6066
WEBSITE: www.kenmore.org

The dining room at Kenmore
COURTESY OF VIRGINIA TOURISM CORPORATION

The unimposing facade of this elegantly simple brick structure is somewhat deceiving, but once you are inside, it becomes apparent that Kenmore is truly an American treasure. The dining room at Kenmore has been designated one of the "One Hundred Most Beautiful Rooms in America." One look at the plasterwork confirms that statement. Thus, it is easy to understand what prompted a few Virginia women who loved history, architecture, and gardens to save Kenmore from destruction back in the mid-1920s.

While still in his twenties, Fielding Lewis was appointed a "gentleman justice" of Spotsylvania County. After the death of his first wife, the twenty-five-year-old Lewis was left with an infant son. He later married his late wife's cousin, Betty Washington, who was a

sister of George Washington. Between 1772 and 1775, the Lewises built their new home near the Rappahannock River. They also located the house close to town, where Lewis was a prosperous merchant.

During the Revolutionary War, Colonel Lewis supported the American cause not only with his leadership, but also with his monetary contributions. He used his wealth to help establish a gunnery to supply weapons for American troops.

In 1922, when it was learned that a developer proposed to demolish the house or convert it to apartments, the Virginia regent of the National Society of the Daughters of the

American Revolution enlisted the aid of a friend in Fredericksburg to form a local chapter. About the time the chapter was organizing, Vice President Calvin Coolidge came to town and described Kenmore as "a national patriotic symbol."

Contributions to save the national symbol came in record time, thanks to private contributors, other D.A.R. chapters, and the Virginia chapter of the Colonial Dames. Between 1924 and 1932, the Garden Club of Virginia restored Kenmore's grounds. The Kenmore project was the club's first restoration project. It was also the beginning of the organization that started the state's famed Historic Garden Week, which is held each spring.

Today, the architecture and interior details of the house give evidence of the Lewises' taste and their preference for English styles contemporary to their times. The richly decorated ceilings are considered the finest in America. Created by an unidentified craftsman, the highly ornate plasterwork offers sweeping circular patterns with flowers and swags in abundance. It is believed that the plasterwork was somewhat patterned after plates in Batty Langley's *City and Country Builder's Treasury*. The plasterwork had to be repaired after the Civil War, because the mansion was damaged by cannon fire.

The woodcarvings, as seen in the mantel in the dining room, are superb. Much of the furniture was made in Virginia during the colonial period.

Thanks to industrious women who were committed to this historic treasure, Kenmore is now a proud and viable part of America's restoration program.

Open daily; an admission is charged.

$\mathscr{S}$tratford Hall Plantation

LOCATION: ROUTE 214, STRATFORD, VA 22558

Stratford Hall Plantation is located 42 miles southeast of Fredericksburg. It is in Westmoreland County, near Montross. Follow Va. Hwy. 3, then turn on to State Road 214.

TELEPHONE: (804) 493-8038

FAX: (804) 493-0333

WEBSITE: www.stratfordhall.org

Because of the role General Robert E. Lee played in leading the army of the Confederate States of America, the last name "Lee" is still revered in certain parts of the South. The gentleman soldier was a bona fide hero, who came from a long line of patriots. The Lees, who set a standard for patriotic duty and courtliness, called Stratford Hall Plantation their home for about eighty years.

Thomas Lee, a prominent Virginia planter and member of His Majesty's Council, built

Stratford Hall Plantation
PHOTO BY RICHARD CHEEK, COURTESY OF THE ROBERT E.
LEE MEMORIAL ASSOC., INC.

the Georgian-style home around 1740. Thomas Lee's grandfather was the royalist Richard Lee, who came to Jamestown from England in the 1630s. Two of Thomas Lee's sons, Richard Henry Lee and Francis Lightfoot Lee, were the only brothers to sign the Declaration of Independence.

When Thomas Lee died in 1750, his oldest son, Philip, inherited Stratford Hall. Philip's five younger brothers are known for their role in leading the fight for independence from Great Britain. Philip's daughter, Matilda, inherited the house at her father's death. She later married her cousin, Henry "Light Horse Harry" Lee. Several years after Matilda's death, Light Horse Harry, who was by then the governor of Virginia, married Ann Hill Carter of Shirley Plantation on the James River. He and Ann Carter had six children. Their fifth child, who was born at Stratford in 1807, was Robert E. Lee.

As a soldier and politician, Light Horse Harry was brilliant, but he was not a farmer.

He went deeply in debt on land speculation and even served a stint in "debtor's prison." Upon his release, he moved the family to Alexandria, and his oldest son inherited Stratford Hall. The son hit upon hard times, too, and ended up selling the plantation in 1822.

On Christmas Day in 1861, while a war was waging and Arlington was occupied by Union troops, the lonely Robert E. Lee wrote to his wife Mary:

"In the absence of a home, I wish I could purchase 'Stratford.' That is the only place I could go to, now accessible to us, that would inspire me with feelings of pleasure and local love. You and the girls could remain there in quiet. It is a poor place, but we could make enough cornbread and bacon for our support, and the girls could weave us clothes. I wonder if it is for sale and at how much. . ."

Unfortunately, the Lees never returned to Stratford. In 1929, the Robert E. Lee Memorial Association purchased the old Lee plantation. Stratford was restored, refurbished, and furnished to greet the many visitors who have toured the house since 1935.

The one-story brick house, with an elevated basement, is built in an H-shape. The bricks of the lower level and chimneys are laid in Flemish bond with glazed headers. The chimneys are clustered in groups on each end.

Added to the Lee furnishings acquired over

the years are various pieces of fine early American and English antiques that have been donated. The Great Hall, with its seventeen-foot ceilings, paneled walls, book-closets, and tall windows with window seats, is a place of wonder. This room is considered one of the finest examples of an American Colonial-period interior. Among the furnishings are an American Chippendale sofa, a spinet, and a harp.

Today, Stratford Hall Plantation is a National Historic Landmark. The Robert E. Lee Memorial Association, Inc., operates the non-profit site. There is a gift shop and small restaurant on the premises.

Open daily; an admission is charged.

*W*oodlawn Plantation

LOCATION: 9000 RICHMOND HIGHWAY,
  ALEXANDRIA, VA 22309
TELEPHONE: (703) 780-4000
FAX: (703) 780-8509
WEBSITE: www.nthp.org/main/sites/
  woodlawn.htm

In the late 1700s, it could be quite advantageous to have a connection to George Washington. For the Lewis couple who built Woodlawn Plantation the connections were extensive. Nelly Custis Lewis, Martha Washington's granddaughter, was like a daughter to the Washingtons. They raised her after the

death of her father, Martha Washington's son by her first marriage. Nelly's husband, Major Lawrence Lewis, was the son of Washington's sister, Betty Lewis of Kenmore Plantation.

In early 1799, George Washington gave two thousand acres of his Mount Vernon property to the young couple as a wedding gift. The Washington family connections came into play again when family friend and architect William Thornton, who had designed the United States Capitol, agreed to design a home for them. The result was a Federal neo-classical home, which they named Woodlawn. The two-and-one-half-story brick mansion features five connected parts that face the Potomac River to the east.

When Woodlawn was finished in 1805, it was decorated primarily with pieces the Lewises brought from Mount Vernon. Later, the house contained the Lewises' own fine things that they acquired throughout their lives. Like other plantations of the period, Woodlawn was

Woodlawn Plantation
COURTESY OF VIRGINIA TOURISM CORPORATION

supported by slave labor. The Lewises were the second largest slave owners in Fairfax County, and in 1820, they owned over ninety slaves, over half of whom were children. The socially prominent and popular Lewises had eight children, four of whom died in infancy. When her husband died in 1839, Nelly moved in with her son and left the house vacant

From 1846 to 1853, Woodlawn was home to a community of Quakers. The house was used as a meeting house, and the two thousand acres were divided into several small farms. It also served as a "Free School," one of the first integrated schools in Virginia. In 1853, the property was sold to a Baptist family who used the mansion as a residence and meeting house for a growing Baptist community. Woodlawn stood abandoned from 1892 to 1901. In 1901, playwright Paul Kester purchased the house and remaining acreage. In 1905, he sold the house to Elizabeth Sharpe. During her twenty years as owner of Woodlawn, Sharpe executed the only major restoration of the structure. From 1925 to 1948, the family of Senator Oscar Underwood of Alabama owned the house and the surrounding grounds.

In 1949, local residents established the Woodlawn Public Foundation, a private non-profit organization, to preserve the declining historic site. The foundation rescued the site from sale to a private owner and two years later, turned the property over to the National Trust for Historic Preservation for operation as a house museum. The Trust became the outright owners in 1957.

Also located on the property today is the Frank Lloyd Wright-designed Pope-Leighey House. The "Usonian" house exhibits Wright's ideas for housing for people of moderate means. The Pope-Leighey is also a National Trust Historic Site.

Woodlawn has acquired much of the original furnishings and artwork, including many examples of Nelly Lewis's needlework. Today this site remains a wonderful example of the customs and culture of Virginia plantation life between 1800 and 1840.

Open daily from March through December; open on weekends only in January and February; an admission is charged.

Mount Vernon

LOCATION: P.O. BOX 110, MOUNT VERNON, VA 22121

Mount Vernon is located at the south end of George Washington Parkway, sixteen miles south of Washington, D.C.

TELEPHONE: (703) 780-2000

FAX: (703) 799-8609

WEBSITE: www.mountvernon.org

Mount Vernon has more than one claim to

fame. It was the beloved home of a remarkable man, President George Washington, but it was also a pioneer project in the preservation movement. When the esteemed Mount Vernon Ladies' Association purchased and restored the property, the nation took an interest in historic preservation. The home remains a testament to the achievement of a group of dedicated women.

George Washington was a multifaceted man who helped to create the United States of America; he was also a planter who loved architecture. During the same period that he was helping to defeat the British Empire in the Revolutionary War, working to forge thirteen independent colonies into one nation, serving as the new nation's first president, and setting abiding standards for patriotism, honor, loyalty, and diligence, Washington was also indulging his passion for architecture.

The first evidence that members of the Washington family resided at Mount Vernon dates to 1735, when George's father, Augustine, is listed as residing in the area. The early history of Mount Vernon is only poorly understood, but it is likely that a house was built on the site of the present mansion at that time.

This structure was passed down to George's elder brother, Lawrence, who substantially rebuilt the house some time in the 1740s. That dwelling was one-and-one-half stories, with

Mount Vernon
COURTESY OF MOUNT VERNON LADIES' ASSOCIATION

four rooms and a central passage on the first floor, and another four rooms on the level above. George acquired the house after Lawrence's death in 1752.

Beginning in 1758, George began expanding the house by raising it to two-and-one-half stories, adding exterior closets to either gable, and upgrading the interior finishes and furnishings. In the spring of 1759, he brought his bride, the former Martha Dandridge Custis, to live here.

In 1774, Washington began a second building campaign, adding a wing to the south that accommodated his study on the first floor, his and Martha's bedroom on the second floor, and storage rooms above.

When he left in the spring of 1775 to fight in the Revolutionary War, the completion of this wing and other planned additions were carried out over the next eight years under the supervision of his plantation manager and cousin, Lund Washington. In 1775, the interior of the small dining room was completely reno-vated, with the addition of an ornate plaster ceiling and an elaborate carved mantel and plas-ter overmantel. The designs for the mantel and overmantel can be traced to English architec-tural pattern books. In 1776, Lund began construction of the north addition, which accommodated a two-story dining room and storerooms above.

By 1777, the north addition was enclosed, but the interior decorations were not com-pleted until Washington returned from the war in December 1783. Also in 1777, the piazza, a highly unusual double-height porch, supported by eight pillars, was added. It ran the length of the east façade of the house. Finally, a pedi-ment and central cupola were added to pro-vide a strong central axis for the extremely long east and west facades, and open colonnades were added to link the mansion with the kitchen and servants' hall dependencies. Many of the elements of the expanded house were clearly influenced by then-fashionable tenets of Anglo-Palladian architectural design.

Today, the passage, or central hall, extends the full width of the house. Washington had the woodwork grained to resemble mahogany, thus creating a huge area that offered the warmth of rich woods.

The rest of the interior is a beautiful com-bination of fine furnishings, outstanding art, and design elements, such as the ornate plaster decoration on the Palladian windows. Rooms are brightly painted in various shades of blues and greens—the front parlor is Prussian blue; the small dining room is green. Most of the rooms feature furniture original to the Wash-ington family. The pieces include Martha Washington's French desk, George Washing-ton's secretary and presidential desk chair, an original terrestrial globe, and a unique "fan chair" which substitutes for the original. There are also important historical documents and personal belongings on display at the estate's museum as well.

After Washington died in 1799, Mount Vernon remained in the Washington family for three generations. The last heir tried unsuc-cessfully to get the federal government or the state of Virginia to purchase the home. In 1853, Ann Pamela Cunningham of South Carolina heard of the plight and pledged to save Mount Vernon as a national shrine. Thus, the Mount Vernon Ladies' Association was founded. In 1858, the association received its charter, pur-chased the historic treasure, and rescued Mount Vernon.

Today, the association operates as a non-profit organization for the maintenance and preservation of Mount Vernon. Approximately one million visitors come to this National His-toric Landmark each year. We can thank the ladies for leaving us this outstanding example of colonial architecture that is such an important part of America's rich history.

Open daily for tours; an admission is charged.

Leesburg

Leesburg has played a role in American history for centuries. During the French and Indian War, the area around present-day Leesburg was an outfitting post. It was during this time that the Virginia House of Burgesses passed a bill authorizing the establishment of a town.

During the War of 1812, Leesburg served the country when twenty-two wagonloads of important documents, among them the Declaration of Independence, the Articles of Confederation, and the Constitution, were stored here when the British burned Washington, D.C.

Today, the old brick-lined streets run past antique shops, historic homes, and the Loudoun Museum. This area is also known for its thoroughbred horses, Christmas tree farms, and wineries. For information on one of Virginia's oldest towns, contact the Loudoun Tourism Council at 1-800-752-6118 or Historic Leesburg at 1-888-777-1758.

Morven Park

LOCATION: 17263 SOUTHERN PLANTER LANE, LEESBURG, VA 20175

TELEPHONE: (703) 777-2414

FAX: (703) 771-9211

WEBSITE: www.morvenpark.org

This grand and gracious late Greek Revival mansion was completed in 1880, although it was begun as a farmhouse in the 1770s. In 1800, Judge Thomas Swann bought Morven Park and began its remodeling soon after. In the 1830s, he added a Greek Revival portico. In the 1840s, Swann's son, Thomas, Jr., a future governor of Maryland, had the house remodeled again. Thomas, Jr., engaged the Baltimore architectural firm of Lind and Murdock to recreate the house, using a combination of Greek Revival and Italianate styles. The Maryland Swanns used the family home as a summer place.

In 1903, Mr. and Mrs. Westmoreland Davis purchased the house, which they used to entertain lavishly. The house came into its own from 1918 to 1922, when Westmoreland served as governor of Virginia.

Once the Davises arrived, the house gained a reputation for hospitality and fox hunting. Morven Park was, after all, in the heart of Virginia's hunt country. The thirty-two-room mansion and its twelve hundred acres provided

Morven Park
COURTESY OF THE WESTMORELAND DAVIS MEMORIAL
FOUNDATION, INC.

a favorite place for foxhunters, and for those who appreciated the lifestyle of the Davises.

Today the interior is as resplendent as it was in its earlier incarnation. Pieces, inherited and collected by Marguerite Davis, are seen throughout. Among these pieces, you can see fine paintings, sixteenth-century Flemish tapestries, silver, and porcelain figurines.

In 1954, Marguerite Davis established the Westmoreland Davis Memorial Foundation. The memorial to Governor Davis assured that the Davises' beloved Morven Park and its spectacular gardens would continue to be a showplace for Virginia. Today, the foundation still runs this Virginia Historic Landmark.

When you tour the home, you can also visit The Museum of Hounds and Hunting, in the north wing of the mansion. It houses art and artifacts of this treasured sport. On the grounds, you can see the Winmill Carriage Collection, one of the country's largest collections of horse-drawn vehicles.

Open for tours Tuesday through Sunday, from April through October; on weekends in November, and in December for Christmas tours; equestrian facilities are available year round; an admission is charged.

Oatlands Plantation

LOCATION: 20850 OATLANDS PLANTATION
　　LANE, LEESBURG, VA 20175

Oatlands Plantation is located on U.S. 15, six miles south of Leesburg.

TELEPHONE: (703) 777-3174

FAX: (703) 777-4427

WEBSITE: www.oatlands.org

It is remarkable that a house built between 1803 and 1810 has been the residence of only two families. Although there was one interim owner, only the Carter and Eustis families have lived at Oatlands. Builder George Carter was a great grandson of King Carter. At George's death, his son George II inherited Oatlands.

Oatlands began as a plain red-brick structure topped by a cupola. In the 1830s, Carter made architectural changes, which included the addition of a two-story portico, supported by tall Corinthian columns, conversion of the drawing room to an octagonal form, and the addition of semi-octagonal stair wings.

The Civil War left Oatlands intact physically, but the Carters' economic woes were mounting.

With few people left to farm the land, George II and his wife ran the grand old family home as vacation rental for city dwellers during the 1870s. It also became a respite for family, friends, and a few emancipated slaves.

Regrettably, the Carters sold Oatlands in 1897 to a founder of the *Washington Post*. The new owner never lived at Oatlands, and in 1903, he sold the reeling and peeling old house to Mr. and Mrs. William Corcoran Eustis. The Eustises had wealth and social position, and used both to refurbish and furnish Oatlands. They turned Oatlands into an English-style country house, complete with popular foxhunts and long weekend visits from Washington friends, who included Franklin Delano Roosevelt.

Luckily, the Eustises were instinctive preservationists who undertook the richly deserved restoration of Oatlands and its four-acre gardens. After William Eustis died in 1921, Edith Morton Eustis remained at Oatlands. Her interest in restoration continued, and her love of fine things is evident in the furnishings and art still at Oatlands. After she died in 1964, her daughters presented the 261-acre estate to the National Trust for Historic Places in 1965. Now, Oatlands is a co-stewardship museum property, owned by the National Trust and administered by Oatlands, Inc.

Today, the terraced formal gardens, some

Oatlands Plantation
COURTESY VIRGINIA TOURISM CORPORATION

of which have been restored by the Garden Club of Virginia, provide a perfect setting for the twenty-two-room Greek Revival mansion, with its pale-yellow stuccoed walls.

Open daily from late March through December; an admission is charged.

Charlottesville

If I could choose any place in the country to live, it would be Charlottesville. It has all the amenities I want: idyllic mountain views, a small-town feel, colonial history, a downtown historic district, culture, commerce, a fine library at the University of Virginia, and the tidy look of the Virginia hunt country.

These appealing characteristics show why Charlottesville is growing by leaps and bounds. Albemarle County appears to be the place to call home for more than a few well-known names in the entertainment and literary world. Let's hope that the wonderful charm remains intact. This is, after all, the home of Thomas Jefferson and James Monroe, so the area should continue to revere its rich history.

And it's history that brings tourists to town in droves. They come to see Jefferson's Monticello, Monroe's Ash Lawn-Highland, and Madison's Montpelier, which is located thirty-five miles to the northeast. But, they also come just to partake of the city's wonderful sites and scenes.

For more information, contact the Charlottesville/Albemarle Convention & Visitors Bureau at (804) 977-1783 or 1-877-386-1102. Their website is www.charlottesvilletourism.org.

*M*onticello

LOCATION: P.O. BOX 217, CHARLOTTESVILLE, VA 22902

Monticello is located approximately two miles southeast of Charlottesville on Va. Hwy. 53.

TELEPHONE: (804) 984-9822

FAX: (804) 977-6140

WEBSITE: www.monticello.org

Since Thomas Jefferson located his home on the mountaintop, he chose to name it Monticello, which means "little mountain" in Italian.

Monticello
COURTESY OF MONTICELLO/THOMAS JEFFERSON MEMORIAL FOUNDATION, INC.

The mansion on the mountain reflects the nature of the man himself—dynamic, compelling, independent from tradition, not easy to categorize, well-planned, and ahead of its time. When you walk around Monticello and view it from different angles, the perfect blending of octagons, triangles, circles, and cylinders is indeed a study in contrasts.

Jefferson began construction of Monticello in 1768 and continued recreating it until his death in 1826. Construction-wise, everything he did took full advantage of the views provided by the blue-misted mountains surrounding Monticello. And to know that the mansion was altered periodically though it appears so unified is another testament to Jefferson's genius for architectural design.

When he was not yet twenty-one-years old, Jefferson inherited five thousand acres of land—one thousand of which he used for Monticello. His mother was Jane Randolph, a member of the prominent Randolph family of Virginia. A few years later, the young Jefferson put his love of architecture to use on the home he designed himself. Monticello became a self-sustaining plantation, with its own brick kiln, nailery, blacksmith shop, and more.

Jefferson's design genius is further noted in Monticello's dome construction. At the time of the house's construction, using small pieces of wood to mold the dome was a very advanced process. As Jefferson recreated the house, he almost doubled its size by removing the upper story and adding new rooms. He also built cellar rooms and rooms in the attached dependencies.

When Thomas Jefferson was appointed Commissioner to Europe in 1784 and Minister to France in 1785, he visited Europe's architectural monuments and no doubt returned to Monticello with ideas galore. Perhaps he got the idea for the dome from the Hôtel de Salm in Paris. He once decided to raise the ceilings of the three main rooms on the first floor to the height preferred by the French. Inside, the pediments over the parlor doors are magnificent.

Jefferson was married to Martha Wayles Skelton, who died ten years later after giving birth to six children, only two of whom sur-

vived. Jefferson never remarried, so it was he who selected the art and furnishings for his home. Some were acquired when he lived in Paris from 1784 to 1789; other pieces were made by cabinetmakers in Williamsburg, New York, and Philadelphia. The house was not without a female presence, however, for his daughter Martha was there with her family.

Thomas Jefferson was a man who loved his work. Even his bedchamber was an alcove between his study and his book room so that he could get up and immediately enter one of his two preferred rooms. His favorite rooms were stocked with books, globes, maps, and writing material.

The Roman Revival-style brick mansion and all its inventive additions confirm that Jefferson was a serious student of architecture. He was also known to have designed many other structures in and around Virginia, including the rotunda at the University of Virginia.

After a long and brilliant career, the statesman, president, and world leader died at his beloved Monticello, where he is buried on the grounds. This National Historic Landmark is owned and operated by the private, nonprofit Thomas Jefferson Memorial Foundation, Inc., which was founded in 1923. A visitors center and museum shop is about two miles west of Monticello, at the intersection of Va. Hwy. 20 and I-64. The winding drive to the property shows off the woods and foliage surrounding the mansion. Cars must be left at the parking lot at the bottom of the hill; shuttles transport the two to three thousand daily visitors to and from the mansion.

Open daily, (first floor only); an admission is charged.

*A*sh Lawn-Highland

LOCATION: 1000 JAMES MONROE PARKWAY, CHARLOTTESVILLE, VA 22902
TELEPHONE: (804) 293-9539
FAX: (804) 293-8000
WEBSITE: http://avenue.org/ashlawn

This home and its surrounding acreage were originally part of the sprawling estate owned by Champe and Maria Carter. In 1793, James Monroe bought the land adjacent to the property of his friend and mentor, Thomas Jefferson. Monroe hoped to move immediately from his farm at the present site of the University of Virginia, but in 1794 he was appointed minister to France. In his absence, Monroe gave Jefferson full authority to locate the house on the property he called Highland. He also asked Jefferson to plant Highland's orchards.

The family moved to Highland on November 23, 1799, and the family considered it home for a quarter century. It was here that their oldest daughter Eliza married George Hay, the presiding judge at the trial of Aaron

Ash Lawn-Highland
COURTESY OF VIRGINIA TOURISM CORPORATION

Burr. Their younger daughter, Maria, who spent her childhood here, was the first presidential daughter to have a White House wedding. The Monroes' only son died at the age of sixteen months.

While at Highland, Monroe experimented with diverse crops and planting methods. He became an early advocate of scientific agriculture. He even tried cultivating Bordeaux grapes for wine.

In 1816, Monroe added the north side of the house. In 1818, he converted the three-room servants' quarters into guest accommodations. Although Monroe frequently talked about retiring to Highland at the end of his presidency, he was forced to sell the estate in 1826 because of pressing debts and his wife's poor health. At the time of its sale, Highland and its 3,500 acres were described as "commodious dwelling house, buildings for servants and other domestic purposes, good stables, two barns with threshing machine, a grist and saw-mill with houses for managers and laborers … all in good repair."

In 1837, Alexander Garrett, a friend of Monroe and Jefferson, purchased Highland and changed the name to Ash Lawn. About 1840, one wing of the house was damaged by fire. In the 1880s owner John Massey built a two-story Victorian section over the foundation of the damaged wing.

In 1974, Jay Winston Johns willed Ash Lawn and its surrounding 535.5 acres to the College of William and Mary. In 1975, the college began research and restoration and reopened the property for public visitation.

Today, you can tour the home, which is furnished with eighteenth- and nineteenth-century furnishings. The furnishings include a dropleaf table made from Honduras mahogany, which was sent to Monroe by the people of Santo Domingo in gratitude for the Monroe Doctrine; a bust of Napoleon that was given to Monroe by Napoleon himself; Monroe's mahogany bed and furniture; and numerous French furnishings the Monroes purchased during two diplomatic missions to France.

On the grounds, you can see a magnificent white oak, which was standing in Monroe's day. It now measures twenty feet in circumference. The oak dominates the boxwood gardens that were planted well over a century ago. The innumerable white ash trees that stretch across the northwest lawn gave Ash Lawn its name.

Open daily; an admission is charged.

*M*ontpelier

LOCATION: 11407 CONSTITUTION HIGHWAY, MONTPELIER STATION, VA 22957

Montpelier is located on Va. Hwy. 20, four miles southwest of Orange.

TELEPHONE: (540) 672-2728

FAX: (540) 672-0411

WEBSITE: www.montpelier.org

Montpelier was the lifelong home of James Madison, fourth president of the United States and the "Father of the Constitution." The Montpelier property was granted to Madison's grandfather in 1723, and his father began building the mansion in 1760.

Montpelier now boasts fifty-five rooms and a spectacular view of the nearby Blue Ridge Mountains. Madison once described the estate, which covers acres of pastures, woodlands, lawns, and gardens, as "a squirrel's jump from heaven." It was at Montpelier that James Madison began to hone his political skills and forge a life in politics.

After graduating from the College of New Jersey, now known as Princeton, Madison began a career of public service that would span more than four decades. He also had a long association with Thomas Jefferson. He served as an official advisor when Jefferson was governor of Virginia and as secretary of state when Jefferson was president. Jefferson also influenced Madison's architectural views. When he was remodeling Montpelier, Madison used builders from Monticello.

At the age of forty-three, the confirmed bachelor met the young widow, Dolley Payne Todd, who was seventeen years his younger. He married her as soon as she consented. Dolley served as hostess at the President's House (we now call it the White House) during the administration of the widowed Thomas Jefferson and during her husband's eight years as president. Her legendary hospitality inspired the term "First Lady."

Madison was well known for his astute political acumen. He played a critical role in framing the Constitution at the Constitutional Convention, authored many of the *Federalist Papers*, and was the chief congressional sponsor of the Bill of Rights. After his second term as president ended, James Madison and his wife Dolley returned once again to their beloved Montpelier. James died in 1836 and was buried on the estate.

In 1844, facing mounting debts, Dolley was forced to sell Montpelier. She died in 1849 in

Montpelier
Courtesy of Virginia Tourism Corporation

Washington, D.C., and was later buried beside her husband at Montpelier.

Montpelier went through six owners between 1844 and 1900, when William duPont, a descendant of E. I duPont purchased the property. He then enlarged the mansion to its present fifty-five rooms. His daughter Marion duPont Scott—an avid horsewoman who was married to the actor Randolph Scott—inherited Montpelier in 1928. She added horse stables, a racetrack, and a steeplechase course, and made Montpelier her treasured home. For much of the twentieth century, Montpelier and its twenty-seven hundred acres of rolling hills and pasturelands was a private hunt-country residence for the duPonts and their friends.

When Marion duPont Scott died in 1983, she bequeathed Montpelier to the National Trust for Historic Preservation. Today, Montpelier is opened to the public. Visitors may tour the Main House, explore the grounds and gardens, visit active archeological sites, and hike through a two-hundred-acre old-growth forest.

Open for tours daily; an admission is charged.

Lynchburg

Lynchburg got its start in 1757 when John Lynch picked the site to build a ferry that crossed the James River. John Lynch also helped the growth of the town by building the region's first tobacco warehouse in 1785. Thomas Jefferson, who was a fan of the town, once said, "I consider Lynchburg one of the most interesting spots in the state."

One of Lynchburg's most interesting attractions is the Old City Cemetery, which contains 2,750 Confederate graves. Another site of note is The Pest House Medical Museum, a restored medical office from the 1840s. The museum shows how medicine was practiced back then and also shows how a house of quarantine was managed.

The Lynchburg Museum at the Old Court House shows off Native American and Civil War artifacts, and items reflecting Lynchburg's early connection to the tobacco industry. Also located in Lynchburg is The Maier Museum of Arts' permanent collection, which features the work of Thomas Hart Benton, Mary Cassatt, and Georgia O'Keeffe.

For information, contact the Greater Lynchburg Convention & Visitors Bureau at 1-800-732-5821.

Point Of Honor

LOCATION: 112 CABELL STREET, LYNCHBURG, VA 24505

TELEPHONE: (804) 847-1459

FAX: ((804) 528-0162

WEBSITE: www.pointofhonor.org

Southern gentlemen placed great importance on their "honor." Legend has it that the perch on a bluff overlooking the James River was often the place where feuding gentlemen chose to settle a "point of honor," which sometimes meant a duel to the death. Thus, the mansion built on this site around 1815 received its name.

Point of Honor followed the trend established by self-taught architect Thomas Jefferson and professional architect Benjamin Latrobe, both of whom favored octagonal designs. Though the name of the builder is not known, the house built for Dr. George Cabell features two octagonal bays on either end of the brick facade. Although he treated many area residents, Dr. Cabell's most famous patient was Patrick Henry.

Several other prominent people have called Point of Honor their home. One was Mary

Point Of Honor
COURTESY OF LYNCHBURG MUSEUM SYSTEM
©THOMAS G. LEDFORD

Virginia Ellet Cabell, one of the founders of the Daughters of the American Revolution. Another was Colonel John S. Langhorne, whose daughter, Elizabeth Langhorne Lewis, was an active and dedicated suffragette. John Langhorne had two granddaughters who also gained fame—Irene was the original "Gibson Girl," and Nancy became Lady Astor. From 1862 until 1872, Point of Honor was the home of the artist Narcissa Owen, a Cherokee "Indian Princess," and her husband, railroad president Robert Latham Owen. Their son, Robert Owen, Jr., was Oklahoma's first United States senator. Indeed, Point of Honor has had remarkable inhabitants.

The restored interior features the classical designs made popular by English designers. Rich colors, mural wallpaper picturing French monuments, and period furnishings are used throughout. In 1928, Lynchburg banker James Gilliam purchased the house. He later donated it to the city, but a bequest from Katharine Garland Diggs, a retired schoolteacher, enabled restoration to begin in the 1970s.

Today Point of Honor has been beautifully restored and furnished by the Lynchburg Historical Foundation, the Garden Club of Virginia, the Katharine Garland Diggs Trust, and the City of Lynchburg.

Open daily; an admission is charged.

Poplar Forest

LOCATION: P.O. BOX 419, FOREST, VA 24551
Poplar Forest is located southwest of Lynchburg, off U.S. 221. Take Route 811, and then turn right on Route 661. It is one mile to the entrance.

TELEPHONE: (804) 525-1806
FAX: (804) 525-7252
WEBSITE: www.poplarforest.org

When Monticello got too crowded with family, guests, and staff—and it was often very crowded due to Thomas Jefferson's popularity and fame—Jefferson retreated to his second home at Poplar Forest. In 1806, at the age of sixty-three, Thomas Jefferson began work on this house. This retreat was located in the remote farming country of Bedford County,

Poplar Forest
PHOTO BY LES SCHOFER, COURTESY OF THOMAS
JEFFERSON'S POPLAR FOREST

about ninety miles south of Monticello, on land he inherited from his father-in-law.

The Palladian-style Poplar Forest once again exemplifies Jefferson's fondness for octagons. The entire structure is octagonal, with four octagonal rooms surrounding a cube dining room. The self-taught architect kept improving Poplar Forest until 1826, when he died. He once said, "When finished, it will be the best dwelling house in the state except that of Monticello; perhaps preferable to that, as more proportioned to the faculties of a private citizen." Referring to both the house and the plantation, Jefferson called Poplar Forest "the most valuable of my possessions."

In Jefferson's day, tobacco and wheat were the major crops at Poplar Forest Plantation. It took up to two and one-half days by horseback to reach the plantation, but Jefferson made the trip several times a year after retiring from the presidency. Poplar Forest was where he went to read, relax, ponder, and seek "the solitude of a hermit."

As well as providing a place to unwind, Poplar Forest gave Jefferson a chance to practice his love of architecture. His sculptor once asked whether he correctly understood Jefferson about an order for the frieze at Poplar Forest's middle room, because Jefferson planned to mix classical orders. Jefferson replied: "I mean to mix the faces and ox-sculls, a fancy which I can indulge in my own case, although in a public work I feel bound to follow authority strictly."

Private citizens, fearing this outstanding property was in danger, formed the nonprofit Corporation for Jefferson's Poplar Forest and bought the site in 1984. Poplar Forest earned the coveted Honor Award from the National Trust for Historic Preservation for the completion of the exterior restoration. The property is registered as a National and Virginia Historic Landmark. Restoration and archaeology continue. There is a gift shop on the premises.

Open daily from April through November; group tours can be arranged by appointment year-round.

Resources

Abbott, Shirley. *Historic Charleston, Great American Homes*. Birmingham, Ala.: Oxmoor House, 1988.

Baldwin, Joseph C. *The Flush Times of Alabama and Mississippi*. Baton Rouge, La.: LSU Press, 1987.

Barney, Howard. *Mister Bill: A Life Story of Walter D. Bellingrath*. Mobile, Ala.: The Bellingrath-Morse Foundation, 1979.

Boorstin, Daniel J. and Brooks Mather Kelly. *A History of the United States*. Lexington, Ma.: Ginn and Company, 1981.

Brownstein, Elizabeth Smith. *If This House Could Talk*. New York, N.Y.: Simon & Schuster, 1999.

Editors of *American Heritage Magazine*. *A Guide to America's Greatest Historic Places*. New York, N.Y.: American Heritage Publishing, 1983.

DeHart, Jess. *Plantations of Louisiana*. Gretna, La.: Pelican Publishing Company, 1982.

Fancher, Betsy. *Savannah: A Renaissance of the Heart*. New York, N.Y.: Doubleday, Inc., 1976.

Gutek, Gerald and Patricia Gutek. *Plantations and Outdoor Museums in America's Historic South*. Columbia, S.C.: University of South Carolina Press, 1996.

Hamilton, Anne Butler. *A Tourist's Guide to West Feliciana Parish*. New Orleans, La.: Habersham Corp., 1983.

Higginbotham, Sylvia and Lisa Monti. *The Insiders' Guide to Mississippi*. Manteo, N.C.: Insiders' Guides, Inc., 1995.

Howell, Elmo. *Mississippi Home Places: Notes on Literature and History*. Memphis, Tenn.: Elmo Howell, 1988.

Kempe, Helen Kerr. *Old Homes of Mississippi, Natchez and the South*. Gretna, La.: Pelican Publishing Company, 1989.

Kennedy, Roger S., editorial director. *Smithsonian's Guides to Historic America*. New York, N.Y.: Stewart, Tabori and Chang, 1989.

Lane, Mills. *Architecture of the Old South*. New York: Abbeville Press, 1993.

_____. *Architecture of the Old South*, (four editions: Virginia, Georgia, North Carolina,

South Carolina). Savannah, Ga.: Beehive Press, 1986-92.

LeBlanc, Joyce. *Gardens of Louisiana*. Gretna, La.: Pelican Publishing Company, 1974.

Legarde, Lisa M. *Frommer's New Orleans*. New York, N.Y.: McMillan Travel, 1997.

Malone, Lee. *Louisiana Plantation Homes: A Return to Splendor*. Gretna, La.: Pelican Publishing Company, 1986.

Martin, Gay. *Alabama, Off the Beaten Path*. Old Saybrook, Conn.: Globe Pequot Press, 1992.

Moore, Margaret H. *Complete Charleston: A Guide to the Architecture, History and Gardens of Charleston*. Mount Pleasant, S.C.: Mills Printing Co., 1997.

Muse, Vance. *Old New Orleans. Great American Homes*. Birmingham, Ala.: Oxmoor House, 1988.

Potts, Bobby. *Historic House of the Deep South and Delta Country*. New Orleans, La.: Express Publishing, 1992.

Porter, Darwin, and Danforth Prince. *The Carolinas and Georgia*. New York, N.Y.: McMillan Travel, 1996.

Rees, James. *Mount Vernon Commemorative Guidebook*. Mount Vernon, VA.: Mount Vernon Ladies Association, 1999.

Rhett, Ann and Michael MaLaughlin, Michael. *The Insiders' Guide to Charleston*. Manteo, N.C.: Insiders' Guides, Inc., 1992.

Roberts, Bruce. *Plantation Homes of the James River*. Chapel Hill: University of North Carolina Press, 1990.

Sansing, David, and Carolyn Vance Smith. *Natchez: An Illustrated History*. Natchez, Miss.: Plantation Publishing, 1992.

Sommer, Robin Langley. *The Old House Book*. New York, N.Y.: Barnes & Noble Books in arrangement with Saraband, Inc., 1999.

Whiffen, Marcus. *American Architecture Since 1780: A Guide to the Styles*. Cambridge, Mass.: The MIT Press, 1986.

Wiencek, Henry. *Plantations of the Old South*. Birmingham, Ala.: Oxmoor House, Inc., 1988.

_____. *The Mansions of Virginia Gentry*. Birmingham, Ala.: Oxmoor House, Inc., 1988.

Additionally, each of the nine states and various cities sent information on historic sites and preservation efforts and general tourism guidebooks. We also used guidebooks from certain sites, among them the *Historic Garden Week in Virginia* booklet; the official guidebooks for Old Salem and Poplar Grove Plantation; North Carolina's Carolina Heritage Guide; Georgia's Antebellum Trail booklet; Tennessee's

Heritage Trail publication; and brochures and press information from many of the homes featured. We also used various articles from the *New York Times* about historic architecture, cultural tourism, and Southern destinations, as well as various guidebooks published by Fodor's, Frommer's, and AAA. My local library—Columbus Public Library—and the inter-library loan system were so helpful in getting regional publications such as the Virginia Landmark's Register and various historic preservation resource books.

Index